SOLOISTS AND SIDEMEN

AMERICAN JAZZ STORIES

Peter Vacher

Soloists and Sidemen:

American Jazz Stories

northway publications

Published by Northway Publications
39 Tytherton Road, London N19 4PZ, UK
www.northwaybooks.com

Edited by Ann and Roger Cotterrell

Cover design by Stewart Aplin, Aplin Clark, London EC1.

Cover photo by Peter Vacher: the Jacques Butler Quintet with Benny Waters at La Cigale, Paris, July 1962.

The publishers acknowledge with thanks the kind permission of copyright holders to reprint the photographs used in this book. Permissions have been sought in all cases where the identity of copyright holders is known.

A CIP record for this book is available from the British Library.

ISBN 978 0 9537040 4 1

First published 2004.

Printed and bound in Great Britain by Antony Rowe Ltd, Chippenham, Wiltshire.

For Patricia, most of all,

and for Louise, Sarah and Amanda, too.

Contents

"Sometimes ordinary speech is banal, and it is always repetitive, but if selected with art, it can reveal the inner life, often fantastic, concealed in the speaker."

V. S. Pritchett

Introduction

I heard a Sidney Bechet recording on a cafe jukebox in France in the early 1950s and was hooked. There and then. Together with some like-minded friends, I began to collect all the jazz records I could – Jelly Roll Morton, Kid Ory, and the great Oliver and Armstrong classics. We played them endlessly and gradually formed the idea of starting a band, prompted as much as anything else by seeing *The Glenn Miller Story* three times in a single week. It was Louis' appearance in the film that did it.

I became an avid reader of *Melody Maker*, anxious to have the weekly news and pick up on reviews, and joined the Jazz Book Club. Like many of my generation, I read *Jazzmen* and *Shining Trumpets* and fell heavily for the romance of the traditional jazz revival. If this music was important so, clearly, were the lives and careers of its practitioners. I devoured everything published about them that I could find (and still do). I also rather liked the music's racier aspects and the colourful characters who played it, and enjoyed filling in parts of the great jigsaw of jazz history.

Back in the 1950s, much of the jazz writing on this side of the Atlantic assumed the primacy of all things American and preferably black American at that. In France, Hugues Panassié was in no doubt; in Britain, writers like Max Jones, Sinclair Traill and Albert McCarthy were following a similar path, as were their friends Jeff Aldam and Jack Armitage, their efforts supplemented by on-the-spot reports from Stanley Dance, the British writer who had re-located to the United States. They would call on any visiting artists – accompanists, dancers, singers, or comedians – who happened to be in town and who had even the remotest of connections to jazz and pursue them for interview. These activities were given greater urgency by the seeming indifference of American writers and researchers to such essential fieldwork; magazines here were constantly harping on about the dereliction of duty evident on the other side of the pond. Indeed, there was something of an evangelistic mood around in those days, a sense of a world disappearing before our very eyes. This work had to be done.

After National Service, our band of jazz friends continued to rehearse and play but gradually it became obvious that the gap between intention and outcome was widening inexorably so my trombone was put away for good. It then seemed a perfectly sensible idea to follow in the footsteps of Max Jones and others and to seek to interview American jazz musicians (of all stylistic persuasions) as they came through London. This began in the late 1950s at a time when bands and groups began to visit and tour here regularly. My photographer friend Ian Powell and I would take a chance and turn up at hotels in Central London at weekends on 'spec', lugging a heavy reel-to-reel tape machine around with us, and try to inveigle musicians into telling us their stories. We met with success at our very first attempt when the pianist Al Williams (from the Buck Clayton All Stars) welcomed us into his room, offered us a Scotch and seemed pleased to talk. With the tape machine set up, it was disconcerting to find I'd forgotten to bring the microphone. Still, we gathered enough material on Al to make a plausible article and this became my first published piece. It appeared in 1960 in the Canadian magazine *Coda*, to which I remain eternally grateful, and it's pleasing to be able to say that I still contribute interviews and features to *Coda* today.

This process continued, quite obsessively, and often on a hit or miss basis, but usually with some success. More and more interviews with jazz musicians were collected here in Britain and later in mainland Europe and I gradually learned how to structure the encounters so that the 'oral histories' had some sort of chronological shape. The resulting articles were usually presented in print on an 'as-told-to' basis and a number of these have been adapted here. Many others were much too long to be considered. Looking back, I can only thank editors like the late Albert McCarthy (*Jazz Monthly*) and Sinclair Traill (*Jazz Journal*) for their willingness to run these life-story features without any strictures about word count or content. Happy days! Indeed, it was McCarthy's interest in running a long feature on Joe Darensbourg that encouraged me to go further and eventually produce a book that documented the Creole clarinettist's picaresque life in full. Their support, and, later, that of Tony Russell (*Jazz The Magazine*), Eddie Cook (*Jazz Journal*), Leslie Johnson (*Mississippi Rag*) and Malcolm Laycock (*Jazz Magazine*) was always vital. My main debt of gratitude, though, is to Max Jones who first prompted me to contribute news items, reviews and feature articles to *Melody Maker*. Indeed, Max became a mentor and very good friend, whose tireless enthusiasm was always an inspiration. It was my good fortune to come into jazz journalism at a time when he and many of these other writers and editors were active and interested.

In some cases, my pieces have been found to be useful by other researchers and quoted in learned volumes and I'm proud of that. Of course, there have been plenty of mishaps along the way. Art Farmer thought my tape recorder too puny the first time we talked, switched my cassette over to his machine and the interview began. Sadly, nothing was recorded as he'd omitted to set the record button. Another piece was taken from memory as my primitive reel-to-reel machine malfunctioned and the speech was unintelligible.

When I made my way to Illinois Jacquet's hotel room by appointment, it was to find that he and his wife had celebrated all night long and there was to be no interview after all. Twenty years passed before we could get together again. Other interviews have been snatched in dressing rooms and on band buses, between sets or after-hours, the potential for narrative flow often scuppered by extraneous noise and interruptions. In some cases, I've had to resort to note-taking using my own rather dodgy version of shorthand. Time is often a constraint. Marshall Royal grumbled, 'How long is this going to take?' and cut me off just as we were starting to make real progress, while the pianist Gideon Honoré asked for five thousand dollars before he'd say a word. When I dropped the names of a few mutual (musical) acquaintances, everything changed and he was sweetness itself, entertaining me to a wonderful lunch of red beans and rice in his South Central Los Angeles home, complete with its walk-in bar and splendid white baby grand. Ed Thigpen politely declined my request for interview, saying that he'd talked about himself often enough, but he did invite us in for tea. And so on.

In a few cases – during several trips to Los Angeles, for example – the illness of a family member or disenchantment with the jazz life and its perils led to a refusal. This is sad because, as a consequence, these men's stories may not have been documented. Inevitably I have missed out on opportunities to talk to key witnesses to this music's development through bad judgment, lack of time, or inertia. Sometimes I have arrived in a city like San Francisco or Los Angeles with a list of potential interviewees only to find that a quarry has just died or left town or deteriorated to the point where his recollections are confused and sadly worthless. There's seldom a second chance in this game.

Quite often, I have been given generous hospitality and invited into the homes of players after only the barest of introductions, turning a conversation with a purpose into an extended and very pleasurable social encounter. For a travelling musician, an interview can be a useful way of whiling away a long day in a strange hotel: as one musician put it, probably tongue in cheek, 'What a pleasant afternoon talking to you about me and my favourite subject.' But I'm still delighted when they do agree to talk. There is also the unspoken sense that a published article may well be of some benefit to an individual for publicity. Indeed, interviews these days will often be set up by record company PRs for that very purpose and I do my fair share of these. As it happens, none of the stories included here came about via that particular route. It's true that there are occasions when a musician is pleased with a piece one has written and will ask whether it can be included in their press kit and that is very gratifying. Indeed, I do know that a couple of veteran players were so delighted that their careers had been documented in a jazz magazine that they had the appropriate pages framed and hung on their walls at home.

There's another unvoiced expectation, of course. It's the assumption of the interviewee that his or her story will eventually appear in print. Suffice it to say that I have as many untranscribed interviews in the filing cabinet, as there are published pieces here. This can sometimes arise because the interview content, once stated and examined, turns out to be lacking in substance or valid detail, or that editors simply can't be persuaded to run a feature because they feel that the subject is of no interest to them or their readers. Blow any documentary value!

I've always been interested in talking to players from the 'jazz backroom', hence the bassists and rhythm men who appear here, as they usually have something interesting to contribute. Prominent soloists and star names have often been interviewed to death and it's sometimes difficult to break through their fund of pre-set anecdotes and routines. In a sense the more obscure the performer, the more ready they are to open up to an interested party like me. I don't mind saying that I prefer to talk to players who have lived a little: men (and it is usually men) who may have started out in minstrel shows yet end up playing bebop, for instance. Their stories of privations on the road can be a window on a long-gone world.

I tend to feel that every musician has a tale to tell, and that the story of the music and its development is still far from complete. Were there enough time in the day, I would be out seeking yet more of them to interview, preferably those who came to prominence in the pre-bop era for, inevitably, they are a dwindling band. I am still desperately disappointed when I hear of the passing of a musician whose story has not been documented. All too often these days, it seems, I'm called on to write their obituaries rather than their career stories.

The pieces included here are adapted and revised from some 40 years of jazz reporting. In all cases, I've preserved the subject's syntax as I heard it. I'm acutely aware of the inadequacies of the interview form itself. So much depends on the relationship between interviewer and interviewee, always a chancy affair, the setting and timing, the choice of questions, informed or random, the interviewer's listening skills, advance knowledge and homework. It's all too easy to think of a good question after the interview is over. And then again, there's the issue of transcribing the resulting tapes. . .

I make no special claims for these pieces – blinding insights may be few – but I do believe they have value in showing how a number of American jazz musicians have spent their lives and served this extraordinary music.

Peter Vacher,
Pinner, Middlesex,
May 2004.

Acknowledgements

My thanks go to the musicians whose stories are included here. I'm grateful to them for the time they devoted to these interviews. Many became good friends. Some have gone now and I'm glad that we've been able to preserve their reminiscences in this more permanent form.

The second group of people who deserve my gratitude are the editors who published some of these interviews in the first place and their successors who have published others, and all those who have sanctioned their publication in a revised and adapted form in this book. They were/are Albert McCarthy (*Jazz Monthly/Jazz and Blues*), Sinclair Traill (*Jazz Journal*), succeeded by Mike Hennessey and Eddie Cook, Leslie Johnson (*Mississippi Rag*), John Norris (*Coda*), succeeded by Bill Smith and Stuart Broomer, Tony Russell (*Jazz The Magazine*), Peter Boizot (*Boz*), Malcolm Laycock (*Jazz Magazine*), Ira Sabin (*Jazz Times*), succeeded by Glenn Sabin, and the editors of *Melody Maker* including Ray Coleman and Richard Williams. My principal debt is to the late Max Jones, 'Mr *Melody Maker*', who encouraged me to write about musicians for his paper and who proved to be a steadfast friend and jazz companion.

Many of the photos reproduced in this book are from my own collection, and some of these have been given to me by musicians during interviews, but I am particularly grateful to Dave Bennett, Berit Bolt, Big Bear Music, Brigitte Charvolin (via Jean-Pierre Battistini), Brian Foskett, Ernie Garside, Ian Powell, Theo Zwicky (mr.jazz Photo Files, P.O. Box 249, CH-8049 Zurich) and the National Jazz Archive, Loughton, Essex, for their generosity in providing photos. It's also good to be able to include images by such leading jazz photographers as William Gottlieb (via Redferns), Duncan Schiedt, David Sinclair and Val Wilmer, and to have had access to the Max Jones Archive (administered by Nick Jones).

Finally, I must mention my wife, Patricia, who assisted this project (and its author) in so many selfless ways, and my editors, Ann and Roger Cotterrell, who kept me up to the mark and supported the concept through to the finish.

Chapter 1

Sonny Cohn

From Chicago to Basie

Sonny Cohn. Photo by Diane Jackson, courtesy Sonny Cohn.

*George 'Sonny' Cohn was on his first European tour with Count Basie when we met
in 1960 at a London hotel to talk about his career. Born in Chicago in March 1925,
he went on to spend thirty years in Basie's trumpet section, travelling the world and
doubling as the band's road manager. We kept in touch whenever he came through
London. Sonny stayed on after the Count died in 1984 and left finally six years later.
He's back in Chicago now and plays locally.*

'How did it all begin? Both my mother and my father had a pretty good conception of music.
When I was small my father used to fiddle around on the piano and he did very well. He
could hear things, like the tunes back then, and he would play them by ear. He didn't study
or anything but in his family they all had good ears. His brother could even do better than
him.'

'There was a certain place my father was working, Sears Roebuck, I think it was, and
it happened that Omer Simeon was there too. Omer influenced him to get a trumpet,
because he was playing saxophone and clarinet. My father used to talk about this all the
time and finally he bought a trumpet. I used to hear him trying to practise, but somewhere
down the line he just got disgusted and he put the trumpet up. The obvious thing to do was
to take it back again but he decided to keep it for me until I was old enough to study.'

'When I was about ten or eleven years old, my father arranged for me to study the trumpet. He was working at the Post Office at the time and there was a fellow there named
Charles Anderson who played trumpet, and he used to come over to the house and teach
me lessons once a week. I'll never forget my father's trumpet; it was an old, old, silver trumpet and it had the weirdest name. It was a Tom Brown Oriole!'

'Charles 'Baby' Anderson was semi-professional and he used to play around town with
the little bands. Now, he couldn't swing so good but he could read very well and he was a
wonderful teacher. At the time I wasn't too interested in the lessons, and, in fact, I preferred
to go out and play with the boys. I wouldn't practise, so when he came over, I'd ask him
about the lesson and he'd play it for me, but since I had an awfully good ear I'd come right
behind him and play it back. Later on, I found it was to my disadvantage to do this and naturally I began to take my lessons much more seriously. I continued to take lessons all the
time I was in school.'

'When I got to high school, I began to really get involved with music and around the age
of thirteen or fourteen I started playing in the little local bands for social affairs, with my
friends. We got paid for these things; it was so little really but at that age it was real money!
Later we formed a group with my sister who played piano, called 'Frances and Her Rhythm

Kings'. We played various dances and after a while we got to feeling that our drummer wasn't good enough and so we got rid of him. My next-door neighbour joined the band on drums. He had originally started out on piano and he could play well, but only in the key of E-flat. Anyway, we converted him to a drummer. He did very well but he's back playing piano now and these days he's a very prominent musician. His name is George Rhodes,

Count Basie Orchestra, c.1960. Count Basie (p); Eddie Jones (b); Sonny Payne (d); Thad Jones (c); Cohn, Joe Newman (t); Freddie Green (g); Henry Coker, Al Grey, Benny Powell (tb); Billy Mitchell (ts), Frank Wess (as); Snooky Young (t); Marshall Royal (as); Frank Foster (ts); Charlie Fowlkes (bs). Photo courtesy Max Jones Archive.

pianist with Sammy Davis Jr. and formerly with the Jonah Jones Quartet.'

'Our quartet finally broke up; my sister had eyes for the boys, and I went over to the King Fleming Band.[1] This was one of the best up and coming bands in Chicago, and working with it really convinced me that music was going to be my life. This was around 1939 and I was still at high school. Although it was a small band it felt a lot more like a big band. We used to work at the Edie Park Theater House as a steady job, every Wednesday from seven till twelve. All the kids from the different high schools would come along and pay their fifteen cents admission; at the end of the evening we'd split the take among all the fellows in the band. When we first started we'd usually go home with fifteen or 25 cents. But it grew and we'd end up with two or three dollars for each guy, which was good when you were going to school.'

'King Fleming played piano. His real name is Walter and I still call him Walter, although he prefers to forget that now. He's about my age and when he started out he wanted to be called 'Keen' but everybody just seemed to take it for 'King' so he adopted that name. He's

Cohn, at his hotel, in London with the Count Basie Orchestra, March 1962. Photo by Ian Powell.

doing very well today with a group of his own that both sings and plays. The singer Lorez Alexandra was with him for a long time. You know, it's a funny thing about Chicago but you can drop out of the public eye and still be working steady. King's one of these.'

'The band continued to work together for a couple of years and then it broke up because some of the guys wanted to join the union and some didn't. I didn't join because I felt I wasn't ready: I was still in high school and I felt a little afraid of the idea. However as soon as I came out of high school in 1942 I joined the union and my first really professional job was with a band working out of Calumet City, about 20 to 25 miles from Chicago; it's where they used to have the strip houses and it was wide open at one time but it's not like that now. The band was led by a guy named Richard Fox, and it was quite an experience for somebody of my age to be with a band like that. Fox had been out there a long time. We were working seven nights a week, from nine till three, but the money wasn't too good and I seemed to spend nearly all my spare time travelling to work. I had to leave home about seven in the evening and ride out to the South Side to this guy's house, go from there to Calumet City and then back after the show. You can do this sort of thing for just so long before you crack up. I lasted four months.'

'The band was used as an accompaniment to acts – Indian acts, interpretative dancers, strip-tease etc. There was a very good bass player and arranger with the band before I joined, Sylvester Hickman, who's been on quite a few recordings around Chicago. Fox himself was a good musician, playing alto mostly; I believe he's still out there working in Calumet City.'

'After Fox, I joined Captain Walter Dyett's DuSable-ites,[2] back in Chicago. Captain Dyett was a teacher at DuSable High School, a coloured school, and he was one of the first to organise a big swing band right there in the school. A lot of your prominent musicians, people like Bennie Green, Jesse Miller, and Lunceford trumpeter Melvin Moore, came up under him and played in his band. Anyway, after these various kids graduated from high school, he decided to get a band together and he got some of the kids that had been in school with him who were pretty good, and called the band the DuSable-ites. They played all the dances and made nice money.'

'Harold Tyler, one of the trumpeters I worked with in King Fleming's band, had been with Captain Dyett and he recommended me to take his place when he had to go in the Service. In fact I worked with Dyett until I went in the Service myself and for a while after I came out. The personnel included Melvin Moore on trumpet.'

'When I started out, the trumpet I really liked the most was Roy Eldridge. Louis was prominent, but Roy was hot then in Chicago and I followed him. But Melvin Moore was such a wonderful player that the experience of working alongside him helped a great deal in forming my style. These days he's out on the West Coast, playing a little violin as well as trumpet. He appeared in some scenes in two pictures, *All The Young Cannibals* and *Walk On The Wild Side*. Tremendous musician, he stayed with Lunceford quite a while after he left Dyett's band and he's still very underrated.'

'I got called to the Service in 1943, and when they found out I was a trumpet player they took me off basic training and made me a bugler. After a while I was transferred to Greensville, South Carolina, where I joined the 770th A.A.F. band. There was also a dance band, led by Poncho Diggs, an excellent tenor player, with some good musicians, but no one that's known today. Diggs is from New Jersey and I believe he's back there working for the union now.'

'I came out in 1945 after eighteen months and rejoined Walter Dyett. One of his sax players got sick and Leon Washington from the Red Saunders Band worked with him for a couple of months. Leon had been with Red for a long time but

Count Basie Orchestra in the US Channel 5 TV production, *The Big Bands*, probably New York City, September 1964, including: trumpets (*left to right*) Sam Noto, Wallace Davenport, Cohn and Al Aarons; Sonny Payne (d); trombones (*left to right*) Henderson Chambers, Henry Coker and Grover Mitchell; Bill Hughes (b-tb); Count Basie (p); Freddie Green (g); Eric Dixon, Bobby Plater, Marshall Royal (as), and Sal Nistico (ts).

Fletcher Henderson's band moved into the Club DeLisa replacing Red's group for a period, so Dyett was able to get Leon into his band. Then Leon told me that Red was getting ready to form a new small outfit; he must have recommended me because Red called me to join him. He had some nice things; he was going on one of those U.S.O. tours, working all the different army camps abroad and over here but I was hesitant, still being young and living at home so the idea fell through.'

'I continued with Captain Dyett for a little longer. Melvin Moore was back in the trumpet section, having left the Jimmie Lunceford Orchestra. He stayed briefly then moved on some place else since he was in demand and had some good offers. Otherwise the band was about the same as before I went into the Service. Red Saunders called me again; he had decided to get another small outfit and start working at nightclubs in the Loop in downtown Chicago. This time I said yes. We then rehearsed and got some little things together. My first job with him was at the Capitol Lounge in Chicago in May 1945.'

'Red used to bill me as the junior member of the band[3] – say I was eighteen and all that sort of thing. Anyway we were at the Capitol for four weeks, then we went over to the

Garrick Lounge in the Downbeat Room and we stayed there for about fourteen months.'

'We did well at the Garrick and we stayed there almost as long as Red Allen did. It was one of the first of the real jazz clubs where people just came to sit down and listen to the music. We'd play 40 minutes on and 20 off. There was no show; we had a little music but we mostly played head arrangements or features for the guys in the band. When the Garrick closed down we went to New York for six weeks and worked the Kelly's Stables. Working opposite us we had the Mary Osborne Trio. I thought she was wonderful because that was the first time I'd seen a girl play [guitar] and sing like that. She had these little things she'd do with her voice, backed up with the guitar harmony. Her piano player was Sanford Gold; I forget the bassist. That was my maiden trip to New York; I was scared at first, you hear so many things about New York but we did pretty well at the Stables. Altoist Porter Kilbert joined us in New York and came back to Chicago with us.'

'When we came home to Chicago we worked the Band Box, right next door to the Downbeat Room, and once again we stayed there longer than anybody else, mainly because we had a little show within the band. We did feature numbers up on the stage but, above all, the kids would love to dance to our music because Red has one of the most phenomenal beats even today. It just lifts you when you are playing so I can imagine how it would be when you're dancing. Musicians used to love to come and play with him because he had one of the fastest foots, beautiful wrists, and he could just swing so well. He's a great jazz drummer, but he's also one of the best show drummers in the country and that's not taking anything from Sonny Payne; he'll say the same thing. He'll make the worst looking act look good. That's why he stayed so long at the Club DeLisa. Those acts would come in without music but when they left they had music!'

'As part of our show at the Band Box, Red's wife, Vi Kemp, would sing; in fact she sang with the band for a long time. She was also a beautiful contortionist. Anyway, she'd do her act and then we got a little thing together where the bassist would join her on the stage and they'd do a real fancy ballroom dance. Then she'd snatch off the skirt of her long gown and I'd go out and do a jitterbug routine with her. This was when the jitterbug was the thing so it knocked the kids out. We stayed at the Band Box for about four months and after that worked in Detroit for about three or four weeks. Just after this, Red reorganised his big band, twelve pieces,[4] to work the Club DeLisa again. This was in 1947. I stayed eleven years at the DeLisa with Red and for the last seven years I was the only trumpet! We ended up as seven pieces.'

'The various acts just loved to work the DeLisa because they knew they were going to have their music played and they were going to look good. Our main idea was to make everybody look good. We broke in quite a few acts; often a new act would come in and they'd want to see how their music sounded. So many times, we'd stay there after we got off work to play their music and help them work out their routines. We played for all the acts and we also played feature numbers. My main stake was always a ballad; I loved ballads and I still love them. But then I had to do everything: ballads, swing, sweet things, high notes; I was just a one-man trumpet section. Show experience is the greatest in the world. With the little tricks you learn, you're home any place; recordings, anything.'

'Talking of recordings, I made quite a few records with Red over the years. In fact, I've recorded in Chicago with just about everybody from the rock 'n' rollers to swing. I've worked for just about every label you can think of, usually in the background of course. To me it was just a few extra dollars in my pocket.'

'I'm on one of Dinah Washington's albums and on some of her things that have not been released yet. Among the blues singers, I've recorded with Big Joe Turner in Red Saunders' band and with Gerry Butler and Dee Clark, both very popular, on the Vee-Jay label. I used to do quite a lot for Vee-Jay because Al Smith and later Lefty Bates, who used to furnish most of their background music, would always call me. I can't remember details of all the sessions but when I was in Paris a guy [Kurt Mohr] caught me and he knew more about me than I know myself; he was telling me people I had recorded with! Here I am thinking I'm a nobody, which to myself

I still am! I'm sort of quiet; I do my job and I hope you know I'm there. I don't make too many scenes or anything like that.'

'If any of the bands came into town short of men, or they made up a band in Chicago, I was often called and this meant doubling from the DeLisa to the Ritz Theater or somewhere like that. I worked with Louis Bellson's band backing Pearl Bailey on one occasion.'

'The two brothers that ran the DeLisa died in 1958 and the club was closed. The place didn't have to close, business was good but the widows felt they were not getting enough money and took it to court. Anyway, the lawyers fixed it so the club couldn't open anymore. After that, we went over to Roberts Show Lounge and I worked there with Red for two years. The group was still the same, seven pieces, that had worked the DeLisa for the last six or seven years.'

'I joined the Basie band in February 1960. I had played with the band before, in October 1959. They were at the Regal Theatre at the time and one of the trumpet players got sick, John Anderson. I came off a three-day vacation and worked in his place. Basie must have been satisfied because when they came back through town I went to work with him again. Thad Jones had to go back to New York to get his teeth fixed or something and I played in his place, with a leave of absence from Red, but just after Thad came back, John Anderson left, and they approached me to join the band.'

'I was very happy to join. I was relaxed

but, naturally, I was a little nervous, coming into the Basie band. No matter how good you are you're still going to be nervous. So I used to tell myself just to be loose, no panic, if you make a mistake keep on going, some of your greatest passages are formed from mistakes.'

Count Basie Orchestra, directed by Frank Foster, 1988. *Left to right:* Foster (ts); Bob Ojeda, Byron Stripling, Mike Williams (t); Kenny Hing (ts); Robert Trowers (tb); Cohn; Dave Gibson (d); Mel Wanzo, Clarence Banks (tb); Clarence 'Ace' Carter (p); Danny House (as); Paul Weedon (g); Bill Hughes (b-tb); Danny Turner (as); Eric Dixon (ts); Carmen Bradford (v); Cleveland Eaton (b); John Williams (bs).

'Back in the King Fleming days, I'd be there on opening day whenever Basie came to one of the Chicago theatres, sitting on the front row. I saw all the bands but his was always one of my particular favourites. I used to look at those trumpets: Harry Edison, Buck Clayton and Ed Lewis, never thinking that one day I'd be in the Basie trumpet section myself. My friend Johnny Thompson had just about every Basie record and I went round his house to listen to them every time I could.'

'My first problem in the band was the fact that I was not used to extensive travelling apart from a few one-nighters, and after only two months I found myself in Europe for the first time. I really enjoyed Europe but my biggest trouble was the money. For instance, you have the night off in one country, next day you fly to Holland or Belgium, then on to

Germany the day after. You're changing money every day. After losing some dollars I learned and now I have a proper exchange book so I'm completely organised.'

'I play quite a bit of lead but Snooky [Young] has most of it. It's even switched about between us in the course of a tune. I have some solos, 'L'il Darlin'', of course; I play on 'Easin' It' with the other trumpets, then on 'The Deacon' and a few others. Every now and then I'll play 'April In Paris'. It's a kick really. It's not easy with the travelling but I've never been as happy as I am now.'

'It's a wonderful feeling, even with concerts. In concert work you're not as close to the people as you are when you play clubs. People moving their heads, snapping their fingers, they inspire you more. You don't hear the band until you hear them at a club or dance. When we play a club like Birdland, we're close to the people, relaxed, and we can do more things. We have well over 300 numbers in the book and in concerts you can only play a few selections here and there.'

Chapter 2

Willie Cook

Trumpet for Hire

Willie Cook with B.B. King's band at Orange, France, 1979. Photo by Brigitte Charvolin, courtesy Jean-Pierre Battestini.

I was intrigued to see the distinguished ex-Ellington trumpeter Willie Cook in blues-man B.B. King's backing band at the Capital Jazz Festival in London in July 1979. Ever approachable, he gave me a very complete interview at his hotel the next day although he was somewhat pressed for time. Willie was an engaging soloist and a charming, handsome man whose creative potential was never fully realised. We exchanged cards and letters occasionally until his career foundered when his health failed. He moved to Sweden in the early 1980s and died in Stockholm in September 2000.

The jazz categorisers cast Willie Cook, like all those musicians who worked for Duke Ellington through the years, as forever an Ellingtonian. True, he was with Duke for lengthy periods in the fifties and sixties, becoming a soloist of note, although somewhat overshadowed by more celebrated artists like Ray Nance and Clark Terry. More to the point, Ellington himself was moved to say of Cook in his autobiography *Music Is My Mistress*: 'He has always been potentially the best first trumpet player in the business,' and, 'his taste as a soloist is quickly proved to anyone who listens to his records.' In Duke's terms then, Cook was a clever all-rounder whose talent repaid critical attention but, for all that, he had largely dropped out of sight in the mid-1970s prior to his stint with B.B. King, which was followed by two years with the Count Basie Orchestra and then his move to Sweden.

In person, Cook's youthful demeanour belied his extensive experience. Like so many musicians of his generation (he was born in 1923), he barnstormed around the highways and byways of jazz, working with a great variety of bands. He told me that he was originally from a small town in Louisiana, although raised in East Chicago, and that he stole his brother's cornet – this leading to his joining the school band and a chance to go on the road early with a family orchestra. His inspiration? 'At that time, I was trying to play Roy Eldridge solos.' Louis Armstrong was an influence too: 'Just seeing him up on the bandstand playing his trumpet, he played it with such ease, the people were so happy. It really impressed me.'

His true professional debut was with the King Perry band (out of Cincinnati) using Fletcher Henderson charts, 'which, at that time, I thought were very interesting.' After forming his own short-lived eight-piece, Cook moved to the 'Bama State Collegians, fronted by the Trenier Twins, this bringing him into faster company, including Sonny Stitt on alto, and Lucky Thompson and Morris Lane on tenors. Cook remembered this as 'one of the most inspirational bands I've been with,' and talked of excellent original material and the fine quality of Thompson's playing: 'I couldn't believe what was coming out of his horn.'

Although the band worked alongside such major stars as Louis Jordan and Maxine Sullivan, money hassles led to the break-up of what was obviously a superior aggregation.

A friendly contact then led Cook to pianist Jay McShann's renowned band. 'That band used to astonish me. Jay, he'd start off playing and he would wait until a groove got set real good and they were swinging, then bring the band in. I loved playing with Jay's band. That rhythm section, they played so good, they just fit together. They could do everything, they could play soft and swing, they could play heavy and swing. They could build to where the band would come in, and it would be just like a roaring freight train – no stopping it!'

After recording with McShann, Cook was among a group of Jay's bandsmen 'liberated' by Earl Hines during a long lay-off. 'I figured I was moving up a stage,' he explained. The

Dizzy Gillespie's big band at the Orpheum Theater, Los Angeles, 1949. *Back row, left to right*: trumpeters Benny Harris, Willie Cook, Elmon Wright. Personnel also includes Al McKibbon (b), Ernie Henry (as) and Yusef Lateef (ts). Photo courtesy mr.jazz Photo Files (Theo Zwicky).

Hines Orchestra was arguably past its very best – no longer a forcing ground for experimenters like Charlie Parker and Dizzy Gillespie – but Wardell Gray and other top men were on hand. Long residencies eventually gave Cook a chance to write arrangements, too: 'You really enjoy hearing something you write. That's the greatest feeling in the world.' Hines encouraged his sidemen to persevere with new ways of musical expression and recorded a few of Willie's tunes. The band, in the trumpeter's view, was superb, but it broke up in 1948. After brief experience with the Jimmie Lunceford band, Cook joined the shouting

Cook with Paul Munnery's band at the 'Ellington '85' Conference, Oldham, Lancashire. Photo by Tony Warwick, courtesy Peter Carr.

Dizzy Gillespie Orchestra, staying two years.

'It was a challenge to get up there and play the parts. I didn't think about solos. The band had such a positive feeling about everything – it was very experimental. The reception we had was overwhelming in that first year. The music was accepted most by the students. In the large cities, it was more of a cult thing. At that time, it was raw. Later it was commercialised. Dizzy opened the door to listening to the different parts of the chord progression. For me, at that point, it was most inspiring. You had to have relaxed chops, so much stuff to play, high and fast. I played all the lead.'

In Cook's opinion, the Gillespie band – with John Coltrane playing lead alto – got better and better, but it ran out of work in mid-1950, leaving the trumpeter available for a new Gerald Wilson orchestra, organised to back Billie Holiday. In 1951, when Duke

Ellington came through Pittsburgh, Cook was introduced to the great man and was then called to Detroit to join his orchestra, ostensibly to replace Shorty Baker. To Willie's consternation, Baker reappeared on Cook's opening night! But no matter, for Baker left again and Cook became a Ducal employee for the duration.

'In that band, I used to just sit and listen to the music. I should have bought a ticket for myself. I felt like I'd reached the pinnacle of success. In the trumpet section then

Cook at 'Ellington '85' with Alice Babs, Bob Wilber and Jimmy Hamilton.

we had Clark Terry, Cat Anderson, Ray Nance and myself. The music was intriguing because Shorty's book, which I played, would have the lead and Duke would have Cat on a higher part. If you listen closely, you'll see that the lead is right down in the meat of the arrangement.'

'Duke was always courteous, kind and understanding. He made you feel as though you were a great person. Always. Anyone could talk to him on any level. In fact, he liked to talk to the fellows. I used to ask him different things about the writing. Duke was a painter, and he was doing the same things with the instruments that he would do with his paintbrush, using different tones and shades. He knew each person's sound and he would utilise whatever talent he had in the band to best advantage. Like when we made our South American trip and Johnny Hodges was out for some reason, I would play Johnny's parts in a felt hat, sitting with the saxophones. It sounded so good.'

'One highlight for me was when Duke wrote out 'Black Beauty' for me to play. I knew that he liked [Artie] Whetsol's lines on this. Anyway, Cootie [Williams] said, 'You oughta feel good playing that because Duke doesn't usually let trumpet players play on that.' That made me feel very good. To me, Ellington was such a great man. Besides being suave and sophisticated, he was a big man with big ideas. He looked at things in a big way.'

Cook worked continuously for Ellington until 1958 when touring took its toll and he decided to come off the road. However, his respite was short-lived for he was back with Duke from 1959 to 1961, rejoining in the mid-sixties and returning to the band for the last time in 1968, staying for two years until, re-married, he settled in Houston, Texas. He refers to the sixties as a bad period and talks of scuffling around New York, with Duke's rescue calls as the only pleasurable aspects of a depressing decade.

Once in Houston, Cook worked in an instrument store for eight years, virtually dropping out of professional music. He appeared occasionally with tenorist Arnett Cobb in a small group and managed Cedric Haywood's workshop big band. He explains this hiatus by underlining Houston's limited opportunities for any music other than country and western. Calvin Owens, B.B. King's bandleader, sensing Cook's frustration, invited him to join King's travelling road show in late 1978, thus allowing the trumpeter to return to active profession-al performance. He was enthusiastic about the great bluesman: 'I knew what he'd got in him and it knocked me out that the people could understand this and receive it that way.'

After a full season with King, the trumpeter formed a small group with some young Texan players but was soon snapped up by Count Basie, making a number of fine record-ings with him, notably a Kansas City session on Pablo, before settling in Sweden in 1982.

When I asked Willie Cook to summarise his own stylistic preference and comment on the future, his remarks were characteristically modest yet suffused with real optimism.

'I've always tried to stay between the modern, which to me is bop, and the Roy Eldridge style. I don't want to go too far in either direction. I want to keep a basic foundation in there and I like the people to know what I'm saying. I'd like to speak through records and say the things I want to say. I believe that there'll be a chance for the very young people to discov-er that old jazz and bring it back up. It's gonna be like a new thing for them'

Chapter 3

Harry Edison

Basie and Beyond

Harry Edison (*left*) with Illinois Jacquet in the film *Jammin' The Blues*, August 1944. Photo courtesy mr.jazz Photo Files (Theo Zwicky).

I can't claim to have been close to Harry 'Sweets' Edison, the stylish former Basie trumpet star, although he was always up for interview. His affection for Basie and the classic band in which he played such a significant role shone through every time we spoke. He seemed never to tire of talking about the old days and was unfailingly co-operative and cordial.

Not long after I conducted the following interview with him in London in October 1996, I was told of Edison's prostate cancer. Later, in 1998, it was reported he had been invalided back to the United States mid-way through a tour of Germany. Then came the news that, with the cancer in remission, Sweets had died in his sleep, back in his home town of Columbus, Ohio, early on the morning of 27 July 1999, tended by his ex-wife and their much-loved daughter, Helena. He was 83.

I was fortunate to hear Edison play in a pleasing variety of settings. On solo tours in Britain, in combos with Eddie 'Lockjaw' Davis and Red Holloway, back in the Basie band, with the Philip Morris Super Band supporting B.B. King, and at many festivals. I interviewed him a number of times and was in his company on social occasions in Los Angeles. It was fun to watch him playing cards there, quite intensely, with his regular companions, the pianist Gerry Wiggins, attorney Jimmy Tolbert (nephew of Lee and Lester Young) and Al Alvelino (saxophonist Vi Redd's husband). I also heard him play at the Biltmore Hotel in downtown Los Angeles in front of his enthusiastic 'home' crowd, fronting a cooking quartet with the underrated Art Hillery on piano and the impressive drummer Paul Humphrey.

Wherever and whenever one encountered Harry Edison, he was the epitome of suavity. He enjoyed the company of women and always dressed well. His Cadillac was usually a low-mileage current model distinguished by its 'SWEETS' customised number plate. I have a mental picture of Harry sitting watchfully, half-smiling, before injecting a wry comment or two. His sense of humour chimed well with the British preference for irony and Ernie Garside, his English tour organiser, told me that he 'had more fun on the road with Sweets than anyone else.'

My talk with Sweets started with him describing the period after he left Count Basie in 1950, or more accurately, the band left him. 'Due to economic reasons, Basie had to break the band up. He was broke. At that time we weren't making too much money anyway. You could book the whole band for five or six hundred dollars. I wouldn't have left the band because that was home to me. Even after I left it was still home to me. I went back when he needed a trumpet player. I'd stay for a year or something like that.'

In New York after the break-up, Edison hooked up with Buddy Rich, also taking tours with Jazz At The Philharmonic and short-term jobs with Coleman Hawkins. It was while he was with Rich that he met the celebrated dancer Josephine Baker, newly returned from Europe, and this led indirectly to his re-location to Los Angeles.

'Well, when she first came back to New York Buddy Rich had the band in the Strand Theater. Of course, I played with Buddy quite often and she worked with the band. Her and I worked up a little act together on the stage. I'd play a solo while she'd dance and so on. It became quite popular so I travelled with her quite a bit, to Mexico City, to California, and she was just drawing huge amounts of people everywhere she went. I stayed with her for about three years. She and I became very close friends because I'd lived in St. Louis for a long time and she was from St. Louis. She was a great performer and a wonderful human being. Between her and Billie Holiday, I think they were the two easiest people to work for.'

When Sweets had first travelled to Los Angeles with Basie in 1939 he had been unenthusiastic about the city. 'At that time I didn't like too much of L.A. Then I went there with Josephine Baker in 1952 or '53 and I began to realise I could do better in Los Angeles. When she went to Argentina I stayed in California and I started making records with Sinatra, Nelson Riddle, just about everybody. I can't think of one singer

of any note I haven't recorded with. Then I went to Vegas, had a band there for a while. I just didn't go back to New York until the late fifties. Started a band, went to Birdland. The quintet with Jimmy Forrest, that's the first band I had, with Tommy Flanagan, Elvin Jones and Joe Benjamin, and then I got Tommy Potter, and Jimmy Jones played piano for me. I just migrated back to New York for a while.'

Edison's quintet became successful, and recorded often, before it teamed up with the ex-Basie singer Joe Williams. 'Basie decided to handle both of us. He was very instrumental in us getting together and he used to tell Willard Alexander, who was the agent, that different clubs would put us on. We made records. I think we made a couple of albums together, then Joe finally got himself a trio and I went the same way that I was going before. I was like a house band at Birdland – Roulette Records owned Birdland – and most people that recorded for Roulette could go in there just about any time they wanted. Art Blakey, Sarah Vaughan, Basie, Billy Eckstine, Maynard Ferguson; they had just about everybody. You worked all the time. There were many clubs in New York at that time. Then you could go to Chicago, Washington, Philadelphia, Detroit; there were clubs all around. We could go to California and play in two or three clubs round there. You could go to San Francisco and then head back to Los Angeles. Sort of like a circuit.'

In any conversation with Edison, Basie is never far from his mind. What were the

Count's special qualities? 'He always knew how to handle musicians. He never said anything, he respected your masculinity. He knew everybody in the band was a man, they had
responsibilities. He never got mad when you were late. Of course, the band was so great
you couldn't wait to get to work. It was always a pleasure to get up there on the stand and
start playing. Basie never fired anybody. He rode on the bus just like we did. There weren't
no cliques in the band, we were all just havin' fun.'

'Basie was subjected to the same thing we were subjected to in the South. You had to
really want to play to take trips through the South. Oh, they just belittle your masculinity

Count Basie Orchestra, 1941. *Rear, left to right*: Walter Page (b); Eli Robinson, Dicky Wells, Robert
Scott (tb); Buck Clayton, Ed Lewis, Al Killian, Harry Edison (t). *Front*: Jo Jones (d); Freddie Green (g);
Count Basie (p); Buddy Tate (ts); Tab Smith, Earle Warren (as); Jack Washington (bs); Don Byas (ts).

down there. You couldn't stop in a restaurant; sometimes they wouldn't even give you a
drink of water. We'd have to have the bus driver go get us something to eat. The thing
about it, they loved your entertainment, but after you got through playing with them they
didn't want to speak to you. You couldn't be a part of their friendship at all. When you
played for black dances, white people would be upstairs in the balcony. Sometimes at
dances they'd raise hell to get down there among the black people so they could dance
but, after the dance, they were ready to run you out of town. It was really humiliating.'

Because Edison lived through a period of extraordinary change, not least for African-Americans, he had interesting views on younger players and on the values prevalent in his early days. 'Musicians had different attitudes towards each other in those days. It was more of a brotherly thing. They had a camaraderie. They just loved each other. More than they do now. Well, that's because they have no big bands now. They don't know what it is to sit beside somebody day after day and have a friend. Nowadays guys become stars overnight, before they have proved themselves. I think Wynton Marsalis is the best of the lot because of his musical knowledge. A great concert trumpet player – he has adapted himself to playing jazz. He's going to tell you the truth because he's well-versed on music. He writes wonderfully. He has educated the kids and he's a good example for the youngsters to follow. Wynton has a lot of respect for the older musicians. That's the class that he has.'

'When I was, coming up in New York, nobody wanted to copy anybody. Nobody wanted to be an imitator. Although there was a lot of guys that tried to play like Louis Armstrong, they had their little things that mixed in with the Louis Armstrong style. Louis was the ambassador of the art form. He took jazz all over the world. If it had not been for Louis Armstrong I wouldn't be playing trumpet – I wouldn't be *trying* to play. He inspired me. And I think he inspired all trumpet players. Because, like Dizzy used to say, if you want to play a decent solo you have to play something

Louis Armstrong has [already] played. During my era, everybody wanted to be originators – I have always kept that in mind. If you've got a sound which you can be identified by, and a style you can be identified by, that's very important. Of course, you have to mix a little new in with the old but don't go to the extreme that you forget yourself.'

He remembered his early New York days with enthusiasm. 'Everything was in Harlem when I first went to New York. There was nothing downtown. I think they had two joints in the Village – the Vanguard and Cafe Society. Everything else was uptown, around 110th Street. Harlem was the centre of entertainment. Billie Holiday was singing on 138th Street, at a place called the Yeah Man Club. Don Redman was playing at Connie's Inn up there. Art Tatum was playing on 132nd Street at a place called the Birdcage. I couldn't go to sleep, I was afraid I'd miss something. You got off work at 4 o'clock in the morning and then you'd go to an after-hours spot, everybody crowding in. Monroe's Uptown House, or Dickie Wells, so many joints had music, live music. Charlie Shavers, Dizzy, all of us, we used to run around together.'

'I lost so much rest in New York, I just fell out one night there on Seventh Ave. Had to go to Harlem Hospital. Just needed some rest. Daytime, you'd see Duke walking down the street, you'd see Louis Armstrong on Seventh Avenue someplace. In the night-time, Tommy Dorsey, Harry James, Benny Goodman, all of them came uptown. It was safe, you could sit down on

Ethel Waters singing in the film *Stage Door Canteen*, 1943, accompanied by the Count Basie Orchestra including: Buck Clayton, Ed Lewis, Edison (t); Eli Robinson, Dicky Wells, (tb); Buddy Tate (ts); Jimmy Powell, Earle Warren (as); Jack Washington (bs); Don Byas (ts); Freddie Green (g); Walter Page (b); Jo Jones (d) and Count Basie (p).

the sidewalk and go to sleep. Nobody would bother you. I used to live on 110th Street and Seventh and it would be so hot you'd have to go over to Central Park and sleep!'

Edison had early links with Kansas City, the birthplace of the Basie band. 'I [first] went to Kansas City when I was very young. I was playing with a band in St. Louis called Jeter Pillars and we used to drive down to Kansas City. That band produced some good musicians. Jo Jones played with the band quite some time in St. Louis, and when Bennie Moten died, Basie got Jo Jones and Walter Page – they were both playing with Jeter Pillars then. [Bassist] Jimmy Blanton and [drummer] Sidney Catlett took their places. Of course, I had heard of Sid Catlett because he had played with Fletcher [Henderson] but I had never heard of Jimmy Blanton. He was only about twenty years old. We knew the importance of playing your instrument [well] but we had no idea that he [Blanton] was going to be that big an influence on the [other] bass players. His mother was a musician and he was an Indian too. [Edison is part Hopi Indian.] I think both of his parents were Indians. Well, you could tell, it was very obvious from his appearance.'

'I went to the Reno Club one night and heard the Basie band. Oh my goodness! He had Hot Lips Page, Jo Jones, Walter Page. He had Jack Washington, and Fiddler [Claude Williams], who was the first guitar player with the Basie band. He had Dan Minor, trombone player; he had Joe Keyes. Oh, he had a helluva band. That's the band John Hammond heard on the radio, caught 'em playing and went right down there and signed them up. Hot Lips Page, he was a great trumpet player. Whew, he was a giant.'

In those far-off euphoric times, many of Edison's peers fell prey to alcohol. 'That was the only thing everybody did in those days, was drink. There was no dope at all, everybody went to the bar because it was so cheap. You could get two drinks of whiskey for forty cents. I never was a drinker. I tried, but the aftermath was so horrible, with the headache and everything. I like to have a glass of wine but, otherwise, I don't care for alcohol. Drugs? I had a mother who I didn't want to upset; I know she would have just had a heart attack if

Edison with Buddy Tate and Lester Young. Dicky Wells (tb) is at far left. Count Basie Orchestra, 1940s.

she had ever heard I was using dope. She just passed away about two years ago; she was 92 years old. I thought maybe, if I stayed out of trouble, it would prolong her life. She is really responsible for my success because she taught me, in a rude way, right from wrong. When I did something wrong, I got beat up! They're talking about the cane now; that was an exercise in my house, the cane. Of course, I didn't have any father, they separated when I was five months old, so she was my everything.'

'I had to leave Columbus because my mother's mother passed away and I had no baby-sitter, so she sent me to Kentucky to live with my uncle and aunt. I stayed living on

Edison with bassist Len Skeat, Pizza Express, London, February 1988. Photo by Andrew Kirk, courtesy Ernie Garside.

their farm from the time I was five until I was twelve. He was a musician, never had no professional training – he worked in the coalmines. In fact, my uncle taught me how to play the scales on the trumpet. Kids around the neighbourhood, he used to try to get them interested in music. He had never had any lessons formally and neither have I, but whatever he taught me stuck with me.'

A recurring theme for Edison was always his appreciation of Billie Holiday. 'People didn't realise what a talent she was, what a stylist she was, until she had passed away. I think if she had been loved in those days like she's loved today, who knows? Men were her downfall. She chose those kind of men. That was her life. They were on the [same] self-destruction rampage themselves. The only one she had that was a square was Joe Guy, the trumpet player, but he ended up just like her. That's the life she wanted to lead and if she had wanted to change she would have. She loved everybody. She was generous to the point she'd take the clothes off her back and give them to you. She was a great buddy of mine. Plenty of times I didn't have any money, she had some, and we'd go to all the bars and hang out. She was just a great girl. And very voluptuous when I first met her, beautiful colour on her; she was a very attractive woman.'

Another musician whom Sweets always championed was tenor innovator Lester [Pres] Young. 'He had something that nobody else had. Everybody knew it, all the tenor players knew it, he had a different sound. Lester liked a lot of tenor players. He liked Bud Freeman, and Frankie Trumbauer was his idol. Pres respected all other players like Coleman Hawkins, Chu Berry, even Herschel [Evans] who was his counterpart in Basie's band. Pres didn't like Herschel's playing but, as a person, he would have gone to war for him. In fact, when Herschel first got sick, Pres was the first one to go to his room and start rubbing his legs.'

'I'm just not talking to you from what I've heard. I've been personally affiliated with these people and we've maintained a friendship over a period of years. When I first joined Basie's band, Lester Young was my room-mate. I miss his little anecdotes; he was very outspoken in his quiet way. He had a drummer one time and Pres didn't like the drummer. Anyway, after the job, the drummer asked Pres, "Pres, when was the last time we played together?" And Pres says, "Tonight. That's the last time we played together." What changed him? The army, he just *hated* the army. He didn't want to go, they put him in a padded cell there one time. Wouldn't let him play. They destroyed his future. He was unfortunate enough to be sent down south and they just broke him down. After that he was never the same. They even made him change the way that he played. Pres was just like all the rest of us, just liked to play. That's all we had to live for. You drive five or six hundred miles on the bus to the next job, get out without going to the [hotel] room, change on the bus, play the dance, get back on the bus and go to the next town. You had to love to play to do that.'

Would Edison consider retiring? 'What am I going to retire to? Golf or the pool? That would drive me crazy. You know, I got my doctorate this year from Holloway University, right outside of Syracuse, and I was among the first to be put in the International Jazz Hall of Fame in Florida. That makes up for a lot of humiliation you've been through. It's quite a consolation to feel that you have accomplished something. I've been blessed.'

Chapter 4

Art Farmer

Serious Art

Art Farmer, London, 1999. Photo by Berit Bolt.

Although Art Farmer's serious demeanour might have seemed off-putting, he would give his time freely once he knew that your enquiries were sensible. We talked first in London in 1985 and it was obvious that the trumpeter's attention to detail was special. Always modest, Art was scrupulous in answering letters, loaned photographs and dealt with questions carefully. I think this piece, based on a 1999 interview conducted a few months before his death, largely speaks for itself. He was an important musician and a dignified, erudite man. I liked him a lot.

In March 1999 Art Farmer came from his Vienna home to play a three-week season at the Pizza Express jazz club in London's Soho. This basement location had been doubled in size a few years previously without losing its qualities of intimacy and comfort, and it regularly provided a showcase for the best players of the day.

Rather than land Farmer with a moveable roster of accompanying musicians, club manager Peter Wallis decided that the Stan Tracey Trio should work with him for the duration of the engagement. Farmer and Tracey knew each other from earlier encounters at Ronnie Scott's Club in the sixties. Tracey, now in his seventies, has often been rated in awards and polls as the best British pianist and is renowned for his creativity. His partnership with Farmer appeared to promise plenty.

Tracey's trio, with his son Clark on drums and the young bassist Andy Cleyndert, can produce the kind of vibrant backdrop that any modern soloist should relish. Rather than the usual format of a visiting star teamed with local support this was to be a meeting of equals. But it was clear, when I visited the club during that 1999 stay, that Art was less than well. The 70 year-old brassman seemed frail, his instrumental command sometimes unsure. He sat more than he stood and kept his flurries short, the tone less centred than in the past, his playing a matter of sudden bursts. That's not to say that there were no real rewards, just that there were fewer than expected, with Tracey in surging form and Farmer showing flashes of brilliance only on standards.

Interestingly, much of the press coverage drew attention to Farmer's use of the flumpet – a specially created hybrid of trumpet and flugelhorn made for him by Dave Monette of Chicago, an innovator in the brass instrument world. (Monette made the streamlined trumpet used by Wynton Marsalis in the USA and in the UK by Guy Barker.) 'The trumpet gives you more projection than the flugelhorn and the flugelhorn has a warmer sound,' Art said. 'The flumpet mixes both qualities together.'

Did the idea for the flumpet originate with Farmer or Monette? 'Monette's idea,' he confirmed. 'It's made for a certain sound. It wasn't copied after the trumpet or the flugelhorn but it still has some of the properties of the trumpet and flugelhorn. Does it suit me? It depends on how long I keep it out of the case. I'm still working on it.'

Over the years, Farmer was a regular visitor to the UK, often touring as a single, play-ing one-nighters and concerts. These visits provided opportunities to spend time with him and he seemed happy to answer questions in his considered and patient way. He filled in the details of his period in Los Angeles for my research into the story of black jazz in California and contributed to the research of others published in *Central Avenue Sounds*.[1]

Lionel Hampton Orchestra, Switzerland, October 1952. *Left to right, standing*: unknown; Quincy Jones (t); Curley Hamner (d); Gigi Gryce (as); Monk Montgomery (b); Buster Cooper (tb); Farmer (t); unknown, unknown; Jimmy Cleveland (tb); Clifford Brown (t). *Seated*: Billy Mackel (g); unknown; Anthony Ortega (as); Clifford Solomon (ts). Photo courtesy Art Farmer.

He guarded his privacy closely but he was invariably courteous and co-operative to seri-ous interviewers.

It was obvious that he valued discretion. When I asked him whether he might write his autobiography, he said, 'I have ruled it out because there is so much personal that I would-n't want to talk about that a bio would seem to be dishonest with so much omitted. Maybe later.' He answered letters and lent photographs, and seemed thoughtful and cultivated, critical and well informed on the issues of the moment. Urbane yet modest, he was happy to draw praise away from himself while paying warm tributes to his peers.

When I arranged to see Art on his 1999 visit, at the flat in Dean Street provided for him by the club's owners, he appeared weary, asking, 'How long will this take?' He spoke in a monotone, keeping his comments brief, leaning back in the couch, but summoned up a smile when I took his picture. For no particular reason, Charles Mingus was the first name that was mentioned.

'I knew Mingus [in Los Angeles]. I met him. He was one of the first guys I heard about

Farmer with Gerry Mulligan in the film *The Subterraneans*, 1960.

when I first went to L.A. in 1945. I was told there was this fantastic bass player but he's temperamental.'

Apropos Mingus' reputation for smashing his bass to pieces in temper, Art said laconically, 'Yeah, well sometimes we would go and buy one for $10 in order to smash it just to impress people. I performed with him a little later on, just a night here, a night there. We recorded.'

Another player who impressed Farmer in those early days was trumpeter Benny Bailey. 'Well, he's still on the Continent. He used to come over here a lot with [the] Clarke-Boland

[Orchestra]. Well, I guess he's over 70 now. [Bailey was born in August 1925.] Benny and I do cross paths from time to time and he was, and is, an inspiration to me.' Altoist Jackie Kelso was another old colleague whose story is covered in *Central Avenue Sounds*. 'I saw him in Austria a couple of months ago with Basie. We were in Floyd Ray's band [in Los Angeles] in 1945 to '46. He could always play. . . still can.'

The much-admired Clarke-Boland band combined European musicians with expatriate Americans like Farmer and Bailey. 'I don't know how it came about,' said Art. 'I guess it had to do with Gigi Campi and Kenny Clarke and Francy Boland. They were the ones that desired to do something. It was a good band. I'm sorry it doesn't exist any more. Sometimes we would only play for a couple of weeks. If you'd get a string of dates you'd do them. Very, very special peple in that band. Like Ronnie Scott and the alto player Derek Humble.'

'What do I make of Stan Tracey? He's a wonderful player to play with. It's not just cliché, cliché; he always does something to interest the soloist. We're having fun. I'm just very happy to be here to play with him. A lot of times you have to play with this guy tonight, and that guy tomorrow night and that's really difficult. Well, he's fine. He's a serious musician from the word 'go'. He's always putting the best thing in that he can, and it's always interesting. His son plays good too. I'm glad to work with him.'

What was Art looking forward to? 'Oh, the same stuff. I'm all over the place. I go from the States to Kuwait. I spend half the time in the States now. You don't get anywhere if you don't travel. I have a couple of health problems. The doctors said I should stay home but I still want the challenge. I don't want to sit at home watching TV all day.'

'I can't say there is someone I'd like to play with; I also can't say that there is someone I don't want to play with. You know, whatever the circumstances, you can always learn something from whoever it is. So I guess, take it as it comes. I just want to keep my health, play better.'

What would he still like to achieve? 'I would like to make a good record. Gerald Wilson and I are talking about doing one. With his big band. That's about it. Man, I'm going to cut out now.'

With that our chat was over. He needed to rest. He showed me to the door, smiled and said good-bye. Less than seven months later, in October 1999, came the news that Art Farmer had died suddenly in New York. His British manager Ernie Garside filled in some of the background details about Art's poor state of health: 'You know what he was like on that last visit. I had a hard time with him. He couldn't even fix his own cuff links. He was confused and disoriented. He had a strange heart rhythm, had it for years. His hips were arthritic and he needed two hip replacements. Only, he said, for the first time in his life he'd made some money and he didn't want to give it away. He had these problems with short-term memory – he'd go a couple of streets away and couldn't remember how to get back. Maybe he'd had a mini-stroke and not realised it. Anyway he was released from hospital in New York and the woman he lived with said he seemed to have recovered his old self. He was sweeping up leaves and wanted to mow the lawn when suddenly he was taken ill and died from a heart attack.'

Garside and Farmer got on well. 'We were really best friends. We had lots of fun. We'd sit around laughing. He'd smile and I'd know he was laughing inside. That moustache made him look downbeat but he was very nice. We never had a wrong word. He was very kind. When he got slightly annoyed he would blush. I'd look out for that.'

'Like me, he was a real jazz fan. One time I was touring with Freddie Hubbard and we arrived at the North Sea Festival and here's Art Farmer in the lobby. He's extolling Freddie's greatness and Freddie looked at him and said, "Just play me a ballad." He knew that Art could wipe him out at that.'

Garside appreciated Farmer's loyalty and generosity. 'He made a lot of money out of that *Great Day in Harlem* film, doing talks and playing concerts. He was due to do a tour for me and I said he could cancel if he had some better things but he said, "I've been doing this for you since '64. It's not about money." We'd talk about the rhythm sections he'd get. He said, "When it's a bad rhythm section, it's a learning night. The next night you put the learning into practice. They all have the right to play."'

'Art played with Lester Young's quintet for a while. Lester wouldn't let him play solos, only the themes at the start and finish. Art was fascinated by Lester's vocabulary – he had his own language. This one time, Mr. Heath brings his son 'Tootie' [drummer Albert Heath] to play for Lester. Afterwards he said, "Mr Young, how did he go?" Lester says, "That bitch vonces nice." Art had no idea what it meant and we asked around and nobody else could ever tell us.'

It's good to remember Art as a kind of amused bystander, enjoying the small nonsenses of the jazz life, unphased by success and loyal to his friends. He had suffered many sadnesses – the loss of his treasured twin brother, the bassist Addison Farmer, troubled him, as did the deaths of his wife and his son – but he remained true to himself and generous in his appreciation of others.

His music was always distinctive, none of it tawdry or ill-considered, much of it profound, tinged by sadness perhaps, but ultimately life-enhancing. Of course, much the same can be said for the character and personality of the man himself.

Chapter 5

Herbie Jones

Ellington Extra

Herbie Jones rehearsing with Duke Ellington's orchestra, BBC-TV Theatre, London, February 1964. Photo © Val Wilmer.

Herbie Jones proved a willing if serious interviewee when photographer Ian Powell and I called on him at Fleming's Hotel in London, on the off-chance, in March 1964. He had joined Duke Ellington just months before and his story is valuable for the light it throws on the Florida scene, an under-researched area, and on the day-to-day world of jobbing musicians in New York. Although Duke described him as 'a great asset', Jones left the band in October 1968 to be with his family. He became the first director of Arts and Culture Inc, an alternative school in New York, and later directed the Bugle Corps of the Police Athletic League in Harlem. He died in the Bronx on March 19, 2001.

Herbie Jones joined the trumpet section of Duke Ellington's Famous Orchestra in Ceylon (now Sri Lanka) in October 1963. This somewhat unusual start to an Ellingtonian career came in the middle of Duke's Far Eastern tour, when Ray Nance had been taken ill and returned home. Happily, Herbie was well prepared for this Ducal emergency, being familiar with the book from previous brief stays with the band. As a long-serving member of Mercer Ellington's band, he had been 'loaned' to the senior Ellington on a number of occasions.

Born in Miami, Florida, on March 23rd 1926, Herbert Robert Jones later moved to New York. From his story, taped during an Ellington visit to Britain, it will be seen that a wide variety of activity was required of a musician in that city – particularly, if he wanted to eat regularly.

Herbie's childhood and early career were spent in Miami, where his father was drum major with a local band. He wanted his son to share his interest in music, and as both Herbie's parents were Seventh Day Adventists – a religion that forbade sports of any kind – young Jones was able to devote plenty of time to musical pursuits. His trumpet playing, which began when he was fifteen, was influenced by marching music and light classics.

'I mainly played church music and marches and it was not until I attended college that I really got the influence of jazz, particularly the big band style of the thirties. I was lead trumpeter in the collegiate orchestra, other members being Cannonball and Nat Adderley, who, though younger than me, were a tremendous influence. We played light classics and the jazz only came when a swing band was being organised. Being a lead man, I was needed in this band. I was pretty advanced as a reading musician, but never considered as a soloist.'

'After leaving school in 1944, I went on playing with the college band and we played for soldiers a great deal. It was wartime and Camp Gordon Johnson and Camp Dale were nearby. The band was Basie-style – four-teen pieces. Cannonball was a major part in all this – he liked Lester Young a lot in those days. Nat wasn't playing anything, but he was very outstanding as a vocalist. The Adderleys are a talented family and their father, a cornetist, had a great influ-ence on his kids. My main influence at this time was Roy Eldridge; I liked him a lot.'

Herbie left college before graduation, and, torn between commercial art and music as a career, decided that music offered the best openings. Musicians were in short supply due to the draft and Herbie soon found a job with the Rockland Dictators at the Rockland Palace in Miami. He was also encouraged to write for the Dictators – a fine house band playing for dancers. A line-up of two trumpets, two tenors and rhythm suggested interesting tonal possibilities and Herbie soon learned to exploit the full potential of this combina-tion. He remained with them from 1945 to 1949, the year he left for New York City.

'It was a very good job because I had the opportunity to write anything I wanted and to try a lot of different things with the band. Willis Jackson, the tenor player who has since had a big success, was in the band and Blue Mitchell played trumpet with us for a long time. He developed while he was alongside me at the Rockland. Funny thing, you can never tell, a man starts with you not playing well and all of a sudden he blossoms into something great. There were other fine musicians in the band who never had the chance to play with name bands. Miami is a very competitive town. The musicians who frequent it are of the best calibre, so you always have competition for the jobs you hold. [Bassist] Sam Jones was also in the group for a while and the Adderleys came down now and then to sit in. The band had two leaders: Richard Smothers, a trumpet player, and his suc-cessor, Sammy Williams, pianist and organist.'

Herbie also worked with Frank Brown's orchestra in Miami. Brown, of whom Herbie speaks highly as musician and man, had played with Louis Armstrong's and Cootie Williams' big bands. A trumpeter, he was also a good pianist and an outstanding writer whose arrangements were used by Armstrong, Williams and Lionel Hampton.

The move to New York resulted from Herbie's desire to progress and he enrolled at Juilliard, but after a year found it more practical to study music by practising the art in public. 'I started playing small dates like the Club Savannah downtown and the Savoy Ballroom with the Lucky Millinder Orchestra. When I joined in early 1950, Lucky had such wonderful names as Lammar Wright Sr., Jimmy Nottingham, Leon Merion, trumpets; Harold Johnson, tenor; Hilton Jefferson and Jimmy Powell, altos. I was with him whenever he played the Savoy, two or three weeks at a time, the bands changing rather frequently. Otherwise, I'd work with the bands of local dance musicians, not name players, and I managed to stay very busy that way. I was then lucky enough to start writing for the local bands – to supply them and keep their repertoire up to date. This kept me so occupied that I could stay in New York, avoid travelling and thus be among good musicians and learn their devices for arranging, and improve my ability. I was one of the type of musicians who'd work with you when you were in town but when you left town, I'd stay home. [But, doing that,] there's no opportunity to gain a name by leaving town.'

From 1951 to 1955, Herbie concentrated on his arranging but at weekends he led his own group (with Eric Dixon, tenor; Rick Henderson, alto; Buster Cooper, trombone; pianist Herman Foster; bassist Don Byron; and drummer Dave Bailey) keeping this band together for about four years, not working regularly but coming together whenever he found sufficient work. Their biggest break came with a season at the Savoy, a year before it closed. Drummer Ed Thigpen and a little-known but excellent tenor, Benny Brunswick, were with Herbie for this engagement.

In 1955, Jones met Mercer Ellington and began an association that was to last until 1960, renewed, of course, in the trumpet section of Duke Ellington's Famous Orchestra. 'I got the opportunity to play with Mercer on one or two dates. He had a wonderful band and we became very friendly. From that time I stayed with him as lead trumpet. In the band when I joined were Hilary Pritchett, a very good tenor player from Fats Green's local band; George Barrow, tenor; trumpeter Jimmy Harris, who had been with Mercer for years, and his regular trombonist Candy Ross. Joe Harris was the drummer and the

great Tom Whaley, copyist for Duke, did the arranging. It was a tightly-knit octet and Mercer's material was tremendous. It was the first time I became accustomed to that type of voicing. Mercer was very influenced by his father – the two of them voice differently from anyone. With Mercer we mostly did high society jobs at large ballrooms in Washington DC and New York.'

'At the same time I was working with Cab Calloway's band, at least from 1954 when I joined his Cotton Club Show. I was with Cab and Mercer at the same time. Whoever had the job [first], I was with him. I never broke away from one to go to the other. They both gave me the type of experience that I needed because to play lead in a show band and then go right into a jazz orchestra really takes some adjustment. I also worked with local bands, particularly with Frank Anderson's Panamanian band, playing Spanish music. Luis Russell's widow, Carline Ray, who plays great bass, was with Frank at the time and we had a very good tenor player, Walter Wheeler, a musician from the older era of jazz, and Clinton Thorburn, a great altoist, clarinettist and flautist. These were men you could marvel at how well they played without having a reputation. They all had day jobs.' Throughout this period Herbie kept the arrangements flowing, and was also copyist for Cab and Mercer.

Jones was called upon by Duke Ellington to play lead in the band at the 1956 Newport Jazz Festival, without rehearsal and without having heard the band in person before. Duke's band didn't necessarily put parts on the music stands, but Herbie remembered the wonderful feeling as the band blended right into his lead, although his sketchy special parts sometimes resulted in them continuing when he had stopped! Duke kept him on for several more days to listen to him play lead and then Herbie returned to New York to fulfil engagements to which he was committed. From 1960 until he joined Duke permanently, he worked with such bands as Buddy Johnson or Andy Kirk's weekend outfit. Otherwise he played with gig bands for one-night stands where no rehearsal time could be arranged. Only musicians whose performance is predictably professional are picked for such dates. Jones' lead playing made him much in demand, even with the exotic Spanish orchestras that abound in New York.

'At the time Duke Ellington called me to join his band in Ceylon, I had been writing more and more small group material, but I was in a rut to the extent that I thought I would form my own unit again and stop writing. Many of the men who played with me, even though in the big-time now, looked forward to me forming my group again. I was just on the verge of setting up things financially when the call came. I took over Nance's fourth book. It's called the fourth book, but it contains something of everything. You just sit down and play, because with Duke you may have four bars of lead and the next four bars you're playing fourth. Most of the lead is played by Cat Anderson because that is the sound of the band and he does very well.'

'Back from the tour, it was more or less up to Ray Nance to come back or not – he decided not, which was a big step because the names of Nance and Ellington have been synonymous for so long. Since then, I've been trying very hard to get some of the old standards up to date – ones they no longer have music for. I've written my whole book over so that I'm prepared if they call anything they haven't played for the last twenty years. I also did one of the things that was featured on my first English tour with Duke; it's called 'The Prowling Cat', an original by Cat [Anderson] which he gave to me to make an arrangement for the band. There are also two things for Cootie [Williams] – he gave me some arrangements he did with his large band, 'Caravan' and 'The Opener'. I recreated these arrangements for him and they're now in the book. Billy [Strayhorn] and Duke don't say too much but they wouldn't play them if they didn't meet the band's requirements.'

Chapter 6

Grover Mitchell

From Sideman to Front Man

Grover Mitchell, 1995. Photo courtesy Count Basie Enterprises Inc.

The following piece is based on two interviews with trombonist and bandleader Grover Mitchell. He was the perfect interviewee, thoughtful and good on detail. I wrote a number of magazine articles about Grover over a period of thirty years and interviewed him quite often.

The earlier interview, in May 1967, led to the first feature article about Mitchell to appear in a jazz magazine. Photographer Ian Powell and I had dropped in on him at the Green Park Hotel in London where he was staying with the other members of the Basie band and we hit it off with him straightaway

The second interview took place in 1998. After leaving Count Basie in 1970, Mitchell spent ten years playing in the Los Angeles studios. By 1980 he was ready to re-join the Chief and stayed on board until Basie's death in 1984, after which he set about forming his own big band. This was successful and the band played for President Clinton's inauguration. Even so, when Count Basie's organisation called him to replace Frank Foster as Director of the Basie Orchestra, Mitchell jumped at the chance.

Grover was enthusiastic yet demanding, and the bandsmen responded well to his leadership. The album to which he referred in the 1998 interview, Count Plays Duke, *won a Grammy, as did a live album with the New York Voices. The band toured and re-visited Ronnie Scott's Club in London in 1999, and everything seemed to be going well. All too soon, however, Grover was diagnosed with cancer and was forced to undergo a series of painful treatments. He stayed with the band, determined to carry on, his ex-wife Jamie and daughter Gail often travelling with him to help. We spoke regularly on the telephone and I was moved by his desire to continue in harness despite the onset of this terrible illness. He died on 6 August 2003 and I lost a true friend.*

Grover Mitchell was born in Alabama on March 17, 1930. His family was poor and they moved to Pittsburgh in 1938 where his father became a foundry supervisor. His original musical impetus came from his mother who could sing and play the piano. A kindly neighbour gave him a bugle and, at twelve, the trombone and tuition came free at public school. To a boy from a large family, this must have seemed a dream fulfilled.

Mitchell had been raised on the blues: his parents and brothers had records by Bessie Smith and Blind Lemon Jefferson. For years he had assumed blues to be the limits of music. School now opened his eyes to the immense possibilities of instrumental study. 'When I first picked up the trombone, I didn't even know what to call it – didn't know what the hell it was – I was very tall for a twelve-year old with long arms and they figured I could manipulate the instrument. This was at Westinghouse High. Albert Aarons, Mary Lou Williams, George Hudson and Erroll Garner all started their music there and the same teacher that helped them, Carl McVicker, has done a lot for many in professional music.'

Caught up in music from that very first day, the young Mitchell listened and learned from

Mitchell, in London with the Count Basie Orchestra, May 1967. Photo by Ian Powell.

Mitchell with Ike Bell, (former trumpeter with Mitchell's Bay Area big band), San Francisco. Photo courtesy Ike Bell.

Will Bradley, Jack Teagarden and the prettiest player of them all, Tommy Dorsey. Soon he began to play in the kid bands that sprang up and he gradually became aware of other names such as trombonists Benny Morton and J.C. Higginbotham. His friends introduced him to records and he listened to the big band broadcasts that had a seminal influence on so many musicians, including quite a few by Count Basie and his orchestra. The music of Eddie Heywood with, first, Vic Dickenson, and then Henry Coker, served further to inspire the young trombonist. Then, at sixteen, there were Bill Harris and J.J. Johnson to upset everything: turning the horn inside out, as it were.

Mitchell played with youngsters from his own and other schools, including later professionals like Stanley Turrentine, Tommy Turrentine, Al Aarons and the pianists Ahmad Jamal and Horace Parlan. The bands, of varying sizes, usually played stock arrangements and Dakota Staton was often the vocalist. Mitchell was now fairly proficient and receiving payment for regular weekend work around Pittsburgh. 'Then I ran off with a couple of bands and got stranded down in Texas. I was supposed to be in school but I joined a band led by a woman bandleader, Amora Wilson, ex-baritone player with the [International] Sweethearts of Rhythm. Everything went wrong and the tour folded in San Antonio, 1500 miles from home.'

Only seventeen and scared, Mitchell sent home for his fare. Then he set off for Indianapolis and joined the big band led by Chicago trumpeter King Kolax. 'He was known for these young bands; [they] probably weren't particularly good but they gave us a training ground. We used to ride in the bus to these funny little dance towns. I can recall some fine musicians: Benny Powell was there, and we had a saxophone player from Detroit named Emmet Mitchell, and a good pianist, Charlie Cottrell. You know, Kolax had been with Billy Eckstine's band, with Fats Navarro, Miles Davis and the others so that made him look even more illustrious to me. This band was new and the arrangements he had were out of Billy's band. We couldn't play the things, but we tried.'

While in Indianapolis, Mitchell saw trombonists Slide Hampton and J.J. Johnson for the first time, and emulated Johnson by working for a few months with Snookum Russell, Johnson's early employer. This band was another touring territory unit, and while such ensembles could scarcely afford top arranger's fees, Mitchell regretted their passing. As a training ground for aspiring instrumentalists and arrangers, they were invaluable. There were also kindred spirits among the musicians: trumpeter Fats Ford and a trombonist, Billy Davis, who should, according to Mitchell, have made it, were with the band.

Touring down in Kentucky, Tennessee, Alabama, on into Arkansas and Texas, Mitchell had his fill of segregated dances and grinding travel. Almost a seasoned professional, he decided to return at last to Pittsburgh to job around with local bands: particularly that of Walt Harper, a respected leader and musical entrepreneur.[1]

In 1950, at the age of twenty, Mitchell joined a Marine Corps infantry unit in South Carolina. After a year, he transferred to California and was able to play music again. 'Most military bands did a lot of civilian appearances and you couldn't appear in public in South Carolina with an integrated group. They were usually pretty diplomatic about it – they'd say you failed the audition and, naturally, you knew what was happening. So I went to California. They looked through my records and asked why I wasn't in the band. I was moved to the marching band right away and I bunked next to Oliver Nelson – who was playing and writing as well as he does now. A few people must have liked us because they took Oliver and me out and put us in the Camp Pendleton Post Radio and TV Band. We had a weekly programme encouraging people to enlist.'

Posted later to Treasure Island, near San Francisco, Mitchell, like many more before and since, fell for that city. Oliver Nelson, meanwhile, was in Japan and Mitchell began a pleasurable period of jamming around town. 'I used to go out and jam every night with Alex Nelson, a good baritone player and a friend of mine. Gerald Wilson had a little band at a place called the Champagne Supper Club with Teddy Edwards on tenor, and the alto player Pony Poindexter was at another club. I was soon pooped up in the bebop movement and I played like a cross between Bill Harris and Bennie Green. After my discharge, I could never get this place [San Francisco] out of my mind – it seemed like everybody had somewhere to play, everybody was working.'

Back in Pittsburgh in 1953, Mitchell concentrated on an education that had been interrupted by his earlier musical travels. He had taken correspondence courses while in the marines and finished high school but hankered now for a college course and entered business school through the G.I. Bill of Rights. He took entrance examinations to Pittsburgh and Duquesne Universities and passed both. Taking classes in business administration might seem unusual for so dedicated a musician, but Mitchell visualised better employment opportunities from such stud-

ies. As for music, private tuition continued as did jobs with Walt Harper. These, combined with a day-time truck driving job, nearly led to a breakdown in health. He married in 1955 and began to realise that a choice was inevitable. Full-time music won and the books were put aside. Satisfied by good marks in college, Mitchell felt that he had proved his academic ability, at least to himself.

In addition to working with Harper, he had played with other bands passing through Pittsburgh, notably Tiny Bradshaw and Paul Williams. With Bradshaw, there had been the tenor player Red Prysock.[2] Bradshaw, primarily a showman, kept himself remote as far as the sidemen were concerned. He functioned as front man and entertainer and according to Mitchell, was a mediocre pianist.

Mitchell also worked with Williams – the 'Hucklebuck' man – on much the same casual basis but once replaced Buster Cooper for a rather longer period pending Cooper's return.[3] In the band was Lammar Wright Sr. on trumpet, a musician who kept his ability to play high and strong throughout his career. But Mitchell turned down Williams' offer of a permanent job. He was already intent on California and moved there for good – settling in San Francisco, of course – in 1957.

Once there, he found work a little scarcer than he remembered. Taking a day job on the Chevrolet assembly line, he joined two good local rehearsal bands, led by Eddy Walker and Bruce Salvine. Not long after, he started a rehearsal group of his own in partnership with pianist and arranger Cedric Haywood, an excellent but completely underrated musician, according to Mitchell. Haywood later left to tour Europe with Kid Ory, and frequently recorded with him.

At this stage a few house-band jobs began to come Mitchell's way, usually from Facks nightclub where bassist Vernon Alley augmented the resident trio to accompany big name singers. Mitchell now realised his original ambition and became a full time musician. At first,

Vocalist Mary Stallings with Mitchell in London for the Count Basie UK tour, May 1967. Photo by Ian Powell.

things went well but inevitably the irregular pattern of casual dance jobs and club dates meant that he needed a day job again. This time it was carrying mail for the Post Office, while still taking every musical opportunity going. A three-week road tour with Lionel Hampton provided a brief lift but helped little in achieving Mitchell's main objective, to establish himself in San Francisco itself.

Earl Hines now began to use the Mitchell rehearsal band for various local engage-ments.[4] 'We all had day jobs and we'd just go out and play gigs. Earl Hines used us as the Earl Hines Orchestra: it was such a good band that he considered recording it.'

Nor was Hines the only admirer. Duke Ellington and Johnny Hodges came to listen and brought other Ellingtonians. When Hodges was sidelined by an ulcer attack, Mitchell was invited to play his book on trombone, sitting in the illustrious Ellington reed section for the complete two-week engagement at Facks. Later, when Juan Tizol left the band, Mitchell joined them in Las Vegas – briefly, as it turned out, as the band broke up soon after due to Duke's absence during the making of the film *Paris Blues*. Mitchell had missed out on a permanent Ellington proposition and was back to the casual routine with which he was already so familiar. He ran a small group with Jimmy Lomba doubling on tenor and baritone; trumpeter Len Haggard, pianist Cedric Haywood, and Ray Fisher on drums.[5] The band played dance jobs, Haywood's fine arrangements making them sound like a miniature Basie orchestra.

Mitchell's disappointment over the frustrating near-job with Ellington now began to make him doubt his continued career in music. At this point, in September 1962, he received an unexpected call from Henry Snodgrass, Basie's band manager, inviting him to join the band the following January. The band would then have four trombones. Elated, Mitchell accepted, and was further surprised to hear three days later that the offer was now immediate – Rufus Wagner having suddenly decided to leave. Wagner, who suffered from high blood pressure, died only a short while later.

Mitchell joined the band in New York, playing lead straight away. Whether Basie intended this is not clear. Certainly Mitchell had the range and read well. Perhaps more to the point, Henry Coker was happy to hand him the privilege of playing first. Mitchell retained a healthy admiration for Coker's jazz playing and Benny Powell, Coker and Mitchell formed a considerable trio, apparently enjoying many good times together. Powell left shortly before the 1963 European tour, to be replaced by Bill Hughes on bass trombone, back from retirement and the joys of domesticity.[6]

Mitchell also had his own solo features with the Basie Orchestra: often ballads including Benny Carter's 'Sunset Glow', and 'If I Should Ever Leave You' from *Camelot*. Asked for a personal view of the Basie band and its boss, he reflected on his good fortune: 'I keep reminding myself you can't go any higher as far as playing in bands on the road. I try to keep separated the respect I'm getting because of my musicianship and the respect because I'm with Basie.'

'He's always been fair with me about money,' he added. 'A lot of people underestimate Basie the man – it's still his band and if you want anything done concerning yourself, you got to go to Basie. He's the boss – whether you stay in the band or leave depends on how he hears you in there. When I came in it was to play a jazz chair – to Basie I was no jazz player but I guess he just liked my tone. As long as Basie lives, I'm afraid you're going to have that band and he'll shuffle the personnel around till he gets what he wants to hear.'

'As for the trombones, well, we're always trying to do a little better every night – it's a good band, no complaints about that. . .'

* * *

When I interviewed Mitchell again, in March 1998, 30 years after those comments were made, Basie had gone but his band was still travelling the world. Grover was now leading it for a two-week sojourn at Ronnie Scott's Club. Audiences were enthusiastic, and sufficient in number to justify a speedy return booking for the band. What's more, this sometimes lacklustre collective seemed to have rediscovered its true self: there were smiling faces on the bandstand and a palpable sense of musical joie-de-vivre. Just like the Basie band of old, in fact. Or as one breathless fan put it, 'They've brought back the excitement.'

Mitchell with the Count Basie Orchestra, New York City, 1995. *Standing, from left*: Cleveland Eaton (b); George Caldwell (p); Charlton Johnson (g); Dave Gibson (d); Manny Boyd (as); Bob Ojeda (t); Bill Hughes (b-tb); Alvin Walker (tb); Derrick Gardner (t); Chris Murrell (v). *Seated*: Brad Leali (as); Clarence Banks, Mel Wanzo (tb); Kenny Hing (ts); Mitchell, Mike Williams, Scotty Barnhart (t); Doug Miller (ts); John Williams (bs). Photo courtesy Count Basie Enterprises Inc.

An avuncular taskmaster, Mitchell had succeeded Frank Foster as Musical Director in July 1995. And this at a time when he had been busily promoting his own first-class big band. So why had he succumbed to the Basie office's call? Mitchell leaned forward and smiled: 'I went down there with the intention of saying no, to be honest with you. However, I really wasn't making it on my own and I needed money. Aaron Woodward [President of Count Basie Enterprises] offered me a goodly amount of money, and proper control. He said I could do anything that I wanted to do. That was a big factor.'

Mitchell set to work: 'I'd been through some good versions of Basie's band and I had a pretty good idea of what it should sound like. I wasn't happy with the way the band was sounding, or some of the people in it. To me, they were misfits – people who, in the days of Count Basie himself, would not have been there. It was kinda difficult at first: two or three of them were telling me how it was going to be, not asking me how it was gonna be. You've known me a few years so you know how that went down!'

One decisive factor in the band's resurgent spirit was the return of Butch Miles, who worked for the Chief in the seventies. 'I've always loved Butch Miles – he is one of the best drummers this band ever had. I didn't think I could get Butch, but he was interested in coming back. Butch is a natural – he brings fire, excitement and dedication. Butch was born to play with this band.'

Having enjoyed a degree of success in running his own orchestra, Mitchell had clear ideas about the Basie band's shape and direction. 'I want to upgrade the bookings back to the level that we were doing when Basie was here. We have to record more, especially this version of the band. It has to be recorded,' he urged. 'I want to do two recordings a year: well thought-out organised projects on which we can tour. I've been doing very well based on the old things I've dug out, but that's got its limits. I don't intend to come back next year doing the *same things*.'

Mitchell handled musical policy but took soundings from his senior sidemen when it came to selecting material to play:

'Actually, they have been very, very happy that I pull out all these old things. I've not had any complaints about the way things are going. Until now, for a lot of the younger guys, the old charts were just records that they had heard, and they're tickled to death to be playing these things. You see some kid, he's real happy to be playing a part that Joe Newman played, or Thad [Jones], or Snooky [Young].'

And how did Mitchell see the band's future? 'We have a project that even Basie wanted to do: to play Ellington-Strayhorn tunes, not like Ellington, but like we play.[7] There's a really good stack of music in there. We should have recorded that by now. We did a symphony programme with the Detroit Symphony for four days to standing ovations every night. I can't tell you how beautiful I thought it was. I want to do more of that.'

'We have to find other venues. We can't just keep doing what we're doing. We have to stay fresh and invent new ways to present this band to people. I'd like to do an album with Benny Golson – he's a great writer and I'm keen for J.J. Johnson to write an album for this band. There are others. Jimmy Heath, he writes really well, and a couple of guys in the band, Bob Ojeda and Doug Miller, they're good writers. I'll maybe do a couple myself. Frank Wess is still around. . . I'd love to utilise him.'

Grover was bullish about the band's solo strengths. 'Kenny Hing is probably as good a tenor player as there has ever been. All of the trumpets are good: Bob Ojeda can really do it; Scotty Barnhart, he's a young, new talent, he's always ready, and Shawn Edmonds is really moving. The trombone player, Alvin Walker, has developed very well. Manny [Boyd, alto sax] is an excellent soloist, Brad [Leali, alto sax] is a coming giant and tenorist Doug Miller is an excellent player. As for the pianist, Terence Conley, I don't want anybody coming in here trying to be Count Basie; he was too special for that. Sure, there's some kinds of generic licks Terence has to play; otherwise I want him to be Terence Conley. He's got so much talent.'

As for Grover's own position: 'I'm able to be the bandleader I wanted to be. All of the things I fantasised about in terms of how to run a band, I've been able to exercise here. You don't have to force evolution on this band, it just grows. And that's still happenin'.'

Chapter 7

Warren Vaché

Modern Mainstreamer

Warren Vaché at the Pizza Express, London, January 1997. Photo by Berit Bolt.

Cornetist Warren Vaché was once described to me by drummer Oliver Jackson as 'a genius'. That may or may not be true, but it's safe to say that he's one of the most creative jazz musicians at work today. Although pigeon-holed early on as a dixielander, Warren is far more than that as evidenced by his recent inclusion in top-level touring groups. He's the epitome of the modern mainstreamer: focussed and determined to make his mark.

Since we shared a morning's conversation at the Hogarth Hotel in London's Earls Court in May 1993, Warren's career has gathered pace and momentum. He has recorded with trusted associates, been through some personal turbulence, and works regularly in the UK where he is a particular favourite. As can be discerned from the interview reported below, he is a stimulating companion with a sharp intellect who is seldom slow to voice his views. It's always a pleasure to hear him play and to catch up on his news.

Warren Vaché is the consummate professional, travelling to every corner of the jazz world, cornet case in hand and portable laptop computer slung over his shoulder. He'll print out his schedule at the drop of a megabyte and, when asked for information, consults his well-programmed electronic organiser. It's all a long way from the romantic view of the jazz musician as hapless itinerant.

Swathed in a Middlesex County Cricket Club sweater, the fruit of a first-ever visit to Lords with British musicians John Barnes and Roy Williams, Vaché talked, during his 1993 London stay, about his recording plans. 'I've just signed a record deal with Muse, out of New York. Joe Fields is the guy who produces. It's been three years since I did a record for Concord – they're never writing, they're not calling, so I had to take the bull by horns. Frankly, I'd been fallow for too long.'

'I'd done a record with a guitarist named Joe Puma for Muse, and after we did the recording, Joe [Fields] called and asked would I be interested in a deal. I said yes, because he seems a little more tuned in to what I want to do these days. I wanted to record with a more modern rhythm section: with a different sort of drummer like Billy Hart; with Michael Moore [bass], and pianist Richard Wyands – top sorts of guys.'

The cornetist believes that working with someone of Wyands' calibre is an aid to progress. 'Richard Wyands, first of all, is an amazing musician, an unsung hero really, absolutely magnificent. He's also one of the world's best compers. If I'm playing a solo and I'm starting to – what's the word? – extend myself, Richard will find just the right combination of notes to play. In other words, he's listening to my line rather than just pounding away, and very often will justify exactly the way I intuited the harmony. Rhythmically, he doesn't lock things in; he swings like mad, yet he does it with the minimum of fuss.'

Anyone who has followed Warren Vaché's musical development since the mid-seventies knows that he hates to be confined. His playing continues to evolve: 'This is not one of those things where you can say I'm going from A to B. It has a lot to do with what I was

Vaché at the Concorde Club, Eastleigh, Hampshire, 1990. Photo by Ian Powell.

able to accomplish with the instrument ten years ago, as opposed to what I can accomplish with it now; what my harmonic sense was ten years ago and what it is now. It's all very different.'

'You constantly learn. I'm not studying formally, as I'm on the road eight months a year, but I went back to some of the books I looked at in college, like Rimsky-Korsakov on orchestration and the Piston book on harmony. Also, I took piano lessons in the early eighties with a guy named Tony Aless so I have a lot of material from that, and I'm going back through my notes. I could always hear the colour of a chord; a major chord is a much different colour than a minor as opposed to a diminished chord. What I didn't have together was all the nuts and bolts to go with this.'

Vaché's mobile version of the jazz life sometimes allows him to attain artistic heights that other musicians seldom achieve, but it isn't easy. 'When it's right, it's a very communicative thing. It doesn't happen all the time, but that's all we play for – that 35 seconds when you really get it right. You can imagine doing these one-nighter tours in Europe in the summer, hitting every night, getting up and getting a plane every day; the energy level drains away. It's not a question of being fit, it's more a question of having the energy to concentrate. In my particular situation – I guess it's the same with most jazz musicians – we're pieces of a human jigsaw which promoters play games with, so that very seldom do we have the opportunity to put something together, and stay with it, and develop that sort of intuitive feeling into something you can count on. Most of the time, we're pieces on the human chessboard,' he emphasised.

'These days, there's more damned marketing than there is playing music. Everybody I

Vaché with veteran British trumpeter, Nat Gonella, Concorde Club, 1990. Photo by Ian Powell.

know has got a fax machine and a computer and we're all busy hustling up the next six months. That's the way it is.' Vaché knows that new recordings matter too, hence his frustration with Concord, the label with which he was associated for fourteen years. He says that Concord were unsympathetic in his attempts to push for better distribution of his records in Europe. More recent recordings have been with independent labels: 'One was with André Villeger, that was done in France. That was a very good band. We toured for a summer with André, Richard Wyands, Reggie Johnson [bass] and drummer Alvin Queen. I was really interested in learning some bebop heads and tunes, and playing more in that way.'

All of which prompts a question about Vaché's present playing. Are we talking about a closet bebopper here? 'That's never going to happen because my sound concept isn't quite that way. It ain't gonna work. Doesn't translate like that. What I'm going to try to do is to take some of the harmonies and some of the flavour. I love those [bebop] records, always did. What's not to love? I mean, I'm still a Blue Mitchell fan. And there ain't no trumpet player worth his salt, in my estimation, that's not going to tell you he loves *both* Louis Armstrong *and* Clifford Brown.'

Vaché finds that many promoters are insensitive and lack awareness. 'It's one of the battles I have to fight almost on a daily basis. It's to get people to let me do what I would like to do. Why don't you just let me play? I'll tell you who I want, and I'll put it together and we'll make a budget. But no, they want to put together these magic all-star bands, as if we're going to have this unique-sounding little big band just because we're all individuals. It don't work that way. We end up playing 'Undecided' or 'Take the A Train' and everybody steps on everybody's else's toes, hunting for an inside part. That's why I quit the Newport All-Stars in 1992, after ten years. It was a very nice experience and I was very happy to do it, and it was fun working with Clark Terry – it's just that it's not very satisfying to play in yet another jam session nine-horn front line.'

Earlier versions of the Newport All-Stars band teamed Vaché with saxophonists Scott Hamilton, Norris Turney and Harold Ashby. 'Basically, that worked a lot better than the current edition of the band, I think, because Harold had that Ellington experience and he could find that fourth note. He could harmonise anything – find that note on the bottom, the 'out' one, that makes the whole texture. Without Harold the band lost

that flavour and for me it was never the same. Harold was the one that sparked that band, not only for his musicality but his personality. Harold's a real pistol.'

Mention of Hamilton, an early companion on Concord sessions, and frequent touring partner, led, inevitably, to a question about their current association. Would they play together again? 'Of course we will. It's just a question of economics at the moment. We're both in the same position, in that, musically, if we really tell the truth, all we want to do is play alone. That's where the most growth is going to come from, and the most satisfaction. I'm sure the two of us would be happy to work together: it's just that we'd both have to take a pay cut in order to do it.'

Vaché admitted that his chosen role placed exceptional burdens on both himself and his family. 'Sure, there's a downside. When I first started doing this, what was I? 25 or 27, full of piss and vinegar, and ready to go out and conquer the world. I'll preface this by saying I don't have any regrets, I've met a lot of people and made a lot of great friends and got a lot of satisfaction from what I'm doing. But when you reach the magic age of 40 and you have a couple of children, then every now and then you want to sit down in that chair at home. The armchair by the hearth, a cup of tea and a book, that's all I really want. I don't get much time off and when I am home, I'm always on the phone hustling.'

'There's always a process of adjusting to circumstances. If I'm home for two weeks and then I go away for a month or

Vaché with Scott Hamilton, Pizza Express, London, December 1996. Photo by Berit Bolt.

two months at a time, I've got to adjust to being alone, which takes a week to three weeks. OK, then you go home and now I'm used to being alone. My wife is used to running the house without me and it takes two weeks for us to figure out how to step around the house without annoying each other. It's a constant state of flux. I do have a great commitment to music but if I could find a way to get off the damn road, I think I would tomorrow. But I've been saying this for at least ten years.'

'Opportunities? They're rapidly closing. There used to be a thing in colleges where a person with a certain reputation could get an adjunct professorship or a full professorship with tenure, and still have a light enough schedule to take off on tour, three months a year maybe. Kenny Barron has a very good job at Rutgers, sort of artist in residence. That's the ideal, Kenny's situation. But academia has been hit by the same depression as the rest of us, so these jobs are plums, and they're not necessarily available.'

For all that, Vaché is determined to continue the process of artistic growth. Encouraged by his father, bassist Warren Vaché Sr, he listened to all the jazz greats on record as a youngster, absorbing their influence, and remembers advice given by trumpeter Buck Clayton in a 1940s magazine article. 'Asked, "Do you have any advice for an aspiring trumpet player?" Buck said, "Listen to everybody and steal. You can steal note by note, because you're never going to sound like them anyway. This way you get some new words in your vocabulary." Yes, I'll take things from others like phrases, the ways around a set of changes, attack, dynamics, vibrato, little signature things, and use them in my own way. I think that's allowed. No, I'm not where I want to be yet but I'm much closer along. At the age of 40, I can realistically expect another twenty years of playing. After that, unless you happen to be someone who's a physical marvel, like Kenny Baker, you're gonna have a little trouble making the effort to get there. Physically, it's a demanding instrument, so it's time for me to hunker down and concentrate 'cause there's only twenty more years to do it. I'm a little more sure of myself now and a little less prone to the cheap shot to get audience approval. There will be no shark-skin outfits, no iridescent pants and no jumping up and down!'

Political correctness being the hot topic it is in the USA, I was interested to know Vaché's views on the question of the racial divide in jazz. Is it appropriate for white players to operate in an arena where black musicians have made all the running? 'I don't find anything wrong with that. Music is there for anyone. If I've been given the ears to be able to hear and appreciate this music, why shouldn't I be able to use it and incorporate it in my tiny little career? As to Roy Hargrove and Wynton Marsalis, God bless them, Wynton can fill a football stadium and I have trouble filling the Pizza Express! OK, so I'm not flavour of the month: I have to put my head down and keep working to feed my family, and I manage to do that with what I consider to be a fair amount of artistic integrity.'

'Wynton is a very, very, good trumpet player artistically but, when it comes to jazz, I have some differences with him. I've read and heard lectures that Wynton's given where he says white people can't play jazz. If that's the way he feels, I'm very sorry for him. I grew up playing at Condon's with the likes of Vic Dickenson who I'm sure never made a pile of money, but had a wonderful time. I've been playing with black musicians, admittedly mostly older ones, all my life. It's never been an issue until recently. Why? Here my cynicism comes to the fore and I'm going to tell you: I think a great deal of it has to do with marketing. It's a lovely point of sale and as long as they can get the guy in the street buying it, then OK.'

Vaché's bassist father was a dedicated dixieland and dance band enthusiast who earned his living as a salesman but always maintained a stake in the music business through his involvement with weekend club work. He raised his sons, Warren and clarinettist Alan, to stand their corner when it came to divergent musical opinions. 'In high school days, we'd have these violent dinner table arguments because I became enamoured of Miles, and more modern things, and he was telling me why that was off. It was a real knockdown drag-out thing. But at least that forced me to develop some sort of aesthetic of my own. I didn't have to agree with him, but I had to be damn sure of what I was saying.'

In his latter years, the elder Vaché became a much-respected author and journalist, publishing fine biographies of trumpeter Pee Wee Erwin and pianist Claude Hopkins. His son admired his commitment: 'He's so directed. At the age of 78, he gets up every day and just works at that typewriter from sun-up to sundown. Right now, he's doggedly pursuing getting a publisher for a new book based on a series of articles on the great songwriters.[1] And he keeps his band going, the Syncopatin' Six, although the recession is hitting him like everybody else. He's quite a unique individual. He had this huge room with wall-to-wall 78s and, at ten years old, if I wanted to get a record down and play it, he said go ahead. I'd come home from school and I'd put Louis Armstrong records on and do my homework. It was a lovely direction for my life although it sorta kept me out of the mainstream among my generation.'

At the Pizza Express, June 2001. Photo by Berit Bolt.

This orientation towards traditional jazz and swing later allowed the fledgling cornetist a chance to play regularly alongside many of the great jazzmen then coming to the end of their careers. After playing his fair share of Polish weddings and 'Your Father's Moustache' jobs to fund his way through college, Vaché was 'doing seven or eight gigs a week, anything that came up and paid a dollar I went out and did. The kind of music didn't matter – as long as I was playing the horn, it was OK. During that time my old man got me to take lessons from Pee Wee Erwin, and one of the deeper and more satisfying relationships of my life developed then. Pee Wee was a magnificent trumpet player who was very well trained. At the age of nine, he could play the 'Carnival of Venice' with his father's brass band in Nebraska! Also, Pee Wee would recommend me for things he couldn't do. I'd get way over my head but I'd get by. Then there were some auditions for a Broadway show called *Doctor Jazz*. Sy Oliver and Luther Henderson were doing the music and they wanted a white dixieland band and a black dixieland band so my brother and I went over and we auditioned with a bunch of people we knew. We got the job and it, of course, failed miserably, and ended about two days after it opened.'

Abortive or not, this experience led to a call from Benny Goodman and, 'The next thing I knew I was on a plane up to New Hampshire and standing on a stage with Hank Jones, Slam Stewart, Connie Kay, Urbie Green, Zoot Sims and Benny Goodman. I was very scared but a set of brass balls and a big mouth will get you through a lot! After that, I just spent the next ten years really scufflin' 'cause I did not know a lot of those tunes. I hadn't really played jazz. All those Polish weddings may have helped the chops but they didn't help me get into what the idiom was about.'

'Although I was with Benny for ten years, he didn't work quite as much as you would have figured. So, at the same time, I'd be working six nights a week at Condon's and then Benny would get a night or two on the road so I'd put a sub in Condon's and go out and do it. Sure, the guys were helpful: Urbie would take me in the backroom and teach me the melody if he'd see me scuffling. Zoot was very helpful, only his idea was more to give you a drink. Hank always had the patience to tell me what the [harmonic] change was, with a smile, when in fact he knew damn well I should have been hearing it for myself.' Goodman's musicianship and creativity impressed Vaché, and he told me appreciatively of the great man giving him impromptu lessons on breath control and dynamics.

He also recalled Vic Dickenson taking time to spell out his melodic responsibilities as lead man in a dixieland band. It's clear from all this that Vaché himself was always a perceptive student of the jazz life, convinced of the genuine contribution he could make to the music's furtherance. What of the future for Warren Vaché? 'Well, there is certainly more to be done in terms of communicating through music, in terms of harmony and approaches to music. I'd like to start writing songs, I'd like to put a band together; I'd like to be more in control of the musical situation and I'd like to get my career to the point where I can guarantee myself at least a month off a year to be with my kids.'

Speaking about his British musical companions, Vaché enthused over 'marvellous musicians here: people like Brian Lemon, Colin Purbrook, Dave Green, Allan Ganley, Dave Cliff and Alec Dankworth. The level was always high – it was just a question of whether I could get to play with them or not. After ten years of stamping my foot and acting like a petulant child, they give me the people I ask for now,' he laughs.

It's little wonder our local musicians vie so willingly to play with a man for whom jazz creativity is about 'conveying a good feeling, displaying some emotion and intelligence and testing yourself all the time.'

Chapter 8

Britt Woodman

Mingus and the Duke

Britt Woodman with Duke Ellington's orchestra, 1951. Photo courtesy Britt Woodman.

I first conducted a lengthy interview with trombonist Britt Woodman at the North Sea Jazz Festival in 1983 and was surprised when he told me that he was very nervous about playing as a soloist. After all, he had tasted jazz fame as an important member of the Duke Ellington Orchestra. Surely there was nothing to fear? Reassured by his wife Clara, Britt went on to play superbly that night.

We met up again at the Nice Jazz Festival and then in London when Britt began to tour each summer with the Mingus Big Band, and spent very happy times talking about his career and early days in California. The interview on which this piece is based dates from the band's 1999 visit to London. Soon afterwards, Britt rejoined his brothers in California and, sadly, suffered a chronic breakdown in his health. This lovely man died in Los Angeles in October 2000.

When Britt Woodman laughed, which he did often, his face exploded in a minor tornado of glee. Mirth appeared to engulf him momentarily as he recalled his time with the Duke Ellington Orchestra and the strength of feeling aroused in some of its members by their forceful band mate, the trumpeter, William 'Cat' Anderson.

'Sam Woodyard kept a pistol, Clark Terry kept a knife, and Juan Tizol kept a knife – all for Cat Anderson!' You sensed that this genial man could regale you with stories like this all day, highlighting the foibles of his past associates without ever becoming judgmental. The California-born trombonist, whose career started in the mid-1930s, left his New York home during the summers of 1998 and 1999 to return to the road in his late seventies. 'There weren't too many one-nighters, so I thought I could make it,' he said, midway into the Mingus Big Band's one-week stay at Ronnie Scott's Club in London in August 1999.[1]

Just as he had the previous year, Britt joined the band for its annual European tour. He grew up with Charles Mingus in Watts, south of central Los Angeles and could recall their childhood days, early musical experiences and continuing associations seemingly at will. 'If Charles could hear this band he'd be very proud. He never had a big band sound like this,' he affirmed.

Far more than a mere custodian of the Mingus past, Britt was a powerful stylist whose take on the blues could still the noisy Scott's crowd and bring a warm smile from his section leader, the dread-locked Akili Jamal Haynes, a trombonist of formidable talent, then barely into his mid-twenties. In turn, Britt much appreciated Haynes, a young veteran of Illinois Jacquet's big band and Lester Bowie's Brass Fantasy. 'Jamal is wonderful, such a talent,' he said. For all that, it was clear that Britt was taking stock of his future, and he told me that he expected to leave New York for good to return to Los Angeles: 'That's where my family is. I don't have any family in New York.'

He lost his wife Clara in 1991, and his brothers – Coney, the former Les Hite pianist, and the fine tenorist William Woodman Jr., always known as 'Brother' – lived in Los Angeles. One can imagine that Britt's decision to move back to California (finally accomplished in early 2000) prompted quite a family celebration; a case, for sure, of the prodigal returned. When I suggested that this move might lead to his retirement from music, he shrugged off the idea, saying, 'Oh no, while I can still hold the horn I'll play.'

Britt was the son of William Woodman Sr., a pioneer jazz musician who re-located to California from Texas in 1918, working with early jazz groups (including Jelly Roll Morton) and theatre bands until he joined Teddy Buckner's dixieland unit in the 1950s.

William Woodman was a strong figure, much admired by his sons, and a resourceful

Woodman while in London with the Mingus Big Band, July 1998. Photo by Peter Vacher.

Flier for The Biggest
Little Band in the
World, Watts,
California, 1937. *Left
to right*: Britt
Woodman, George
Reed, Willliam
'Brother' Woodman Jr.
and Coney Woodman.

provider. At various times he operated a dance hall and set up a barber's supply business
while maintaining a busy professional schedule. 'My dad had a chance to go with a lot of
bands but he didn't want to leave. He raised us, working at the Follies [burlesque] Theater.
At that time, $21 a week – that was a lot of money. During the depression we were blessed
– my mother never did have to work. My dad didn't drink and my mother didn't set foot in
a theatre, didn't put a foot in any clubs, yet she wasn't that strict; not to say you can't do
this, you can't do that. She was a Sunday school teacher and we was raised up with
Sunday school every Sunday, the whole family.'

Woodman Sr. turns up on a number of Sonny Clay's 1920s recordings, and was clearly a player of considerable proficiency. Britt told me: 'I'm still not the musician my dad was.

He had the ear, which is supposed to be in jazz. In fact, if you have that ear and you can execute – well, you got it made. He could play fourth part harmony. If he had gone out with a jazz orchestra, he'd have been recognized as great as Lawrence Brown. In some respects he was greater than Lawrence Brown 'cause he could arrange and he could read. Lawrence Brown, after he play it a couple of times, he got it.' William Woodman was offered and declined a place in Duke Ellington's trombone section in 1932. Brown, who had already starred with Paul Howard's Quality Serenaders and the Cotton Club Orchestra,

Les Hite's orchestra in the film *Pudgy Boy*, late 1941 or early 1942. *Rear, left to right*: Ellis 'Stumpy' Whitlock, Joe Wilder, Walter Williams (t); Oscar Bradley (d). *Middle*: Allen Durham, Alfred Cobbs, Woodman (tb); Frank Pasley (g); Benny Booker (b). *Front*: Sol Moore (bs); Rodger Hurd (ts); Floyd Turnham Jr (as); Quedellis Martyn (ts); Coney Woodman (p); Hite. Photo courtesy Britt Woodman.

leapt at the chance. Ironically, Britt Woodman was Brown's successor with Duke some twenty years later.

Each of William Woodman's sons learned three musical instruments, and eventually the youngsters formed the Woodman Brothers Orchestra, usually billed as 'The Biggest Little Band In The World.' Britt played clarinet, tenor and trombone; William Jr. played alto, clarinet and trumpet, and pianist Coney, the leader – he was the eldest – doubled on banjo and guitar. George Reed, succeeded by Jesse Sailes, was on drums. Later, bassist Joe Comfort (doubling on trumpet); saxophonist Jewel Grant (Buddy Collette sometimes subbed for him), and trumpeter Ernie Royal were added. Collette subsequently recalled, 'It was such a good band, man! They could get any combination of sound and could make all the music you could imagine. They were playing jobs on a professional level when they were fourteen and fifteen. They were an important inspiration for all of us.'[2]

Audiences loved the way the Woodmans switched instruments as they played. The boys attracted widespread attention, tackling three or four engagements a week, often playing for parties at the homes of movie actors and entertainers. Their father was the band manager and paymaster, training the musicians and providing the arrangements (with assistance from saxophonist Maxwell Davis). 'We had a little studio in Watts where we rehearsed and also gave a little dance once a week. It so happened someone told Maxwell Davis that we were rehearsing on this particular day, so he came down with his horn, and said, "Hey fellas do you mind if I toot with y'all?" "Toot" – that's the word he used. Anyway, when he finished playing his solo, it taught us a lesson. Who do we think we are? My brother [William Jr], he was a good soloist [on saxophone] because he had a good ear, but he was nowhere near Maxwell. He was one of our

greatest musicians in Los Angeles. Nice arranger and everything.'

Thus launched, Britt was soon proficient enough to take his father's place on trombone at the Follies Theater, while attending Jordan High School where he had befriended Charles Mingus. 'We were like brothers. He was in the junior orchestra playing cello and I was in the senior orchestra. He was two years younger than me. I met him when he tried out for the senior orchestra. He was a bow-legged, shy person, and he didn't have no friends. He was very awkward. Actually, I didn't have a friend that played basketball, or horseshoe, ping-pong, paddle tennis, so I was teaching him all that, and we'd go to playgrounds and we hung out quite a bit everyday. I'd go to his house and eat or we'd go over to my house and eat. I went to his church – he lived on 108th Street and his church was on the corner of Compton. My church was down on 54th – sometimes he'd go to my church, sometimes I'd go to his.'

'One day he said he'd sure like to play trombone. I brought my trombone to his home, I found out he was playing cello by ear. I used to learn some of the jokes during playing [at the Follies] and teach them to Charles during recess. We'd have kids around us. I brought him out of his shyness. I told his mother he'd be a great bass player with that ear he had and she said, "We can't afford it." Anyway, two weeks later he called me and said he'd got a bass, so I went by his house and we took the bass to school. That bass brought him out. Before I graduated, he came to school with a beige zoot suit, the long coat, the chain and the peg-leg pants, and [began] jamming with the fellas [including Jay and Bobby McNeely] during recess. I knew he had something then. I graduated in late '39. He was two semesters behind me, see, so he graduated in late '40. I left home in 1940 [with Les Hite's orchestra] and then I was drafted in 1942. He was play-

Lionel Hampton with his trombone section, San Francisco, September 1947. Woodman is second from left
Photo by Chester Gau Studios, courtesy Britt Woodman.

ing bass then, he hadn't started doing any writing yet, and that's when I saw him. By '44 he was really playing, he had that bass down. You know, I'm fortunate to have been around a genius, and didn't even know it!'

After two years with Les Hite, Britt spent four years as an army musician before return-ing home to play with Collette, Mingus and Lucky Thompson in the Stars of Swing. When this unit foundered, Britt was snapped up by Eddie Heywood before he joined Lionel Hampton in September 1946. 'In '47, that's when I worked with the Lionel Hampton band, and I recommended Mingus in the band in '49. He [had] started writing in the forties and

Woodman soloing with the Mingus Big Band, Brecon Jazz Festival, August 1999. *Left to right*: Bobby Watson (as); Woodman; Alex Foster (as); Eddie Henderson (t); Jamal Haynes (tb); John Stubblefield (ts); Alex Sipiagin (t). Photo by Peter Vacher.

he had a big-band rehearsed. Damita Jo, she was the singer in the band, and I can remember so well: Charles made an arrangement on 'Body and Soul' – he would invert those chords so you couldn't hardly recognise 'Body and Soul'. She amazed me, where she could still hear the melody; she had that kind of ear. I was also playing with Benny Carter's band and he asked me did I know any female vocalists. So I drove her to the dance and Benny was very pleased with her. Later, I understand she left home, went up to San Francisco and got tied up with a quartet. She married the lead singer. That's when she went on her own, until she got sick.'

'I was playing with [trumpeter] Red Mack at an after-hours club when Duke Ellington called my mother – I was staying with my mother – and I got home about 4.30 a.m. and she said, "Duke says call him any time you come home." I was recommended by Cress Courtney, the manager of Boyd Raeburn's band, from when I recorded and played with him: that was in '46 [and] '47. Truthfully, I was a little frightened when I found out I was taking Lawrence Brown's place. I didn't have any fear of reading – I was a very good sight reader – but improvising? To me Lawrence Brown was the greatest. I knew the band was built up on soloists so that was a little frightening. I started asking everybody – I called Buddy Collette, all my friends – and they said, "You better go." Naturally my mother and dad was thrilled about it.'

In February 1951 Britt travelled to San Francisco to join the Ellington band. Brown had stayed on to 'school me about the book.' Britt asked Brown how he composed his solos 'so they match so perfectly in the arrangement? So he said, "I think it out, I hum it." I tried that but when I get up to play the things I had thought about, it goes some other kind of way. Then he made another statement: "I want to give you a nice advice – don't stay in the band too long, 'cause you too good a musician. I stayed there too long." Of course, he was leaving to go with Johnny Hodges, Sonny Greer and Al Sears.'

'Anyway, we got to the rehearsal and they played the number 'Harlem' where the trombone has a large space to work with. I wasn't frightened, I didn't have a solo, just [had to] play the parts. After I played that, all the fellows applauded. I didn't know they were very particular until the alto player [possibly Tommy Douglas] was so nervous, he couldn't play, he couldn't read. Johnny Hodges had heard him play, recommended him, 'cause he sound so much like Johnny. So in an emergency they had to call Floyd Turnham, a very prominent [Los Angeles] alto player, and he came in and played the gig at the Thunderbird [February 1951]. Duke didn't like his sound, he didn't have

the velvet sound, so he made some kind of arrangement and [trombonist] Juan Tizol, [drummer] Louis Bellson and [alto saxophonist] Willie Smith, they joined us from the Harry James band.'

Gradually Britt conquered his fear of improvising as Duke began to write specific pieces for him, usually designed to feature his exceptional instrumental command and culminating in the remarkable 'Sonnet for Hank Cinq' from *Such Sweet Thunder* (1957). Never daunted by demanding written parts, Britt had developed his technique while studying 'harmony, solfeggio, arranging and conducting' at Westlake College in Los Angeles, benefiting from the GI Bill, from 1949 through to 1951. 'There was a trumpet book I used to play out of, and they had short versions of things, and they had the 'Bumble Bee' in there. So I wrote an introduction for the clarinets and I'd come in on trombone. See, I was a very fast trombone player at the time. They were amazed to hear a trombone playing single-tongue – most musicians double-tongue on those fast things,' he recalled.

Because Woodman worked closely with two towering figures in twentieth century music, Ellington and Mingus, I asked whether they were similar in their approach to music creation. He laughed and said, 'The only comparison that you have is this: it's in the music, staying up all night writing, ideas, being creative. That's the only thing to compare. Other than that – Charles – he didn't have no qualities of Duke. His mind was as great as Duke's, though. I wish he had some of the class of Duke, but

Charles' music wouldn't be like it was because that's the way he was. Like he'd stop the band and tell the audience, "Listen, and you'll learn something about music." I did three months in the Village with him [in 1960]: there was Eric Dolphy, Ted Curson and myself. Anyway, we came in one night and he said, "We're closing. We ain't playing anymore. This is it." He had an argument with the manager, something about the money. So he said he was going into the Five Spot about a week later, so I made an excuse. . . I just couldn't go through with that. He was in the Five Spot about a week, when he broke the piano. That incident barred him from working in New York for about a year.'

Heeding Lawrence Brown's advice, Britt left Duke in September 1960 (replaced by Matthew Gee) and embarked on a 40-year freelance career split between New York and Los Angeles. This took in any number of recording sessions, small groups (including Mingus of course) and big-band gigs, film and soundtrack appearances, special concerts and ice shows, club dates with Meyer Davis, and overseas tours and festivals with Clark Terry and Benny Carter. There was also membership of the New York Repertory, Smithsonian and Lincoln Center Jazz Orchestras, and stints as a pit-band musician for hit shows in Los Angeles or on Broadway. As a first-call session player, Britt was known for his exemplary musicianship, his willingness to rehearse, invariable good humour and, yes, his improvising skills. Confident in his technique but modest about his solo capabilities, Britt always enjoyed the company of radicals like Eric Dolphy, Mingus, and, later, the tough-minded players in the Mingus Big Band, of whom he said, 'I feel very honoured, very blessed that the fellows accept me. I realised a few years back that I was the oldest one in the band, but they really respect me. Sometimes, I think they just jive with me, but they seem to be honest, and they like my playing. So it's a pleasure for me.'

Forever enthusiastic, always animated, Britt Woodman was one of the surviving links with the great days of Los Angeles' Central Avenue. I'm pleased to have captured some of his memories but above all, I feel privileged to have known him and to have experienced his music at first hand.

Chapter 9

Kenny Davern

Out of the Tradition

Kenny Davern, January 2000. Photo by Berit Bolt.

Anyone who knows New Yorker Kenny Davern will confirm that his opinions, although usually masked by humour, are often hard-edged and trenchant. Kenny sees no reason to veer away from controversy and he enjoys the cut and thrust of debate. He visits Britain most years, has many friends here, and is an artist of consummate skill who will recall past eras and individuals with evident relish.

The interview on which this piece is based took place while Kenny was playing at the Brecon Jazz Festival in Wales in August 1994 and his comments are typically honest and direct. It's always a pleasure to talk with him and to hear him play. He has created a distinctive style and almost single-handedly kept interest in the clarinet alive. Kenny and his wife Elsa have recently relocated to a remote part of New Mexico in their quest for peace and calm.

Kenny Davern is a familiar presence on the jazz world's many bandstands. Whether as a soloist or in combo line-ups, he seems always to give of his best, developing clarinet improvisations of matchless beauty and intensity. Yet he's also an acerbic humorist, with something of the late Lenny Bruce's mordant wit, as he reflects on the vagaries of life.

For all his emphasis on the comedic, he is never more serious than when he plays. He has clear ideas about the presentation of his music. Witness his stance on acoustic sound, with Davern eschewing the use of microphones to allow the true timbre of his instrument to come through.

In modern parlance, he is highly focused. He has little time for cant or pretentiousness and after 40-plus years of jazz activity, sees no reason for compromise. He concedes that his mainstream kind of jazz is an endangered music with little or no relevance to the broad mass of the American public. It relates, 'only to a handful of people who show up at these so-called jazz parties which, I think, is a redundancy in terminology. It's neither jazz nor is it a party – it's more like a rush of adrenalin. Like Flip Phillips says, "If you wanna earn a dollar, you gotta make 'em holler." The people are of a silver-haired vintage. They're very nice, they all have some bread, they're sorta like groupies. They go from party to party because they're the only ones who can afford it.'

Davern laments the passing of what he calls 'a higher plane of culture, when today there's a complete lack of culture. In the so-called big band era, sixteen guys in a ballroom, working together like bunnies to get a blend, created an energy that three guys today can get by turning up the volume. Back then, there were songs, arrangements, a great deal of art and craft. I think the culture was higher. The people who get the short end of the stick now are those young guys who get hooked on the older music and start to play real instruments. There are no places, no clubs, for them to test their mettle.'

He dates his first awareness of jazz to wartime days. 'We used to have block parties when a group of servicemen were released from duty. The whole block was cordoned off, loudspeakers were set up, the beer kegs were put out, every neighbour prepared some food. The music was always Glenn Miller's 'In The Mood', Benny Goodman, Jimmy Dorsey, Artie Shaw's 'Stardust'. I just remember being washed up in this great tidal wave of excitement.'

'I was born in Huntington, Long Island, but I was in nine foster homes before I was six years old, the product of a broken marriage. In 1941, when I was six, I had to go to school so my mother finally had to establish me in residency. She gave me to her folks in Woodhaven, Queens. My grandfather was a red-haired, blue-eyed descendant of Austro-Hungarian army people and my grandmother was a little peasant Russian woman from the then-occupied Lithuania. They were Jewish, and my father's side was Irish-Catholic.'

'I pleaded and begged for a clarinet until my mother saw an ad in the newspaper that said [that] up the block a man had one for sale for $35. She bought it, not knowing anything about the clarinet, and it turned out to be a C Albert system clarinet. Teachers would look at this and say, "We don't know very much about that," until I finally found an old Italian man named Louis Bruno who knew both systems and he taught me to play the Albert clarinet. Finally, I got a Boehm system and started to switch over.'

'In those days, I was listening to Ted Husin's *Bandstand* [radio show] and for fifteen minutes of each day, he'd play dixieland jazz. One particular day, I heard this thing and, whack! It was like a baseball bat between the eyes. I stood transfixed. I said, 'I want to spend the rest of my life doing that.' It was Pee Wee Russell playing his two choruses on 'Memphis Blues' with Muggsy Spanier's Ragtimers on Commodore. That was my true emotional experience in jazz. I was about eleven years old. I remember it like it was yesterday.'

'So-called dixieland grabbed me and I listened to everybody. At high school, I got into the band. One of the kids who played the drums in the marching band was Bobby Grauso, who was Joe Grauso's son, and he liked the way I played. We had a little dixieland band in school and Larry O'Brien was the trombone player – he went on to lead the Miller band, the Dorsey band, and so on. Joe would take us to the old [Eddie] Condon's [club] on West Third Street and there'd be my idols standing there. I was in love with these guys and the music they produced. I didn't care about any of that other stuff, although I had the opportunity to hear Charlie Parker play on several occasions, in the bleachers [musicians' tables] at Birdland. I was very impressed – he was the only one who moved me – but I still didn't want to go that route.'

'Guys like Bobby Hackett, Ernie

Caceres and Red Allen – the most dynamic musician I've ever met – hired me when I was sixteen years old, and I'd go sit in with the McPartlands [Jimmy and Marian] or with Dicky Wells and Buck Clayton. They were very sweet to me. Buster Bailey, every time he'd see me coming, he'd say, 'Come on, do you want to play, kid?' Cutty Cutshall and those guys used to say, "You guys got the mantle now." That was me, and [Johnny] Windhurst, and [Dick] Wellstood, and [Bob] Wilber, and [Ed] Hubble. "You gotta keep this stuff going." We thought we were on a mission, a crusade.'

'Now, I don't really give a shit if my music is pigeon-holed or not. I love the songs I play: there's always room to do something different if you can possibly mix or scramble those twelve notes and three octaves you have to deal with. The fascination is, you never know what you're going to come up with, whereas in the older forms, unless you absolutely stick to the tried and true clichéd traditions, you're dead. That's why when Ornette Coleman hit town, I suddenly went, "Isn't this a breath of fresh air?" See, it transcended bebop. I could hear the older influences but not in the form I was used to. Unfortunately, the only one who's taken it to another step is Steve Lacy and I see where he turned it into an entity unto itself.'

Lacy and Davern were fellow traditionalists in the fifties. 'I was in one of Steve's bands. We called it the ill-fated Steve Lacy band. In 1951 we went to Boston. We got hired through Joe Glaser's office. I played baritone saxophone; Steve played clarinet and soprano; Dick Schwartz, who became Dick Sutton, played trumpet. Our drummer was Eddie Phyfe; the bass player was Billy Goodall, and our star was Elmer Schoebel, the pianist with the original New Orleans Rhythm Kings. We rehearsed at the old Condon's for one day and drove up to Boston where we got shut out after a week because I was playing the saxophone! The woman that owned the place, Mrs Donohoe, hated the saxophone, any saxophone, because it didn't belong in a traditional jazz band. We hung around to see who was going to take our place, and who did they bring up but Hot Lips Page with Paul Quinichette, a tenor player! She took one look at his tenor and locked it in the basement. Poor Paul had to play those charts that Lips had on the clarinet, trying to transpose it an octave lower. He was scuffling. . .'

Davern had taken up alto and baritone saxophone alongside the clarinet on the advice of seasoned local musicians. He auditioned for popular bandleader Ralph Flanagan ('60 one-nighters in 90 days') earning 'great money' until an opening with Jack Teagarden beckoned. When Flanagan, a pianist and jazz devotee, heard that the nineteen-year old Davern had been hired by Teagarden, he asked, 'Do they need a piano player?'

Davern remembers Teagarden as 'a splendid, gentle guy. When I was with him, he hadn't had a drink in two years, so he was really quite the family man. His wife even cooked us Thanksgiving dinner.

Davern with Al Casey (g), Brian Lemon (p), Len Skeat (b) and Ronnie Verrell (d). Pizza Express, London, 1980s.

Really nice. I was only with them a couple of months and then I got a call from [trumpeter] Phil Napoleon to join his Memphis Five. But the music was too slick and commercial. I hated it. On our Capitol sides, where we had Sonny Igoe on drums (a swell guy who still plays wonderfully), we did thirteen takes on one tune until Phil got his set chorus the way he liked it sounding, without him flubbing.'

Perhaps as a reaction to Napoleon's over-facile approach, Davern became enthused over the more primitive New Orleans music of people like George Lewis and Wooden Joe Nicholas, and returned to the Albert system for a while. Even so, as a 'journeyman musician' he still had to take big band jobs with the likes of Tommy Tucker, Johnny Long, and Billy Butterfield before finally selling all his saxophones and assorted woodwind in the late fifties to concentrate solely on jazz clarinet.

'I played jazz all the time, regardless. Even on those rotten bands, I was still the guy who played the jazz clarinet. Like I was hired to play a month with Ted Lewis at Roseland [New York City] with Jack Lacey in the trombone section. When Jack played a tune like 'Tenderly', it would make your flesh crawl. He was wonderful. Always had a music stand in front of him but no music, because he couldn't read. This was in '63. Then I got the call to join Louis Armstrong after Buster Bailey died. But I was working at the Ferryboat [in Brielle, New Jersey] with Jack Six and Dick Wellstood. We had a great band, I was a mile from my house and I was courting my wife. I would have had to go out for six months with Louis, but I had too many wonderful things going for me, so I turned it down.'

Davern has always considered himself a freelance, sometimes taking long-term gigs such as a five-year stint at Nick's or one-nighters at New York's Central Plaza. He counts himself fortunate to have known and worked with so many superb black players: 'To gain acknowledgement from Rex Stewart, Tommy Benford (he was like a father figure), Joe Thomas, Vic Dickenson – they were a wonderful generation of guys who made it in spite of many horrible things that happened to them and managed to keep their dignity and their humanity. We played in mixed bands – like for Princeton reunions – and I'd be the only white guy in Red Allen's band. To me, that was the big time. It seemed like it would never end. There was a better *esprit de corps* among blacks and whites in those days. Then I got in with the Eddie Condon crowd. He was a cut-up, one of the fastest-witted, one of the brightest guys I ever met in my life, no matter what condition he was in.'

One of the happier outcomes in recent years for Davern was his renewed association with fellow reedman Bob Wilber. As co-leaders of Soprano Summit back in the 1970s it was well known that they did not always agree. But 'we see eye to eye now,' Davern told me. 'When we play together, it's really a joy. We have the same frame of reference but a different point of view. It's become more of a bond,' he emphasised, adding that Wilber's 'retirement' would not preclude their getting together on special occasions.

As for the real value of his music, Davern says, 'In a not-so-beautiful world, if I can relieve people's anxieties for a brief moment, then I've done something. I'm still hopeful I'll be able to do something definitive. I'm hoping that happens while I'm still conscious! In other words, I hope I'm still striving until the day I die.'

Chapter 10

Teddy Edwards

West Coast Hot

Teddy Edwards, Los Angeles, 1990s. Photo courtesy Don McGlynn.

This piece derives from my first encounter with the fine tenor player Theodore 'Teddy' Edwards, backstage at the 100 Club in London in February 1984. Later, I met him many more times here and in the USA. Teddy came to my home and I went to his in Los Angeles. When he picked me up there at the Blue Line rail station he looked around and said, 'Welcome to my town!' He always knew that he had received less recognition from the jazz establishment than his talents merited, yet he remained loyal to his Californian fan base.

We went on to spend lengthy periods taping his reminiscences for a possible book about his life. He was a rich source of jazz anecdotes as well as a distinctive modern stylist. But any chance of progressing the book project was stalled when he became ill. Although we spoke of starting work again, it never happened. Teddy died in April 2003, aged 78.

Howard McGhee Sextet, Billy Berg's Swing Club, Hollywood, 1945. *Left to right*: McGhee (t); Vernon Biddle (p); J.D. King (ts); Bob 'Dingbod' Kesterson (b); Edwards (ts); Roy Porter (d). Photo courtesy Roy Porter.

Teddy Edwards had the kind of flypaper memory for facts that made him an asset to jazz historians. He was an eager talker, pleased to recall moments and musicians that might otherwise be forgotten. And his experience was unusually wide-ranging, including the long-gone world of territory big bands, the California bebop scene of the forties, and small group work in Florida and elsewhere.

Streets of Paris Club, Hollywood, California, 1946. *Left to right*: Chuck Thompson (d); Edwards; sculptress Julie MacDonald; Wardell Gray (ts); unknown; Freddie Threats (p). Photo courtesy Teddy Edwards..

Edwards was from Jackson, Mississippi, born into a musical family, and after mastering the alto saxophone, he soon moved into full-time music, working in Detroit and Alexandria, Louisiana. Later, he was based in Tulsa with the Ernie Fields Orchestra before settling on the West Coast, where he took up tenor sax to join trumpeter Howard McGhee's new group. After that, his base remained in Los Angeles, where he appeared as a soloist or combo leader while also functioning as a composer-arranger. He was one of the finest tenor saxophonists in jazz.

His reminiscences were recorded for the Library of Congress oral history project. He told me, 'They paid me $2000 and I talked for five hours. And I only got as far as 1952! What they like is that I can talk about people in music who you haven't heard of, people who never made it but who were so talented. I talked about Central Avenue [the main

Edwards when he was a member of Ernie Fields' orchestra, c.1945. Photo courtesy Teddy Edwards.

thoroughfare of black Los Angeles] in the forties. When I arrived in L.A., things were really jumping there, all kinds of music going on along together. People just don't know what it was like. No-one even has a picture of Central Avenue from those days any more.'

What about some of those lost talents? 'Did you ever hear about Harry Pettiford? That's Oscar's elder brother, and he was just one of the greatest saxophonists that ever lived. When I was with the Ernie Fields band, we'd go through Tulsa a lot and that's when we'd run into Harry. There'd be guys from about four bands there and we'd jam the whole night. At the

end, it would be just Harry that was playing. He was fantastic. Then there was Booker Green from Florida. I ran into him when I had my own group in Tampa. I was playing alto then and Booker was an inspiration. He never left Florida so nobody knows him.'

'During my Florida days, the Adderley brothers were around listening to our sounds. Cannonball was kind enough later on to say that [Eddie] Cleanhead Vinson and I were his earliest influences. Another cat who said he always liked my sound and tried to play like me was Sonny Criss. I told him he had his own style but it was a nice compliment.'

Edwards was involved with bebop's greatest practitioner, alto saxophonist Charlie Parker, during the latter's notorious California sojourn. 'I know things about Charlie that nobody else knows. We were very close during Charlie's California days. Why, I was sitting right next to him when he started to have his breakdown. We were rehearsing – that's Howard McGhee's band, the one with the sax section of Charlie, Gene Montgomery, Sonny Criss and myself – when Bird took ill. There's a whole lot of stuff that hasn't been told about Charlie. Now it seems like they're going to make the film of his life.[1] I had a call just before I came over to go talk to the production people about my memories of Charlie. So something may come out of that.'

Mention of Howard McGhee triggered some observations that emphasise how the jazz community supports its casualties. 'Howard takes time to get to know you but when he knows you're on the level he's a

Edwards with the Gerald Wilson Orchestra, Los Angeles, 1964, recording for Pacific Jazz. Photo Pacific Jazz Records.

true friend and will do anything for you.' He described how, just before the ex-Basie trumpeter Waymon Reed died, 'Howard took him home and gave him something to eat and put some money in his pocket. Howard didn't have much money for himself but he could see Waymon needed help so he did that. That's how Howard is.'

Edwards went on to talk about another trumpeter, Harry 'Sweets' Edison: 'Harry's another great friend and we have worked together. These days, George Wein and Norman Granz use him so we don't have a chance to make records or anything. I've never worked for George or Norman. It's not that I've ever had problems with either of them. They just don't use me. I guess it could be because I don't come from either the Hawk or Pres tradition. I don't sound like either school so maybe this is difficult for them.'

Aside from his exceptional gifts as an instrumentalist, Edwards had an enviable track record as an arranger. Like many, he started young. 'I could arrange for a big band by the age of fourteen. I just did it by watching other people and reading a few books. I never had a lesson. These days I can write for a 100-piece orchestra without any problems. This trip, I had arrangements to do for Belgian TV and in 1980 I did a TV special for the Dutch TV orchestra when the BBC in London was co-producing. It seems like I could spend all my time writing but I like to play as well.'

That pleasure in performing was evident from the moment Edwards took the stand. His appetite to play remained strong and he'd seek out his peers whenever opportunity allowed. 'Red Callender has a regular Sunday gig at a club in North Hollywood. It's just a trio, with Gerry Wiggins on piano and the drummer Kenny Dennis. When I just want to stretch out and blow, I go up there and sit in. We have a really good time.'

Ever the man to give credit where it was due, Edwards mentioned another talent deserving wider recognition. 'I was just out at [trumpeter/organist] Red Mack's house before coming over here. He was giving a party for Clora Bryant, the trumpet player. You know, she's as good as any man. She has range and ideas and enough talent to go to the top. She can hit the high notes too. You ask Clark Terry and Diz. She scares them. She hasn't made many records but if she visited Europe, she'd be sensational.' In fact, Ms Bryant debuted on the European festival circuit in 1986, appearing with the Johnny Otis Rhythm and Blues Revue at both the Nice and North Sea jazz festivals.

While we talked, Edwards was organising himself for the evening ahead. Neatly labelled folders were laid out side-by-side, one each for tenor, piano, bass and drums, the manuscript sheets inside faultlessly prepared. He travelled with a complete book of quartet arrangements, trusting his accompanists to do them justice. As he checked the charts over, the young English drummer with whom he would work that night started to look at the drum parts, explaining nervously to the American that his reading was not up to much, but he'd do his best. Teddy, a true professional but an understanding colleague too, closed the books, smiled, and said: 'That's OK. We'll just play standards and blues. Just so that you feel comfortable. That's what I want, and that way, we'll *all* have fun.' And they did.

Chapter 11

Herb Hall

London Session

Herb Hall at the Nice Jazz Festival, 1980s. Photo by Bill White, courtesy National Jazz Archive, Essex.

It was instructive to watch clarinettist Herb Hall, observing how calm he stayed, at the recording session in March 1981 that is described here. Later that month we met at Dick Cook's house in Southall to tape his (unpublished) career story and Herb talked readily about his beliefs in vegetarianism and yoga as an aid to inner peace. He returned to Britain the following year with Bob Greene's 'Tribute to Jelly Roll' and was much encouraged by the reception he received.

In his final years, Hall stayed close to his home in Bourne, Texas, near San Antonio, just playing occasionally. His recording with clarinettist John Defferary, drummer Trevor Richards, bassist Alyn Shipton and pianist Bob Barton is still unissued. Hall died in Bourne in March 1996 just short of his eighty-ninth birthday.

It's a March night in London's Soho. Downstairs at the Pizza Express, the red chairs are piled on to the marble-topped tables. The basement jazz room is devoid of its usual bustle and lit only by a pair of spots. A small gathering of musicians and friends is there, the talk a little desultory as instruments are unpacked and microphone placements checked. Dave Bennett is seated at a four-track tape machine, cans on, establishing a sound balance. Unbeknown to the diners upstairs, a recording session is about to get underway.

The producer, reedman John Defferary, positions the instrumentalists – clarinet, piano, and drums. Herb Hall smiles, fiddles momentarily with his Albert system clarinet and asks, 'What are we gonna attempt first, John?'

A list is passed around and after a whispered consultation with the rhythm section, it is decided that 'My Funny Valentine' should be tried. Hall sits facing the other players, the mike positioned near to the bell of his clarinet. He is barely a yard away from pianist Bob Barton and the two confer frequently over tempo and harmonic niceties. As the familiar song unfolds, it's evident that Hall is in the line of the great New Orleans clarinettists, men like Noone and Bigard, who favour a full-toned sound, with a warm low register and a feeling for the elegant turn of phrase: in his own words, he 'embellishes the melody'. Surprisingly for someone whose lengthy career has encompassed extensive big band work and much lead saxophone playing, his clarinet style is pure New Orleans, with few swing-era overtones. Perhaps his Albert system clarinet, which formerly belonged to his brother Ed, is the key to this. After Ed died, his widow passed the instrument to Herb.

A second take of 'Valentine' is decreed – 'just in case'– the theme unwinding attractively in this trio setting. Barton's solo is a trifle more florid and the overall effect is languid. Opinion has it that the first take was better although there is no playback. Hall agrees but

Don Albert and his music: San Antonio, Texas, 1934. *Rear, bus top*: Lloyd Glenn (p, arr); William 'Geechie' Robinson (tb); Sam Birt (vln). *Seated on top of engine*: Alvin Alcorn (t); Jimmy Johnson (b); Ferdinand Dejan (g). *Standing, front*: Frank Jacquet (tb); Albert 'Fats' Martin (d); Don Albert (t); Louis Cottrell (ts, cl); James 'Dink' Taylor (cl, as); Floyd Snelson (in window, reporter for the *Pittsburgh Courier* who travelled with the band and sent back reports); Hiram Harding (t); Herb Hall (cl, as, bs); Henry Turner (v-tb).

doesn't force his views on his colleagues. His temperament is as sunny as his playing style – he seems always to seek the discrete solution and to avoid confrontation. In conversation, he'll tell you of the impact yoga has made on his life and talk enthusiastically of his exercises and consequent calmness of disposition.

'Wolverine Blues' is to be next. Herb wants Barton to run through the bridge and Defferary answers a harmonic query or two. The take starts. This time, the tempo is medium-up and drummer Trevor Richards comes into his own, playing a series of breaks that recall the style of his teacher Zutty Singleton. Richards is using a kit that was largely Zutty's, purchased from his widow. There's also history in the snare drum that he plays, formerly used by Alec Bigard, Barney's brother, and according to Trevor, 'Just the best snare I've ever played.' There's something pleasing about this because these instruments could so easily rest in the homes of collectors or in a jazz museum.

A second take peters out. The third is too slow; everyone is agreed on that. Defferary

Hall playing at Shoreham Airport, solo British tour, March 1981. Photo courtesy Sid Bailey.

worries about the bass drum. 'Is it booming too much?' Yes, so Richards makes adjustments. A fourth take, brighter this time, is completed. Despite reservations about the harmony on the bridge, it seems as though the first take was best. Ah well!

'St Louis Blues' follows, the theme briskly assertive and the tempo spot on. No second take is needed. Defferary calls a break, amid general approval. A few go in search of refreshment while one or two hang on to chat. Trumpeter Clive Wilson, who brought Hall from America to England for this, his first visit, is warming up quietly in a corner; he's expecting to take part in the recording later on. He goes out while Hall stays to talk to the bystanders. Asked about his instruments, Hall says, 'I sold all my saxophones: that's my alto, my tenor and my baritone. I sold them all except my soprano and I gave that to my nephew but he never did anything with it. See, there's so many saxophone players that unless you're in the class of a Lester Young, you don't get any work. I'm just listed in the Union book now under clarinet. I don't take any jobs except on clarinet.'

Naturally enough, conversation turns to Herb's late brother. Earlier, he had seemed disinclined to speak much about Ed and it was possible to sense that the younger man had grown tired of constant comparisons with his famous relative. After all, Herb is a fine soloist and his playing deserves evaluation on its own merits.

Still, he's proud of Ed and shakes his head sadly at the memory of his brother's death in 1967, at the comparatively young age of 66. He tells me about Ed's heart attack: 'He owned some property alongside his home in Boston and he rented this to a business further down the street. They used it to park their cars and my brother would keep it tidy. It was a large open space really. Anyway, it had been snowing heavily and Ed was clearing the snow away. I don't think you realise how tired you are when it's cold. You do when it's hot, because you feel exhausted. He finished the clearing and came back in the house. He told his wife that he was just going down the corner to get a paper. He got in his car and drove about two blocks but had to pull up, just outside a fire station. They saw him and put one of those respirators on him and rushed him into hospital. He was DOA – dead on arrival. There was no saving him.'

Recording restarts with 'Just A Closer Walk With Thee'. The melody, so sweetly expressive, unwinds in its timeless way, Hall giving each phrase its full weight. As the take ends he says, 'Let's do it once more.' The musicians start again. This time, everyone is satisfied. 'We're not going to do it better than that, worse maybe, but not better,' says Barton.

At this point, the trio is to be augmented as Defferary intends to record some clarinet duets. Bassist Alyn Shipton is tuning up while Defferary fits his clarinet together. I'd heard the two reedmen play duets earlier in the tour and had been impressed by their obvious empathy. They launch into 'Blue Skies', with Trevor Richards on brushes, quickly achieving a rapport and stylistic balance that's quite delightful. Clarinet duets are often rewarding and these seem likely to be no exception. The two men put their heads together and work out a routine, alternating melody and structuring the piece to keep it fresh.

They try a take. Shipton needs to check the harmony. Another take follows. Richards uses tom-toms in the introduction and his cymbals pick up the vibrations, spoiling the take. Wendy Stagg, who has taken over the timing from Defferary, sets her stopwatch again. This time the take is perfect.

As the session continues, there's speculation about the music's release on record. The album is expected to be issued later by the musicians themselves, or leased to another label. For me, the clarinet duets make its availability imperative since Hall's lovely playing is complemented most spiritedly by Defferary's fiery and inventive performances. The whole session has the ring of quality about it.

Chapter 12

Scott Hamilton

More Fun Than Ohio

Scott Hamilton with John Pearce (p), Pizza Express, Watford, March 2001. Photo by Berit Bolt.

Scott Hamilton has nearly forty Concord albums to his name and he continues to release albums on the label, often with British friends in a quartet. These days, as well as playing tenor, Scott acts as his own record producer and lives in London much of the time. He works less in the US and travels widely, often visiting Japan where his family is based. There's a refreshing honesty in his playing; he's good at what he does and audiences relate to his swing feeling and creativity. He is, in short, a star.

When we sat down to talk in the Pizza Express flat in April 1992, Scott was about to begin a season at the jazz club in Dean Street, Soho, a regular annual engagement. He has always cared deeply about jazz and about performing at the highest level. Sometimes laconic, he's unfailingly courteous and we've talked often over the years. Although Scott says he has such a low profile that he 'can't get arrested in New York,' it's good to know that he's found a receptive audience here in Britain.

Scott Hamilton's British connections were well established by the time of his 1992 spring season at the Pizza Express. 'I made my first record in '76 and I first came here in '79. The last five years, it's been really an important part of my life. What fixed things for me was when Brian Peerless went into business and took Warren Vaché and Kenny Davern over for tours. They started telling me how much easier it was, that all I had to do was get on the telephone. It opened up a whole lot of work for me.'

'Things have gone so well in the last few years that I'm able to come here for two months a year: one in the spring, one in the summer. I hope we can keep doing it. Not only do I love Soho but I'm comfortable here, and also the room – the Dean Street Pizza Express – is comfortable. I like the staff down there and the musicians can't be beat.'

'I play as much with Brian Lemon and Dave Green and Allan Ganley as I do with anybody. In fact, more than I do with a lot of guys back home. I'm able to work things out with these guys. It's not only that I get to play with them for extended periods of time, which helps – but it's also that they're so good, and they're free of any kind of attitude. In New York, sometimes, people don't always want to play, whereas here everybody's willing to try something new.'

Given that Scott's stylistic preferences are based on notions of jazz that predate bebop, did he feel the need to defend his playing stance? 'No, things have progressed to a point where I don't think most jazz audiences find it unusual that I'm doing what I'm doing. But for a certain kind of person, I've been sort of a political tool and it has very little to do with

Hamilton with Dave Green (b) and Allan Ganley (d), University College School Theatre, London, March 1993.
Photo by David Sinclair.

what I do. They don't mean any harm, they're people who were really disillusioned with modern jazz and pop music. They felt there needed to be some sort of a figure that's gonna carry on what they believe in. I fit the bill pretty well and I've got to admit I profited from it. I probably still do. But it's not really me. I'm just playing this way 'cause I like it.'

'I really don't have any animosity towards any other style. I object when somebody uses me as a way of criticising other kinds of music. In other words, I'm given a good review sometimes just because I don't play the things that those guys don't like. Nowadays, Branford and Wynton Marsalis have to go through all the same nonsense I had to go through, only theirs is on a bigger level. To me, it doesn't make any sense. I don't think either of these guys are condemning anybody like, say, David Murray. They're just playing what they want to play,' he emphasises.

Martin Williams wrote of Ruby Braff: 'He has found a personal challenge in the idiom of his choosing.' Didn't that sum up Scott's position? 'I was interested in meeting Ruby long before I ever saw him because he may have been the first to play something that had its roots in an earlier era but to do it on the absolutely highest level. In other words, he's a musician that's on a level with any of the other trumpet players that were his age, but he chose to do something different. There's been very few people like that.'

'By the time the eighties came around, I was a little bit older and better at what I was doing, so he and I were able really to work together. That's when I felt like I could really keep up with him. I've certainly learned more things from Ruby than anybody, more so than from any of the tenor players I've known. He educated me in a lot of ways.'

Dave Green, Allan Ganley, Scott Hamilton and Brian Lemon, late 1990s. Photo courtesy Dave Green.

Scott's initial prominence came suddenly, when he was still very young. 'I found it difficult. I wasn't ready for all that nonsense but at the same time, you had to go with it. I didn't have any choice. The only alternative would have been to turn things down and when you do that the phone never rings again.'

I reminded Scott that he had been in pretty poor shape at one time. He nodded: 'Oh yeah, I was almost dead – came pretty close. I stopped drinking in 1981 and I've certainly had a few drinks since then, but I haven't fallen into real trouble with it the way it was before. I just have the bad luck to be an alcoholic but at the same time it was aggravated by being in a situation where I had no control. I didn't know what I was doing. I was a good musician and I've got pretty quick ears so I was able to jump into a lot of things. I was used to working in a nightclub where you got [to play for] four hours a night, with people drinking and talking. For that I was always fine. It was no problem to play at Eddie Condon's in New York but getting on stage with Benny Goodman where you're supposed to hit and sound good straight away, I wasn't prepared for that at all. I didn't have the confidence and I didn't have the knowledge. Recording was even worse.'

'The more you drink, the more everything just becomes impossible. It's a cycle you have to break. How? Just by trying a whole lot of times. The easiest part is if you get yourself in a situation where your health is so bad that you don't have any choice. Then it's not so hard,' he said, smiling again.

How did Goodman react? 'I was lucky in the sense that I didn't get sick any of the times I was with Benny. I could always play [while] drunk as long as I had my health. Benny had a great attitude about that sort of thing – he really didn't care as long as you could do what you had to do. He wasn't interested in your personal life at all. I always had good experiences with Benny. He was very friendly and complimentary a lot of the time. I kept my distance but he knew how much I loved his playing. A lot of guys used to come on Benny's band and they had an attitude from the beginning of, "I've heard about this bastard, he's gonna do that to me." And those cats were the ones that would always get it. With me, it was always, "Jeez, Mr Goodman, can I have your autograph?"'

Still a fan at heart, Scott has never concealed his admiration for past and present tenor masters, notably Illinois Jacquet. 'He's been my idol since I was eighteen years old. He was famous when he was young but in the in-between times he's been brushed aside by a lot of players. I could never understand that, 'cause this guy's got everything – incredible technique, intensity of feeling and invention – when he's not playing a set solo routine. Unfortunately a lot of people see him in the wrong situations where he feels obligated to play his famous solos, but there's a lot more to him.'

'I used to see him when he had the trio with Milt Buckner and Jo Jones. One night they'd be miserable, yelling and swearing at each other, telling each other to go home, with Jo's drums falling apart and Illinois screaming. Then the next night there'd be some of the best music I ever heard in my life. Jacquet would play chorus after chorus after chorus, with something different every time.'

'I've been on stage with Illinois once or twice. I just stood back and followed orders. It was a real thrill and he was great. There was a night in Nice, then the next night we went to Italy and played at the Umbria Festival. They put together a group with Illinois as the leader and they had Buddy Tate, Arnett Cobb, myself, John Lewis, Eddie Jones and Gus Johnson.'

'I was in heaven. This was the other side of Illinois, the guy that captivates mass audiences. He had these people crazy. I've never felt anything like that on stage before. I suppose Louis Armstrong was capable of doing that, Buddy Rich too, and there've been others, but it was frightening in a way. I think of Illinois as being one of the first tenor players after Lester Young to really understand what Pres was doing and incorporate it. He didn't have the same sound but his solos certainly had that logic,' Scott explained, adding that he was inspired, inevitably, by players he'd managed to see live, like Jacquet, Paul Gonsalves and Lockjaw Davis.

'These guys were the biggest influences on me, and through them, the others. I never got to see Ben Webster or Don

Byas, but to tell you the truth I didn't expect them to die so fast. I missed Hawk too – he came to my home town, Providence, in 1969, when I was fifteen years old but it was the same kind of crap we always had with jazz clubs where you had to be 21 to get in. I mean, I was out drinking every night really when I was fourteen and I was working in all these places, but if I wanted to get in and see somebody, it was just out of the question.'

Hamilton with guitarist Herb Ellis, Pizza Express, London, April 1995. Photo by Berit Bolt.

Scott's early work was on harmonica, 'doing a lot of gigs in bars and playing college fraternity dates. I met [guitarist] Duke Robillard round '69, and he was the one who got me back listening to jazz. People wonder how I never got into playing like Coltrane. One of the reasons was that I just didn't come from there. I was listening to pop music when I was eleven or twelve: the Beatles, Jimi Hendrix and whatever. Through that music I started hearing Muddy Waters and Little Walter, and I liked that stuff better. By the time you hear B.B. King, you're really not that far away from coming back into jazz but in a mainstream way.'

Did that route preclude bebop? 'That's another annoying thing. When I first started making records, I always used to be accused of playing as if Charlie Parker never existed. But that was kinda stupid – I owe quite a bit rhythmically and harmonically to Bird. I can't imagine what I would have sounded like if I didn't know Charlie's records.'

His discography is burgeoning: is there a grand plan at work here? 'Basically, I've got a free hand with Concord. I think I've got a contract that says two albums a year but we've never even talked about that. That may have been appropriate in 1978 but [I] think it would be foolish for me [now] to make more than one record a year. Sometimes things get a little bit over-booked, so to speak, and in a way it's a mistake because one album is always going to suffer. It happened in 1986 – I made a record I'd been thinking about for a long time and [Concord founder] Carl Jefferson said, "Oh, we really want you to do another record with Dave McKenna and Jake Hanna. And then we really want you to make a record with Gerry Mulligan." Well, these three things came out at the same time – bad timing but each one was something I wanted to do.'

'See, I'm lucky, I've got a record company that's given me real continuity – I mean fifteen years is a long time. Carl is my producer but he lets me do what I want. In the studio, he usually sits there and takes care of his own business while we record. All he says is, "That's great – see you next time." Every once in a while he comes up with a project: he'd like to put me with somebody and see what happens, and, of course, I'll always oblige him on that. Right now, we're talking of an album with strings. Most of the time, I'll go out of my way to do something for him because he allows me to pick the guys I want, to pick the material I want, and even occasionally to tell him what I want on the cover. It's unbeatable really.'

Scott led a quintet for a long time but changed to a solo act, travelling, playing clubs and for private parties. He regretted the lack of young people among the party audiences and liked clubs because they attracted the younger set.

'It's entertainment, and I have no problem with that at all. I'm a professional and my job is to play something different every night. But at the same time I've got to look out for the audience. If I don't keep them interested, how am I going to expect them to come back? I do a little pandering to them, but it has to be exciting for me too. I feel like I can let go and try to push it as far as I can. That's the only way you get anything back.'

At the time of our talk he was content with his career, gratified to know that there was a loyal audience out there. 'Jazz is the only music where you can be world-famous but where you make the same kind of money that some guy in the music department in Ohio State [University] makes. But I'm very happy and we've got enough to live on, so it's real nice. Anyway, it's a lot more fun than being in Ohio State,' he laughed.

Chapter 13

Illinois Jacquet

Flying Home

Illinois Jacquet at the North Sea Jazz Festival, July 1990. Photo by Ian Powell.

My admiration for Illinois Jacquet's prowess as a jazz soloist knows no bounds. He is the very epitome of the heroic tenor saxophonist, hard-driving or fulsome by turn, and quite simply one of the finest jazz performers of all time. The interview on which this piece is based was a long time coming – Illinois had promised me that we would talk about his career way back in 1971 but time ran out, and despite some near misses over the years, it wasn't until July 1992 that we were able to get together.

Jacquet had brought his big band to Birmingham for the festival and allowed me to observe his sound-check, an education in itself. After a storming set, he stayed up talking to his admirers and we then chatted at his hotel over a late-night meal. He was expansive and very relaxed. He turned 80 in October 2002, and continues to front his big band occasionally in the New York area.

Jacquet's big band arriving for the Birmingham International Jazz Festival, Birmingham Airport, July 11, 1992. *Standing left to right*: Randy Eckert (t); Rudy Rutherford (as and cl); Brad Shigeta (tb); Jacquet (as); David Glasser (as); Ravi Best (t); John Gordon (tb); Bob Cunningham (b); Johnny Grimes (t); Art Daniels (ts); Tom Olin (bs). *Kneeling at front*: Irvin Stokes (t); Jamal Haynes (tb); Armadou Divalio (ts). Photo by Mark Hadley, courtesy Big Bear Music Group.

When I met Illinois Jacquet in 1992 he was a reformed character. He had foresworn alcohol, preferred vegetarianism and would not touch what he called 'cancerous meats.' He claimed to have quietened down a bit, off the bandstand anyway, and what's more he even had a personal guru. This surprising metamorphosis had been supervised by Carol Scherick, his manager, who husbanded the saxophonist's energies and ensured that his musical life was stress-free.

It was clear from his performances in England in the summer of 1992 that Jacquet's new-found inner strength was being put to good use. His dramatic improvisations, with their marvellous depth of tone, brought the fans excitedly to their feet, just as they always have. He said he was in top playing form and all the evidence supported this.

Lionel Hampton with members of his orchestra, Los Angeles, November 1940. *Rear:* Jacquet (ts); Marshall Royal (as); Dexter Gordon (ts); Ernie Royal, Karl George (t). *Seated:* Hampton; Jack McVea (as, bs); Sonny Graven (tb); Joe Newman (t). Photo by Apeda.

Even more important to Jacquet was his new role as leader of his own big band, in his view the right and proper setting for his talents. 'I'm *supposed* to have a big band because I do things in front of a big band that nobody alive can do. I can dance, when I'm in good shape, I can play and I can sing. I've developed into what I think I started out to be, the bandleader of today. I don't have to imitate anything that's been here or anything that's gone. I'm more of what I want to be in front of a big band. I'm not doing it for money; I'm doing it because that's what I do, that's what I *have* to do.'

Jacquet enjoyed trawling the generations when picking his band. This time it included 79 year-old trumpeter Johnny Grimes and the exciting trombonist Jamal Haynes, just nineteen and, according to Illinois, a star in the making. 'He reminds me of when I first heard J.J. Johnson. He's got a great range, and he's an arranger. He's a nice person, he's respectable, he wants to be a vegetarian, he don't drink. Jamal is a typical young jazz musician on his way. That really thrills me.'

Jacquet talked about his band's recent activities. 'We have played some of the biggest engagements that any band has played in the past twenty years. We just played the Waldorf-Astoria in New York, we were at the Town Hall 'Salute to Buck Clayton' in June, we played for the Brooks-Astor birthday party at the Armory, and we played for the Bobby Short salute and went to New Orleans. Hadn't been there with the big band. They wouldn't let us off the stage. I had a chance to invite my ex-bandleader Cab Calloway to sit in with the band. Here's the man I played for in his band; now he's singing, in New Orleans, with my big band. When that happens, you gotta feel like you grown up, and you really part of this history.'

Jacquet's career began in Houston (his parents moved from Louisiana when he

was an infant). Another Texan tenor saxophonist, Herschel Evans, the Basie star who died in 1939, was a mentor and influence. 'He was *the* Texas tenor. He was with the Troy Floyd band and they battled my father's band, which was called Gilbert Jacquet's Legion Steppers. Herschel was the top soloist in Floyd's band and my oldest brother Julius had to play against him. Well, Herschel had such a big tone, you couldn't get near him and the only way the battle would be settled is when I would dance in front of my father's band to try to help him to cut Floyd.'

Influenced by their bassist father, Illinois and his siblings all became musicians. Aside from Julius on tenor, brother Linton played drums – 'a helluva drummer,' says Illinois – and Russell played trumpet. The four brothers later formed their own band, the California Playboys. A cousin, Frank Jacquet, 'a great trombone man', was with Don Albert's Happy Pals, another fine Texan territory group. Illinois himself first tried drums and soprano saxophone, before adopting the alto. He took lessons from a good local saxophonist, Lou Fred Simon, who later played in several Jacquet groups in Houston and Los Angeles.

'My father gave me $50 to buy an alto saxophone. I walked from the Fifth Ward to downtown to the music store and back, stopped by Lou's house and he gave me a lesson. Took me though a whole saxophone book before I even got home. I was about fourteen. I was gettin' really hot then. Making gigs, going to school with a little money in your pocket. I was hot stuff, but I was cool with it. Teachers were looking at me because I have a tie on, and a suit; sharp, you know. Sharper than the teachers. I didn't know too much because I was sleepin' in the classroom. I'd come from a gig to the class.'

Another outstanding saxophonist, Arnett Cobb, who gained fame with Lionel Hampton when he followed Jacquet into the band, was a few years ahead of him at the same school. Cobb, Jacquet and saxophonist and blues singer Eddie 'Cleanhead' Vinson, became teenage members of the Milt Larkin Orchestra, Houston's celebrated black big band. 'That

Illinois Jacquet's band, 1947. *Left to right*: J.J. Johnson (tb); Joe Newman, Russell Jacquet (tp); Illinois Jacquet; Al Lucas (b). Photo courtesy Illinois Jacquet.

could have been one of the best bands in the world had he been able to keep it. By the time he got a break to come east, everybody had gone. We used to battle Jimmie Lunceford's band – we'd take their music off a record, and play just like 'em. So when they came to battle us, they would put us on first and we played all their stuff. They had nothing to play!'

Larkin's arranger was Cedric Haywood, the band's pianist. 'He was a genius, one of the greatest. You know, playing this music, you have to be part genius. I mean, who could actually play and hypnotise you, put you in a trance like Art Tatum? Listening to a man like that, he was not an ordinary man, or an ordinary human being. How could that man do that? Where was it coming from? How was it possible?'

A moment arrived when Jacquet knew he had to make a decisive break. 'When I heard the Count Basie band in 1939 in my senior year, I knew I was gonna leave and get out of Texas. This was the band with Lester Young and Herschel Evans, all those great guys. I wanted to see what they looked like, how they walked into a place, set their horns down. All that was fascinatin' to me. That band was just like coming out of heaven, and by the middle of the night, that place would be smokin'. When they left there was nothing. Musically, you could feel it was empty, so I had to go.'

Originally he had New York in mind. His father, a railroad employee, secured him a travel pass but the only destinations available were New Orleans or California. Jacquet settled for the West Coast. 'California was the only new place I could go. I went on a pass, me and my brother Russell and my sister May. I stayed, they went back. I couldn't go back. I met Charles Mingus and we jammed and played every day, became great friends. He fell in love with my alto playing. I couldn't get rid of him. He was knockin' on my door every morning. "Let's go play," he'd say. That helped me to stay sharp because here you got guys that want to play, whether they're working or not. You don't need no piano player, you don't need no

drums, just saxophone and bass. He was so great on bass, the drums would be in the way. We'd even go on gigs with just bass and saxophone. I also played with the Al Adams Band but the work was very scarce and it wasn't payin' nothin' anyway.'

Jam sessions proved to be Jacquet's performing lifeline. 'Art Tatum was living out there then. He'd go on his job every night and get off at two o'clock, and that's when you hear him, at a house party, anywhere, he'd be jammin' all night. Then Norman Granz started having jam sessions at the Trouville and other little clubs on Sunday evenings, and he would book me and Lester Young, like a small-time Jazz At The Philharmonic. Central Avenue then was sorta like 52nd Street. It was really boomin' but I still couldn't get a job, so I'd just go and blow cats out.'

'Nat King Cole heard about all this. He had the trio then, working in Hollywood. There was nothing like 'em; they were like kings out there. I met him and he took a liking to me and became my best friend.' Cole's interest in Jacquet's musical skills led to the youngster's participation in the Labor Day jam session in Los Angeles in September 1940.

'Every Labor Day, the black musicians' union, Local 767, they would have a parade up and down Central Avenue. They would wind up in lower Central Avenue, near downtown, at the headquarters. Now they have the jam session, and that's when Nat got Jimmy Blanton, Sid Catlett, Charlie Christian and himself as the rhythm section. He said, "I don't want anybody else to

RCA Victor recording session, December 1947: Jacquet and Leo Parker.

sit in but you, 'cause we want to *hear* you." And man, we started cookin'. I was playing alto then, and I was playing just as much as Bird. Bird had heard me, he came and got me, kept me up all night one time in Kansas City, when I was with Milt Larkin. Bird couldn't believe that what I was doin' was so similar to him, 'cause I wasn't copyin' nobody. It was that style, that Mid-Western Texas style. He had it, I had it.'

'Now here I am in California, and I need a job. The better I was, the less I got work! Nobody would tell you where they were working; they figure you gonna come out and take the job. Until that jam session. That was one of the big moments of my life. After that, Nat started inviting me out to those clubs, out in Hollywood. Guys like Humphrey Bogart

staggered in, Errol Flynn, they heard me play and I started meeting guys like that. Nat introduced me to everybody.'

Through Cole, Jacquet made his fateful connection with Lionel Hampton, then back on
the West Coast after Benny Goodman had disbanded in July 1940. Hampton was talking
to Cole 'about making the trio his rhythm section. They never did join him but at the time,
it sounded good. The idea was to keep Nat's trio and put it with Hamp, and maybe tour with
him. Nat wanted me there. He said, "I'll introduce you to Hamp: if we goin' with him, we
would like to get you in." I'd join any band, I'd join *your* band if you could get a job!'

Jacquet with Lionel Hampton's orchestra, 1940. *Rear*: Lee Young (d); Irving Ashby (g);
Vernon Alley (b). *Front*: Marshall Royal, Ray Perry (as). Photo by E. F. Joseph, courtesy
Illinois Jacquet.

Jazz At The Philharmonic, Los Angeles, July 1944. *Left to right*: Jacquet, Jack McVea, Red Callender, Shorty Sherock. Photo by Alfred Trella.

"'Hamp's coming down tomorrow for a jam session. Come out with your horn and let him hear you, and I'm pretty sure when he hears what you doin', he'll ask you to join his band," says Nat. Sure enough, Hamp came and we had a jam session, and the stage was burnin'. The more I played, the more Hamp played, the more everybody was playing. This was at the Radio Room on Sunset and Vine, just a little place. So many people there, you couldn't move. Hamp would swing so much on the vibes, they fell off the stage, ended up on the floor. After, he asked me would I like to join his band, "provided you change from alto to the tenor."'

Jacquet moved over to tenor and the new Hampton big band made its debut in November 1940 in Los Angeles. They achieved national popularity, thanks to Hampton's own prominence and to a hit record that made Jacquet's name and played a crucial part in his career. His brilliant solo on 'Flying Home', recorded in May 1942 when he was nineteen, earned him the sort of attention previously only enjoyed by Coleman Hawkins with 'Body and Soul'. As Count Basie put it, 'It was the record that made Jacquet famous. Everybody remembers his solo on that record, and a lot of people can still hum it note for note.'[1] For many years after, when Hampton's road bands played this rousing piece, Illinois' chorus was incorporated in the score, harmonised as a saxophone section feature. Jacquet continues to re-invent his famous improvisation and created a new number around it called 'God Bless My Solo'.

Public attention on such a scale left the young saxophonist exhausted and broken in health. This he attributed to 'drinkin', smokin' pot, hangin'. Dope was getting round. I knew I wasn't going to get on that 'cause my mother would have killed me. We were very religious people, and I think that's what really saved me. The background destroyed the temptations.'

When Hampton reached California, Jacquet quit and stayed home for a year. 'Mingus came around and said, "We ought to get a band. I'll be the bass player."' But this new activity was short-lived as Jacquet joined Cab Calloway's orchestra in 1943, staying for about a year. 'I really formed the band when I left Cab. The first job we had was right across the street from the Paramount Theater. Some white cracker came in and said, "What are you niggers doin' in here?" Mingus was very tense. He took his bass and hit this guy, and his head came right through the bass so that was the end of that job! We only played but one or two songs. Mingus was beautiful really, but he couldn't stand that. I couldn't stand it either but I had to take it out with the music.'

'Next we went into Billy Berg's for one night. He was trying to sell his club 'cause it wasn't doing no business. He'd heard about my little group and he brought us in his club for a Monday night. Billy fell in love with the band and gave us a two-week contract. Business picked up and when it got good, he sold out. The new owners kept us in there a year! That was in 1944. We were in the Swing Club when we made [the film] *Jammin' The Blues*. Count Basie was at the Plantation Club in Watts, and Lester Young and Jo Jones were going in the Army. That's why it's such a helluva picture, because Lester was cryin' inside, knowin' he was going to the army.'

Illinois reached the end of his meal – fish, of course. Reminiscing about some of the best moments in his career had obviously pleased him.

Chapter 14

Eddie Miller

Bix, Ben and Bob

Eddie Miller, 1930s. Courtesy Max Jones Archive

Eddie Miller was playing a gig at a hotel in Derby in 1978 and I went up from London to hear him play. We found a corner to talk and this story ensued. Miller was his usual calm and collected self and coped admirably with a mini-barrage of questions from a local journalist as well as me. He died in April 1991, just short of his eightieth birthday.

The fine tenor saxophonist Eddie Miller occupied a special place in the affection of jazz enthusiasts on both sides of the Atlantic. His association with the Bob Crosby band (1935-1942) undoubtedly contributed to this acceptance, because the band's many recordings provided a vital showcase for Miller's well-ordered melodic playing.

His British tour around the time of this interview (solo, and with the World's Greatest Jazz Band) afforded happy proof that his skill and puff were unimpaired, and, incidentally, probably reminded some listeners that beauty in jazz still has its place in these otherwise fast and frantic times.

Eddie told me of his first idol, the New Orleans clarinettist Leon Rappolo, and of his teacher in New Orleans who insisted that 'sound or tone was uppermost'. The saxophonist Frankie Trumbauer was a major source of inspiration, too.

'When I was coming up,' he explained, 'the one guy I listened to on records was Trumbauer. I think he influenced many saxophone players like when I talked to Johnny Hodges and he told me that he used to listen to Tram. And I think you can tell that Lester Young heard Trumbauer. It was the sound, and the smooth, even flowing way he had.'

'I played alto first, and Frank [Trumbauer] played C-Melody. When I was offered the job to play with Ben Pollack in New York it was on alto, and then it happened that alto man Gil Rodin was going to stay with the band. So Benny says, "Do you think you could play tenor?" I was about to say no, and Ray Bauduc says, "Sure you can, go out and get a tenor." I had never had a tenor in my mouth in my life!'

'Now, the Pollack band was the utmost amongst musicians, so I tried out. I never thought I'd make it but I gave it a stab. In this business the biggest percentage is talent, but there is a percentage of luck also. And that was the turning point of my whole career. But for that, I would probably have been somewhere playing alto and nobody would know me at all,' he laughed.

Jazz history books make much of the Pollack band and its co-operative successor, the Bob Crosby Orchestra (with the Bobcats, its spin-off small group) so our conversation homed in on this period and the great names that derive from it. The appeal of this band arose, in Miller's view, from its 'loose and swingy' feeling, 'like a big jazz band', where

Bob Crosby's Bobcats, Blackhawk Restaurant, Chicago, 1938. *Left to right*: Yank Lawson (t); Ray Bauduc (d); Warren Smith (tb); Nappy Lamare (g); Irving Fazola (cl); Bob Haggart (b); Miller; Crosby; Gil Rodin (reeds).

others from the swing era had a more precise sound. He cited the engagement at the Blackhawk in Chicago as its finest hour.

One now-forgotten soloist from those Crosby days was trumpeter Sterling Bose, who was driven to suicide in 1958, the culmination of a long history of alcoholism. Inevitably, talk of booze problems brought us to the legendary cornetist Bix Beiderbecke, apparently an associate of Miller's in his early days in New York. I asked Eddie to tell me something of Bix's state of mind then.

'The colleges used to hire people like Tommy Dorsey before they ever had a [regular] band, so Tommy and [his brother] Jimmy would get a band together. They always had Bix, and I got to know him at the latter part of his life. He was a very quiet and withdrawn type of guy. Didn't talk much, but a real nice guy. I remember when we played up in New Haven, at Yale. It must have been six months before Bix died. And at intermission, Bix sat down at the piano and all these college kids came up. There was one particular girl who was in awe of this man, so the guys in the band said, "Bix, this girl is crazy about you, why don't you talk to her?" Bix says, "She doesn't like me, she likes my music." That's the way he was.'

'I'll never forget that evening. At that time he was composing all those things: 'In A Mist', 'In The Dark' – that was supposed to be a suite dedicated to members of his family – he told me that – which he never finished. I idolised him, too, as a kid.'

So far, we'd spoken only of white musicians. Had he taken note of the great black innovators? Yes, he was quick to reply, his childhood in New Orleans had enabled him to hear many fine players like Willie Humphrey, clarinettist on the riverboats, and trumpeter Lee Collins. He mentioned Johnny Dodds, particularly recalling his drive and blues feeling.

Members of the Bob Crosby and Count Basie orchestras, backstage jam session, Howard Theater, Washington DC, late 1938. Ray Bauduc (d); Bob Haggart (b); Herschel Evans, Miller, Lester Young (ts); Matty Matlock (cl). Photo by William Gottlieb/Redferns.

Later on, it was Coleman Hawkins that impressed him. 'I think all tenormen tip their hats to him, and later I got to know Hawk pretty well.'

Despite the segregation of the thirties, there were opportunities to cross the colour-lines, often after-hours. 'We were in Washington DC with the Crosby band, and Count Basie was in the other [Howard] theatre. That was in the days of segregation. Anyway, they came over to our theatre, and this one night after we got through we went to their theatre.

When they got through with their show, they pulled the curtain down and with some of our guys – not the whole band – and some of their guys, we had a full band. Besides Lester, there was Herschel [Evans] and Ray Bauduc, too. And we jammed – it was just a great thing.'

'There was two kids from college who had a recorder there. They came backstage the next day and said, "If you pay for the discs, we'll make copies." And we said, "Oh no, what do we want with that thing?" Today it would have been a classic!'

After ten years in New Orleans with dixieland clarinettist Pete Fountain, Eddie returned to the West Coast (where he had previously spent many years as a studio musician) working in clubs with old friends, comfortable in life and disposed to take only the gigs he enjoyed.

Perhaps this explained the unruffled ease of his instrumental performances, so I asked him finally to sum up his playing motivation: 'Pretty notes, that's what I'm trying to think of, not sound effects. Because the guys that I listened to, they played very flowing and melodic.'

'When I was a kid of sixteen, Leon Rappolo came in this speakeasy where I worked every couple of nights, because he was going with a girl who was a hostess there. I'd ask him to play and once in a while he'd play and I'd sit there in awe – almost have a nosebleed. Anyway, one night I must have got on the stand and tried to show him just how many notes I could play. Now this was a man who was supposed to be half-crazy at this time, and he said, "Hey, kid, remember this, it's not how *many* notes you play, it's the notes you play." And that always stuck in my head, to this day.'

Chapter 15

Geezil Minerve

Riding Shotgun for Duke

Geezil Minerve with Harry Carney and Duke Ellington, 1973. Photo by Dave Pochonet, courtesy Harold Minerve.

This piece is based on an interview in 1975 when the Ellington Orchestra was tour-ing Britain. After talking to Geezil Minerve in his hotel room in London, I was allowed backstage for that evening's concert and witnessed an almighty row when one of the trumpeters confronted the band's young bass player who had celebrated too extensively and failed to appear until the final moments of the concert. Geezil observed the fracas without comment, more amused than annoyed.

Geezil's fiery, boppish alto style was like a breath of fresh air and Duke created some memorable pieces for him. He stayed with the Ellington Orchestra when Mercer took over, following Duke's death in May 1974, before touring with the musical show Black and Blue *and playing in the pit for the Broadway version of* Sophisticated Ladies, *again under Mercer's direction. Geezil was a potent jazz soloist whose talents could easily have gone undiscovered but for Duke and Mercer's encouragement. He died in New York in June 1992 soon after his seventieth birthday.*

The late Duke Ellington was once moved to describe the alto saxophonist Harold 'Geezil' Minerve as 'a formidable musician'. Geezil acquired that accolade and a place in the Ducal scheme of things in 1971, after a long apprenticeship in the jazz hinterlands. Four years later, when I talked to him, he remembered his initiation with some amusement.

'September 9, 1971, I became officially an Ellingtonian and on September 11 we went to Russia! I'd already been trouble-shooting for them here and there: I called it riding shot-gun. When I went to Russia I was covering for Paul Gonsalves. I played all over the band with the alto: I've played the trumpet books, the trombone books and I even played the baritone parts. I understood I had to bide my time. Now, with Norris Turney out of the band, I play all the lead alto, have done for two years.'

We were talking in the cheerful disarray of the Minerve hotel room, where the stocky altoist spoke with enthusiasm about the Duke Ellington orchestras with which he'd been associated.

'It's the top. The Ellington band is really the epitome of musical endeavour for any musi-cian. The Duke would create on the scene. He would start something and he'd get a guy's idea and he'd ask him to come out and play. That would give birth to something: he was such a great man, he could hear you play and take it from there.'

Any enthusiast who's heard Minerve in concert or on record with Duke will know his dis-tinctive modern style founded on the blues. Originally a Benny Carter man, yet an admirer of Willie Smith and Johnny Hodges, too, he came to musical maturity in the early forties when Charlie Parker first turned jazz around.

'Blues to me means something like love – not a sombre type of thing at all. I have a type of blues that makes me happy. Guys like the late Louis Jordan and Eddie Vinson all had an impact on me. But I remember when I first heard Charlie Parker I thought he was stumbling on his horn, but as I grew I thought differently. Parker was a natural; I used to hear him and another terrific saxophonist, John Jackson, with Jay McShann's orchestra. Wonderful days.'

Ray Charles at the piano with his orchestra and the Raelettes (Pat Mosley, Margie Hendrix, Gwen Berry, Darlene McRae) in the film *Ballad in Blue* (US: *Blues for Lovers*), 1964. *Rear*: Oliver Beener, unknown, Roy Burrowes, Philip Guilbeau (t). *Centre*: Edgar Willis (b); Sonny Forrest (g); unknown, Julian Priester, Curtis Miller, Keg Johnson (tb). *Front*: David 'Fathead' Newman (ts), unknown, Minerve (as); James Clay (ts), Leroy Cooper (bs).

Geezil's initial musical motivation came from his French West Indian father, an amateur musician who moved his family to Florida in the twenties. His first noteworthy job was with the veteran blues singer Ida Cox. 'I was a child then, just coming out of high school,' he chuckled. 'Johnny Crawford, a tenor player from Atlanta, had the band and they found me in Orlando, Florida.'

Later, Minerve was with the remnants of the Joe Robichaux band, formed by the singer Joan Lunceford. 'This band was from New Orleans. Everywhere we went we got raves: toured all over the USA.' Then followed a period with the Ernie Fields Orchestra, a territory big band from Tulsa, Oklahoma, which built up a fine reputation. After his military service and more time with Fields, he joined the little-known Buddy Johnson Band, staying until 1956. 'They were a rival for Lionel Hampton. Buddy labelled his band as "the walking rhythm" – it was a danceable thing ,and very good too.'

Of course, those were days of segregated audiences, yet Geezil could still lament the passing of the big band era. 'You got a chance to play. You didn't make a lot of money but

Duke Ellington directing his orchestra at the Berlin Jazz Festival, November, 1971; Cootie Williams soloing. *Rear*: Johnny Coles, Eddie Preston, Harold 'Money' Johnson, Mercer Ellington (t). *Middle*: Malcolm Taylor, Chuck Connors (tb). *Front*: Paul Gonsalves (ts); Minerve (as); Harold Ashby (ts).

it was a happy scene. There were so many bands to go to: we've lost a lot now.'

He referred to his time with Fields and Johnson, and a later stint with the Ray Charles Orchestra, as 'backgrounding' – providing the backdrop for singers like Melvin Moore, Arthur Prysock, Ella Johnson, and Charles himself. Later, his work with the Ellingtons, father and son, put him firmly in the jazz limelight, whether as soloist or section man.

'This band is a musicians' band,' he said of the Ellington Orchestra. 'The prime object is to showcase the soloist, the instrumentalist. No, I haven't regretted one minute of it. In fact, I'm out in deep water – I can't turn around now. I'd say that anything before was a preparation for my time with Ellington.'

And what of the Ellington band of the mid-1970s? 'The band has a lot of young fellows now. We have a new type of enthusiasm there, a new vibrance. These guys can all play. They're not tired. We're doing the same titles but Mercer is bringing out new ideas. He has a knack of listening and knowing whether you're capable. I've worked with Mercer's bands before – he's always had a gift for picking out musicians.'

'Naturally, the old man had it too. Like we have a bass player, J.J. Wiggins, who's eighteen years old. You have to listen to this guy. Ricky Ford and Bill Easley too, you got to hear that. Then Joe Temperley is a terrific musician. You have to move aside for newness, so it's a revised type of Ellington music.'

Harold Minerve projected happiness in his own music, and in person. 'I always play happy. You listen to my solos, they're vibrant that way.' No less so than his zest for life and search for friendship in music, I'd say.

Chapter 16

Vi Redd

Central Avenue Blues

Vi Redd, Marla's Memory Lane, Los Angeles, 1980s. Photo by Nareshimah Osel, courtesy Vi Redd.

When alto saxophonist and vocalist Vi Redd appeared at Ronnie Scott's club in September 1967, she was so successful that her engagement was extended until Christmas. Although she toured in Europe with Count Basie the following year, she did not return to London until October 1983 when she played another much-lauded season at the Pizza Express in Dean Street. I taped her account of her career at that time and realised that Vi was a mine of information about the early African-American jazz scene in Los Angeles. We renewed contact a few years later and met up again (recording more reminiscences) when she returned to the Pizza Express in October 1994. Vi had brought her husband Al, and her drummer son Randall, to London with her and the following is adapted from a piece written at that time.

Vi and her family were generous hosts when I visited them in Los Angeles a few years later. Her letters were always positive, with plenty of detail about her many activities, until Randall's sudden death in September 1996 seemed to break her spirit. She has performed only rarely since then although she was very proud to be the recipient of the 2001 Mary Lou Williams Women in Jazz Award.

1994: The London flat is awash with the flotsam and jetsam of tourism. Souvenirs and home-going gifts cover every table. Amid the detritus, Elvira 'Vi' Redd tries to cram a mass of new possessions into cases that seem to have become smaller since she arrived. The deadline for her return home to Los Angeles is looming and time is running out.

But in the midst of all the rush, somehow she manages for a few minutes to push aside the packing to reflect on the ebb-and-flow of her musical life. She's a respected custodian of community values and will talk readily about long-gone musicians from the black California jazz scene. She connects with their relatives and survivors, keeping a watchful eye on old-timers and contemporaries.

When I interviewed Vi on that 1994 visit she still maintained a busy performing schedule. Her son Randall Goldberg, who worked with her regularly at the time and was on hand for her London engagement, was the latest in a long line of percussionists in the extended Redd family. Randall's father, Richie Goldberg (who died in November 1994) worked with Herbie Mann in the sixties, and his uncle, Buddy Redd, toured with the Ink Spots for a time. But it was from Vi's drummer father, Alton Redd, Louisiana-born and a contemporary of early pioneers like Kid Ory and Mutt Carey, that she (and her son) drew their chief inspiration.

By all accounts, Redd senior was an important figure in the black music community: 'He was the most benevolent man I've ever known, always concerned about other people. Papa Jo Jones was crazy about Daddy. He told me Daddy would always come down to the train station in Los Angeles to pick them – the Basie guys – up, and ride them into town two or three at a time. This was when black musicians couldn't get places to stay.'

Oddly enough, the first time Vi and her father played together on a gig was when she

Pops Foster Tribute Concert, AFM Local 47 Auditorium, 1969. *From left*: unknown; Alma Hightower at the drums, Alton Redd, Vi Redd.

led the band: 'He used to call all over town for musicians and mother said, "I don't know, Alton, "Why are you calling this place and that place? Your daughter can do it." I guess he had his chauvinist thing going too. So, finally, I had to hire him and, after that, we used to gig together all the time.'

Vi's first impetus to play came from a legendary teacher, her great-aunt Alma Hightower. 'She was my grandmother's sister and came to live with us when I was quite young. Aunt Alma got a reasonable horn, gave me the mouthpiece and said, "Open your mouth and say 'pah, pah, pah,'" and that's how it started. She had a band with tenor saxophonist James Jackson; trumpeters Arthur Walker and Robert Ross; Melba Liston, the trombonist; and my first cousin, who was a wonderful musician, Lloyd Prince Harrison. He was a great tenor player, went on the road with Jay McShann when he was about fifteen and did get into some difficulties. He died very early.'

'Aunt Alma not only taught music, she taught dancing, too. She could teach dancing and never get up from the chair. She was very, very, short; wasn't even five feet, but a dynamo, absolutely. With her band, we played at every church; played parades, used to sit on the corner of 43rd and Central, and play there. Melba Liston once said she went some-where with Dizzy Gillespie – Iran or some place – and this man came up to her and said, "I remember you. You're the little girl who used to play the trombone on 43rd and Central." I think Melba called him a bad name.'

Central Avenue achieved fame as the principal focus for black entertainment in Los Angeles during World War Two, packed as it was with thriving clubs and jazz joints. Now Central Avenue is run-down, and Mexican-Americans are the majority population. Vi

Vi Redd, late 1970s. Photo courtesy Vi Redd.

remembered its best days in the mid-1940s: 'I'll start at West Washington where the Young family lived, that's Lee and Lester, at one end of Central Avenue. Then there was the Rosebud Theater, the Florence Mills Theater, the Bill Robinson Theater, Gibbs Jockey Club where we used to sit and play. There was a First Market, the Los Angeles *Sentinel* newspaper, the *Eagle* newspaper. There was everything on that street that you'd want: dry cleaners, barbecue places, two or three Victory markets, night clubs, all right there.'

In 1944 to 1946, Vi was a student at Dorsey High School where she encountered fellow saxophonists Herb Geller and Eric Dolphy. 'Eric was child-like – I always say that. Not that he didn't have the mentality. He was so much like a child – that's it, just really, really innocent. We had some classes at City College together, and he was playing flute real good – I had such a hard time with the flute. We lived close to each other; Eric's folks lived up at 36th Street near Western and we were on the corner of 36th and Gramercy. Eric would drop me and come in and jam. Eric was 'out' then, he was into 'free expression', even at that time. Martha Young, my pianist friend, would get so angry but Eric was child-like and lovable; he'd just laugh. He was a lovely man.'

Vi is often categorised as a bebopper but she was something of a late convert to the modernist cause. At high school, she sang a lot, influenced by the church. 'I'm an ecclesiastical hodgepodge – part of my family was Baptist, part was Holiness and most of Daddy's family was Methodist. My grandmother used to go to Holiness prayer-meetings with Charles Mingus' grandmother – his 'Wednesday Night Prayer Meeting': that was for real! The music of the church was very important to me. It's still important.'

'Bebop was just thrust upon me. In 1948 when I went to college, I got a band together. Martha Young was the piano player; she was Lee and Lester's niece, just a lovely person. My brother played drums; I played saxophone; my first husband, Nathaniel Meeks, played trumpet, and we had a bass player named Morris Edwards. We started playing for all the fraternities and sorority social affairs. All of Nathaniel's friends were into bebop and Nat used to play all the bebop songs: he had all of Dizzy's records. Martha and I were just caught up in it and, oh, I loved it.'

'People like Teddy Edwards and Sonny Criss were ahead of me; they were really gigging then. But we all knew each other. Hampton Hawes was a nice, nice guy. I really liked Hampton. He got into the drug scene and then he got out of it, received a pardon from one of the Kennedy brothers. Hamp's father was a Presbyterian minister and didn't approve [of jazz], no, but Hamp used to sneak the guys into the rectory and they'd have jam sessions there. Hamp was something else.'

Charlie Parker is often cited as Vi's principal influence, yet she only saw him once. 'It was at the musicians' union office, Local 767. He was having trouble getting to play because he had come from New York and didn't have his union card. When I saw him that day, he was saying, "Please talk to Elmer Fain [the union business agent]. I gotta work my job tonight." I said, "Is this Bird? He's so humble." I never got a chance to hear him play.'

Vi Redd went on to build an important career as a soloist and vocalist, appearing with Earl Hines and Count Basie, while also finding time to bring up her family and attend to her other interests. Her musical ambitions, as she described them on her 1994 visit, may surprise hard-core jazz enthusiasts: 'I don't want to get out and do, say, a hundred one-nighters. That's not for me. What I really want to do is to play my saxophone in a movie, and I'd also love to play with the Boston Pops [Orchestra].'

'I have an interest at the church which is very important to me. I'm concerned about the injustices, primarily for young black men, and I do what I can in that field through my church. There's so much to be done in this life.'

In the early 1990s she had been busy as a teacher specialising in helping handicapped children. Newly retired from that, she said, 'Now, I'm back to the first chapter – the music, and I'm keen to pursue whatever God gives me to do.' She was also optimistic about the emergence of more female jazz musicians: 'Females are taking up instruments; you see more of it now, but there is, as in business, the glass ceiling. But like all injustices, we're going to have to pursue, pursue, pursue.'

With its upbeat yet soulful character, Redd's music mirrors both her personality and life experience. She is proud of her ability to combine blues and jazz – 'I can't separate them,' she said. And happily for her listeners, she is intent on spreading her version of the jazz message more widely than ever before.

Chapter 17

Hal Singer

Cornbread's French Leave

Hal Singer in France, 1980s. Photo courtesy Hal Singer.

Hal Singer has been living in France with his wife Arlette and their daughters for more than thirty years now. He was one of a number of African-American jazz musicians who chose to settle in Paris, and he still fulfils concert and club engagements around Europe, even though he says he's semi-retired these days. We first became acquainted in 1981 when the saxophonist played a series of solo dates at Pizza Express in London. I drove him around town and we taped a lengthy interview at the club. I've always enjoyed his company (and his music) and we continue to maintain contact. It's just a shame that he plays in the UK so rarely.

Harold Singer was born in Tulsa, Oklahoma, on 8 October 1919. His father was a respected factory overseer and the family enjoyed a comfortable if confined existence given the rigid segregation of the races then in place in the southern USA. Looking back, Hal likened the black section of Tulsa to a 'town-within-the-town, with our own churches, stores, athletic fields and even our own police force. It was rarely necessary to leave our community for greater Tulsa where the whites lived.'

As with so many African-American families, church attendance played a crucial part in Hal's upbringing, allowing him to gain a taste for the vibrant musical display that was key to their religious observance. Even so, Hal's father decided that his son should take up the violin, rather than any other more impactive instrument. 'That was the respectable instrument of respectable families like ours,' Hal emphasised. He took lessons at the age of eight, but was soon aware that the violin was not for him. It took his high school music teacher to turn Hal on to the clarinet and, later, the alto saxophone. In time, he became a proud member of the school band, travelling around the state for football games.

His parents were also pleased to take him to dances in Tulsa: thus the youngster saw the bands of Andy Kirk, Jimmie Lunceford, Count Basie, and most tellingly, Duke Ellington. 'Basically, all the big name orchestras passed through Tulsa.' Hal learned to lie in wait for visiting stars when they came to town, pestering them to give him tips on saxophone technique and inviting them to come to his home where his mother would prepare food for the visitors. Johnny Hodges and Lester Young were among those who dined at the Singer's table: quite a coup for the hero-worshipping novice. Entranced by Young's playing, Hal persuaded his mother to buy him a Conn tenor saxophone (paid for in instalments) and he began to sit in with small groups locally.

Determined to embark on music as a career but mindful of his father's concern that he should prepare himself for a proper profession, Singer elected to go to the Hampton Institute in Hampton, Virginia, to study agriculture while playing with the marching band

and the Hamptonians, the college swing band. Back in Tulsa on vacation, he heard from friends that legendary bandleader Terrence Holder was looking for musicians, and seized the moment.

'My first job was with T. Holder. We were playing at a barbecue stand in Tulsa. I was no more than seventeen years old at the time. Now when 'T' played his trumpet, he kinda shook his head. I guess it was to get a vibrato. That made me so worried 'cause I thought

Hal Singer with Lucky Millinder and his orchestra, Savoy Ballroom, New York City, early 1948. Photo by Moss Photo Inc., courtesy Hal Singer.

he was shaking his head in disapproval. Holder played beautiful sweet trumpet, you know, but he was an incorrigible womaniser and heavy gambler. His game was simple: he pretended to be absent-minded, 'forgetting' to pay the musicians. Because he was so charming his oversight was often forgiven.' Holder was an Oklahoman who, many years before, had starred as the trumpet soloist in Alphonso Trent's popular band and had then formed the Clouds of Joy in 1925 with the one-time postman Andy Kirk on tuba. When Holder played funny – 'forgetting' to pay his sidemen, no doubt – with the money, Kirk had been

Henry 'Red' Allen's band in the 1940s: Allen (t); Eddie Bourne (d); Singer; J.C. Higginbotham (tbn); General Morgan (p); Benny Moten (b). Photo courtesy mr.jazz Photo Files (Theo Zwicky).

persuaded to take on the leadership and later built his version of the Clouds of Joy into a nationally prominent unit.

After completing his second year at Hampton, Hal spent the summer in Oklahoma City where he joined a combo led by Ed Christian, the bass-playing brother of guitar innovator Charlie Christian. 'Since he was the bandleader, Ed decided to play piano which allowed him to be on stage in front of the band and check out the girls in the audience.' Hal retains happy memories of meeting Christian, already renowned throughout the Southwest for his instrumental skills, and he was present at a celebrated jam session when Charlie sat in with Mary Lou Williams and the Andy Kirk band. 'He was going 24 hours a day – he had unlimited energy,' Hal remembered. After accepting a tour with his fellow-Tulsan, the trumpeter Vernon 'Geechie' Smith, Singer realised that he had missed the deadline to return to Hampton for the commencement of the school term, and thus became a professional musician by default, much to his family's disappointment.

Through a childhood neighbour, the excellent saxophonist Luther West, Hal was able to take up an offer in the summer of 1938 to join the touring orchestra of Ernie Fields, then rated among the best of the territory big bands. 'Ernie was a great organiser and trombone player; he also had a strong business sense. He was like a father figure. His wife was a schoolteacher in Tulsa and they were counted among the most respectable folks in our little black town-within-a-town. They lived in a large, beautiful home. I knew they defied the image people had of jazz musicians.' The Fields band sported fine soloists like Luther West and tenorist Buck Douglas; the arrangers were guitarist Rene Hall, later a force in Los

Angeles R&B circles, and trombonist Parker Berry, who also flourished subsequently in California.

In the spring of 1939, Sir Charles Thompson, the pianist with Lloyd Hunter's big band in Nebraska, came to Tulsa looking for a saxophonist. Some of Hal's musical friends from the Booker Washington High School days were already in Hunter's group and had recommended him. Singer asked Thompson to talk to his parents and, within days, Hal was on his way to Omaha. Hunter played like fellow-trumpeter Hot Lips Page and prided himself on his band's brass section. 'The quality of the music was more important to Lloyd Hunter than the business side. Hunter could always swing the best. His bands were rough but they

Roy Eldridge (t); Sol Yaged (cl); Coleman Hawkins (ts), and Singer at the Metropole, New York City, 1950s. Photo courtesy Hal Singer.

could swing.' Hunter's band toured the Mid-West in a raggedy old bus, playing largely for appreciative white audiences. Singer relished the less restrictive ambiance of Omaha. 'It was the first time I felt free,' he said. For all his appreciation of Hunter's happy-go-lucky style, he knew that the Nat Towles Orchestra was the top outfit in Omaha and was gratified to receive an invitation to join Towles, whose band paid better and whose engagements were generally in more salubrious locations. 'Towles was better for musicianship. Neal Hefti was the arranger for Towles then. He was just sixteen and you could hear then what he did later. You could take those charts today, play them, and they'd still be great.'

In late 1939, Singer relocated to Kansas City, happy to be in 'the capital of swing'. On his first night in town he heard the news that Tommy Douglas was looking for a saxophonist and joined his band straightaway, staying for a year. 'Tommy Douglas was one of the greatest alto players that ever lived. He played with great mastery. A well-raised, refined and courteous man. I was with his band when Jay [McShann] came for me in '41. Tommy said, 'I won't stand in your way, go ahead.' He didn't demand no notice or anything. In those days, between the musicians and the union, it was all based on friendship. A man wouldn't stand in your way if you had a chance of making progress. It's not like that now.'

In an interview McShann recalled Hal's arrival. 'Hal was with Tommy Douglas. I think I sent Gus Johnson and Gene Ramey down to catch him. I believe we were in Kansas City too. Tommy was nice enough to let Hal leave with our band. Hal always had a gutty sound. That's the first thing that gassed the cats and of course, the cats told me, "Man, he's got that tenor sound." So I said, "Well, get him." So that was our first chance to work together.' Hal left K.C. the next day with the 'blues-saturated' McShann orchestra, bound for points north, east and west, travelling by train and playing many military bases.

Singer had the opportunity to observe his bandleader at close quarters: 'Jay never should have been the leader. He was too young. He had no authority. He was too keen to hang out with the guys and he'd get drunker than any of them. I found that out myself when I [later] had my own band. You had to keep a gap between you and the guys in the band. I thought I'd be just like one of the guys, but that never did work.'

Tired, finally, of touring, Hal headed for New York in 1942 and settled into combo life, playing with a succession of great musicians on and around 52nd Street. After stints with Willie The Lion Smith and the Hot Lips Page Sextet, he joined Roy Eldridge's big band (teamed on tenor with Franz Jackson, another doughty survivor) for a year. He made his first recordings with Eldridge in 1944 and worked in a Don Byas group with trumpeter Joe Newman in 1945. Always a Byas devotee, Hal relished the opportunity to play alongside his idol. A year later, he was with Red Allen's swingy small group before joining Big Sid Catlett at the Downbeat Club. 'I took Dexter Gordon's job on 52nd Street. One night Dexter didn't show so someone said, "Hal's here," and I got the job. We backed Lady Day.'

Following the run-down of 52nd Street after World War Two, Hal worked briefly with Lucky Millinder's big band in the Savoy Ballroom, staying until he was called in the summer of 1948 to join Duke Ellington for 'the greatest musical thrill of my life. I was the sixth saxophone. Jimmy Hamilton didn't want to play sax at that time so I played his sax parts and he doubled them on clarinet.' Within six months, though, his hit record of 'Cornbread' (the nick-name of his friend, trombonist Clyde Bernhardt) came out and Hal was besieged with offers to tour. However reluctantly, he felt compelled to leave Duke as 'Cornbread' became a national jukebox choice, helping make Hal's name, although its success tended to confine him to the lucrative rock and roll circuit. According to Arlette Singer, 'Hal gave all the rights [to

Ljubljana Jazz Festival 1971. Dill Jones (p); Budd Johnson (ts); Bill Pemberton (b); Oliver Jackson (d, hidden); Singer; Benny Bailey (t). Photo courtesy Hal Singer.

'Cornbread'] to someone else. He never got a cent for the record but the A&R man gave him a Cadillac.' Incidentally, this recording was pianist Wynton Kelly's debut on disc. It also led to a variety of follow-up record dates, many employing Hal's peers from the jazz world although, inevitably, most of their creativity was sacrificed in favour of simplistic riffing and honking. For all that, Hal was able to squeeze in the odd ballad feature, like 'Indian Love Call' or 'Easy Living', which demonstrated his command of the fulsome tenor style epitomised by the better Hawkins followers.

Singer then led his own groups for the next ten years, barnstorming around the USA (often appearing at the Apollo Theater in Harlem) on starry R&B package tours and recording frequently. By May 1958, he was back on the New York scene and joined the raucous regulars at the Metropole bar on Seventh Avenue to work with trumpeters Charlie Shavers and Red Allen. Leaving the Metropole in 1962, he formed an organ trio with Frankie Dunlop on drums and then enrolled for a course in mid-career, at the prestigious Juilliard School, before taking off for Paris in 1965 at the suggestion of blues singer Memphis Slim, then a Paris resident himself.

The rest, as they say, is history. Hal decided to remain in Paris, sensing that European audiences were vastly more appreciative than their counterparts in the US. 'By being in Europe, I think I've prolonged my staying power. It's given me time to concentrate on my musical growth, to be with my family and to find myself as a person,' he told journalist Mike Zwerin in the *International Herald Tribune*. Hal performed with others of the American expatriates who made Paris such an exciting place for jazz lovers in the 1960s, and then led groups of his own, many featuring younger French players. He recorded often, played festivals, galas and shows (notably, *Black and Blue* at the Châtelet in 1985), and criss-crossed Europe with fellow-Americans like Jay McShann, Kenny Clarke, Slide Hampton and Art Farmer. He has made regular visits to Africa and to the States to play with old friends, and he participated in a composition course at the Berklee School in 1972.

Hal also began to visit the United Kingdom, first as a single, then with R&B outfits like Rocket '88. Audiences warmed to what Kevin Henriques, writing in the *Financial Times*,[1] called 'his straightforward, no-nonsense playing', and saw that Singer epitomised the full-toned mainstream jazz tenor style. For all that, he is aware of newer trends and has per-formed often with contemporary musicians like tenorist Archie Shepp. Speaking of John Coltrane, Hal said, 'Sure, I admired John and loved his playing, at least the earlier stuff. We were good friends and I know that he was the most dedicated musician I've ever met. Like when he was playing a club, he'd always continue practising during the break so that in effect he was playing continuously the whole night. That's how he achieved what he did. I was never that dedicated – I value my family and friends too much for that.'

For many years now, Singer and his wife Arlette, who is French, have been based in Nanterre, near Paris, where they lead a contented family life, far from the roistering image that attends so many jazzmen of Hal's generation. They have two daughters, one a lawyer, the other a beautician, and two much-cherished grandchildren. Hal's performance sched-ule is a mix of local concert engagements and foreign tours – he was recently in the Far East and Hong Kong and then in Switzerland – and, happily, there's no shortage of demand for his services. He has been honoured by his adopted country – the French Minister of Culture, Jack Lang, made Singer a 'Commandeur des Arts et Lettres' in 1992 – and the good people of Nanterre marked the thirtieth anniversary of his arrival in their midst with a month-long festival dedicated to him, in October 1995. The subject of a documentary film *Hal Singer: Un Musicien Parmi Nous* by American director Guetty Ferlin, Hal also made a cameo acting/playing appearance in the 1989 film, *Taxi Blues*, a French-Russian co-production which required him to spend time in Moscow. Not to be outdone in the provision of honours for Singer, his home state of Oklahoma inducted Hal into their 'Jazz Hall of Fame' in 1996.

So while he may never have matched John Coltrane's extraordinary creativity – who has, after all? – Hal Singer knows that he is valued and that he has been successful in bal-ancing the rewards of a happy family life with those derived from artistic achievement. Ever open-minded, he says, 'I've got no blocks against any kind of music. Just get in the groove, do something good, and save the rest for the next tune.'

Chapter 18

Eddie Vinson

Cleanhead's Blues

Eddie Vinson, 1980s.

Altoist and blues vocalist Eddie 'Cleanhead' Vinson made a major impact on me at
the Nice Festival in 1978. Although his career in the USA had picked up after a
period in the doldrums, his acceptance by European audiences meant a lot to him
and he toured (and recorded) regularly as a solo artist, often visiting Britain with his
wife Bernice. I was impressed by his candour as he spoke about his drinking and
the virtues of Alcoholics Anonymous when we talked in 1978 at his Nice hotel.

The present piece is based on a lengthy interview recorded at that time. We met
up again after that on several occasions, and I never tired of hearing him sing and
play. Eddie died in July 1988 in Los Angeles, aged 70.

In conversation, the Texan veteran was quietly spoken, reserved even, his reticence at odds with the extrovert manner of his stage presentation. I asked him first about the origins of his alto style, so reminiscent of Charlie Parker.

'I met Charlie in '39 or '40, and he was with the Jay McShann band. I was playing one day down in the car and one of the guys said, "Eddie, have you heard Parker?" I said "No." And he said, "You should hear him 'cause you two are similar."'

'The Milt Larkin band – that was our band – we were a very popular group in Texas at the time, and Jay McShann was in the same town, but their dance didn't do so good so everybody came down to where we were playing. After the dance we had a jam session and that's where I met Charlie.'

'That night I had to go 300 miles back to Houston. So I kidnapped him and put him in the car and took him back there and kept him about three days at my house. Every day before breakfast – well – I'd take him out in the barn and we would run over things together. That's the story of my association with Charlie, and it went on a long time.'

Vinson emphasised that his style and sound were set before he met Parker and talked of their common background in the blues. 'Years ago, you could see anybody on any street playing guitar; walking down the street, just singing and playing. Some guys would sit on your front porch and they'd be playing so you'd give them a dime. It was just one of those things. Then at home we always had the Bessie Smiths, the Ma Raineys, playing on our Victrola. I tell you, the first guy I heard playing the blues that really was modern was T-Bone Walker. He had a different thing going on. But I had listened to Big Bill Broonzy; he's my favourite. I do some of his tunes all the time.'

Earlier, young Eddie had been required to concentrate his emerging singing skills on Baptist church meetings, where his aunt was programme director. The blues were considered suggestive, hardly fit for respectable ears. Vinson focused on ballads, and with his saxophone prowess – he started playing at fifteen – was soon in demand. As he said: 'I knew the old tunes, and I could play them all, so I got a lot of the gigs.' He was usually cast as lead saxophone in the local big bands and, 'during the time we were getting out our set, we would start playing blues.'

'Then I started just singing blues and that would go on for three minutes until the set was ready. Then the people were just asking for the blues. We couldn't understand it, when we had all those good arrangements. But that's what they wanted.'

So, accidentally perhaps, a career that took Eddie from sideman to star was underway.

Cootie Williams and his orchestra at the Savoy Ballroom, New York City, mid-1940s. *Left to right*: Fletcher Smith (p); Norman Keenan (b); Sam 'The Man' Taylor (ts); Williams (t); Vinson; Butch Ballard (d). Photo courtesy Norman Keenan.

He had no explanation for his 'big' vocal sound and when I asked about his characteristic falsetto break he could offer little comment, other than: 'I can make it happen sometimes but usually it just comes on the end of a phrase.' No matter, for the voice was timeless in quality, cutting through to touch the emotions of most listeners, black or white, I fancy.

Instrumentally, Eddie made his start with his career-long associate, tenorist Arnett Cobb, in the Houston big band of trumpeter Chester Boone, before working with the Birmingham Blues Blowers, another unsung territory orchestra. As the youngest man, he was encouraged to front the band and sing ballads – not blues. Then came a lengthy period with the Milt Larkin band, another Houston-based ensemble that was among the best of the black swing-era combinations.

Consider a saxophone section that included, at one time, Vinson on lead alto and the tenors of Arnett Cobb and Illinois Jacquet. Yet Larkin never recorded, despite the band's huge reputation and high quality solo skills. 'It was just a happy band, everybody liked to rehearse. The reed section would probably rehearse at my house one day or Illinois' house the next. Then we'd come together: that's what made the band so good.'

'Hard-driving swing stuff – it would have been a band that would have been known

Cootie Williams Orchestra, Grand Terrace, Chicago, February 1942. Kenny Kersey (p); Norman Keenan (b); Williams (t, ldr); Butch Ballard (d); Robert Horton, Jonas Walker, Sandy Williams (tb); Rostelle Reese, Joe Guy, Louis Bacon (t); Don Stovall (bs); Greely Walton (ts); Vinson, Charlie Holmes (as), Bob Dorsey (ts). Photo courtesy Norman Keenan.

today. It was pushing Basie and Lunceford hard at that time – maybe that's why we didn't record,' Eddie reflected.

Trumpeter Cootie Williams came to Texas in 1941, prompted by John Hammond, and persuaded young Vinson to join him in Chicago. He was reluctant to move but fate must have intervened, for an immediate record date with Williams included a Joe Turner blues called 'Cherry Red' with Vinson's individual vocal its standout feature. Eddie laughed and admitted: 'Man, I couldn't have cared less about records – I just wanted to go back home! The music wasn't as good as Milt's – it sounded like tissue paper to me.'

It was at this time that Vinson assumed the 'Cleanhead' identity that became his trade-mark following an accident with a hair straightener, his unique shaven head making him as distinctive physically as he was vocally.

His singing on the Williams sides made him a jazz 'n' blues celebrity and, in time, led to a solo career. 'Cootie told me it would be best if I got my own band 'cause he could not pay me what he thought I was worth. I always respected him for that.'

Vinson's first big band was packed full of Texans, naturally enough, and travelled extensively by courtesy of Universal Attractions until 'around about '53.' He was proud of his later association with promising young musicians in his smaller groups – notably John Coltrane. 'In fact, I put him on the tenor saxophone. I was mixing everything together then, like bop and the blues. I would play my records, for the hits, but then we would play bebop. I knew Trane was something special when I first heard him in Philadelphia. I had to ask his mother if he could go on the road.'

Record success made Vinson a rich man – temporarily, for as he admitted: 'I drank an awful lot of whiskey then. It was a big problem, 'cause you get to the stage where you don't care and that's what the whiskey will do. In fact, I only stopped drinking about three years ago. However, I'm a member of Alcoholics Anonymous and I live it now. It's my life. I go to the meetings anywhere I can and I'm making little talks. It's the best thing that ever happened to me in my life. My whole outlook is better. Now, I'm free – I think – for today I tell everybody I don't even rub with alcohol,' he laughed.

Eddie's admirable frankness about a hazard familiar to many musicians, and its successful resolution, are worth emphasising. In his later years, he based himself in Los Angeles, working weekends with a rhythm section and travelling to Europe to shout the blues and keep in touch with modern jazz.

'I've got some new things and I'm starting to record quite a bit,' he enthused. 'I have some new blues too. Leonard Feather and I have one called the 'Taxi Drivers' Blues' – based on the truth. I'm looking for things with real truth in them. Why, I can dream a blues, wake up and write it down. For me, the blues has to be a happy thing.'

Chapter 19

Benny Waters with Jacques Butler

Jazz in Montmartre

Patricia and I chanced on La Cigale and Benny Waters while on holiday in Paris in 1962 and went to this raffish neighbourhood club a number of times, returning again the following year. The two articles adapted here sought to report on these experiences and, incidentally, to provide biographical information about Jack (Jacques) Butler and Benny Waters, two interesting jazz musicians who have been somewhat neglected by the history books.

We started a friendship with Benny then that endured until his death in August 1998. It seemed important that he should be known in Britain; eventually this happened and he became a great favourite with English audiences. After leaving La Cigale, he also began to record regularly and to travel endlessly around Europe, appearing as a guest soloist. He stayed with us, played our piano, attempted to teach one of our daughters the clarinet and entertained us as a family whenever we were in Paris.

I continued to interview Benny, wrote many articles, reviews and sleeve notes about him, and heard him play often in Paris and elsewhere. He was always stimulating as a performer, enthusiastic yet never satisfied, generous to his fellow musicians and utterly indefatigable. I admired him without reservation and valued his friendship a lot. I last saw Benny wowing a young audience at a high school in northern California in 1995; he was 93 years of age and totally blind. Everyone loved him. Always canny with his money, Benny Waters left an estate valued at $500,000.

Jacques Butler's early career took him from Washington D.C. to New York and then to Europe where he toured (and recorded) with Willie Lewis' celebrated band in the 1930s. He was lured back to Paris in 1950 after working with Mercer Ellington in New York, gaining additional prominence when he appeared in the film

Paris Blues *alongside Louis Armstrong in 1961. In the late 1960s, he returned to New York for good and took a variety of club engagements with the Harlem Blues and Jazz Band. Known as something of a ladies' man, he had family in both France and America, and kept in touch with them all until his death in April 2003 at the great age of 94.*

Jacques Butler with his quintet, including Benny Waters, La Cigale, Paris, 1963. Photo by Ian Powell.

Benny Waters in Britain in the 1980s.

Visitors searching for jazz in Paris in 1962 tended to look toward the Blue Note, where such well-known names as Bud Powell, Jimmy Gourley or Kenny Clarke were to be found. Other clubs featured fine musicians, both French and American, but certain jazzmen in Paris continued to make music well away from the forces of publicity. Among them were trumpeter Jacques Butler and tenorist Benny Waters, both American expatriates, who played nightly at La Cigale, a Montmartre bar on Boulevard Rochechouart. Their efforts seemed taken for granted; certainly there was no critical comment on their performances in French magazines, and their recordings in France had been few. Here are my impressions of the scene at La Cigale as noted at the time.

. . . The billing for the band is: 'Jacques Butler et son Quintette avec Benny Waters'. The small bandstand is set to one side, away from the bar. As decor, there are large photographic murals depicting musical instruments. Tables and chairs for the listeners. No dancing. There seems always to be a number of genuine jazz enthusiasts present, together with the inevitable tourists and neighbourhood relics. There is no entrance charge but the first drink is expensive. The place is well lit, it's easy to see the band and an amplification system allows everyone to hear. The band works every night from 9.30 p.m. to 1.30 a.m. with an extra three hours each Saturday and Sunday afternoon.

An erect, neat man, dark-suited, Butler leads the band, playing hot trumpet, singing warmly, all with apparent relaxation and good humour. He smiles to many old friends, some of whom call over to shake hands. Shorter and fatter, Waters is the featured soloist, extrovert in his phrasing and confident, with the same underlying good humour and relaxation. Butler previously spent many years with Willie Lewis' band in Europe. Before that he had worked in America with Willie Bryant, Horace Henderson and Lucky Millinder. His style owes much to Armstrong and Eldridge, his tone broad with much vibrato, his playing generally fiery and brassy; on ballads he often uses a felt mute and has a mellow, lyrical quality. His phrasing on the up-tempo riff tunes is in the big-band tradition, building to grandstand climaxes. On occasion though, control is erratic and the striving for effect too marked, but he plays with conviction and genuine heat and can produce solos of quality. His all-round musicianship in ensemble work cannot be faulted.

Waters, his front-line partner, is a jazz phenomenon: at 62 years of age, he can look back on recordings in the twenties with Clarence Williams groups that also featured King Oliver, followed by periods with Claude Hopkins, Fletcher Henderson, Jimmie Lunceford, Hot Lips Page and Jimmy Archey. He came to Europe after World War Two and today he plays with the passion and interest of a youngster, his invention and drive unfailing. Waters is broadly of the Hawkins persuasion with a full rich tone and swinging, turbulent phrasing. He manages to avoid the excesses of romanticism, only occasionally allowing a 'tourist' element to creep into his playing, which is still brisk and sparkling; the pity of it is that his appearances on record have been few since his stay in Europe. There is some solace in the fact that he has just recorded an album with blues singer and pianist Memphis Slim, another Paris resident. Ideally Waters should have an album of his own to demonstrate his multiple talents with the men of his own choice.

At La Cigale, the band occasionally performs traditional jazz numbers such as 'Muskrat Ramble' and Waters plays clarinet in New Orleans style, similar to, say, Edmond Hall. His tone and vibrato are broad, with flaring accents in ensemble work and dynamic command of all registers in solos. On a showcase such as 'Petite Fleur', Waters will play soprano sax, respecting Bechet's conception of the tune but always going his own way. His command of the instrument is complete.

The band plays tightly-knit, small-group swing, something akin to Harlem bands of the late 1930s and early 1940s, mainly choosing standards with neat riff-based arrangements to give added force. Diverse instrumental combinations are featured: open-trumpet/tenor, felt-muted trumpet/soprano, trumpet/clarinet, etc. When Jacques sings on rarely heard pieces such as 'Poor Little Rich Girl', Waters adds a subtle accompaniment on soprano.

The rhythm section swings all the way, with a commendable lack of fussiness. Indeed, when the right groove is there, their pleasure in playing conveys itself insistently. Pianist Jean-Pierre Louis, a huge man, huddled behind a puny piano, has an admirable Hines-Wilson style. Bassist Roger Tripoli plays in the decisive, modern manner and works and swings hard. Young Carl Regnier is a former pupil of American drummer Carl 'Kansas' Fields, another Paris resident. Regnier has caught much of his mentor's infectious drive and his cymbal work, snare drum accents and control of dynamics push the band in stimulating fashion.

A team effort this, not noticeably the worse for tourist requests or the nightly repetition of international 'favourites'. They know that each audience will include people who are hearing the band for the first time. A refreshing reality in performance remains; away from the restraints of the concert hall, a direct and natural communication is always there. The group, as it stands, deserves to be recorded. . .

I spent several evenings listening to the band that summer and on one occasion, talking to Butler, I queried the adoption of 'Jacques' in favour of Jack. 'Well that just helps a little with the tax problem,' he smiled, avoiding any further explanation.

We then talked for a while about the band: 'We've been here at La Cigale for about ten years now. I came in one time when the owner was just getting going with a new dance called the beguine. I played then and I've worked here since that day. Benny Waters has been with me most of the time from 1953, except for a short while ago when he was in Germany. I'm only really happy with Benny in the band!'

'The pianist was born in Bordeaux but his parents originally came from Guadaloupe and the bassist also comes from one of those French islands in the West Indies.' I asked Butler to tell me something of his career. 'Well I was born in Panama, you know, under the protection of the USA but I was really raised and I went to school in Washington, D.C. I first came to Europe in 1929. I was in London in 1934 at the Palladium – I was both a dancer and trumpeter then in a revue featuring people of colour. I enjoyed London and we made plenty of friends. I was caught in Norway when the war started but I managed to get back to America. I came back to Europe in 1950 and I've been here ever since.'

What about other American jazz musicians living in Paris? 'There's Bill Coleman – he's just back from Spain. He was over my house to see me last Monday, telling me that things went very well. Arthur Briggs is still playing good jazz trumpet – he's at Aix-les-Bains for the summer. He usually goes there and is very popular. Kansas Fields is in town, not working regular, playing a few concerts. I've been trying to get him in the band – without any success so far. Maybe he'll join us later on. We see Mezz Mezzrow and Albert Nicholas now and then, they do a few concerts around Paris. You know Mezz's son Milt junior is going to be a fine drummer.'

'Who else? There's George Johnson, an excellent alto player from around Detroit who lives in Paris now. There are two other names that you should write down, two Frenchmen:

Jacques Butler (t) with his quintet, including Benny Waters (ts), at La Cigale, Paris, early 1960s. Photo courtesy mr.jazz Photo Files (Theo Zwicky).

Filiberto Rico, a fine alto saxophonist in the Afro-Cuban style, and Robert Mavounzy, an alto player of the Charlie Parker type, really something special. These are guys that you are going to hear from one day.'

There we left Jacques Butler, an American in Paris, married to a French woman and raising a French family. He seemed very content with Parisian life, enjoying good food and a little wine, and leading a band playing relaxed, rocking jazz in the mainstream manner.

* * *

A year later, in July 1963, we returned to La Cigale. It was a Saturday night, the eve of Bastille Day. Naturally there was a relaxed and festive atmosphere. Apart from new red uniform jackets, with Butler resplendent in a pale blue suit, the immediate changes were a new rhythm section and the fact that Benny Waters had added alto to his tenor, clarinet and soprano. It being holiday time, a Cuban singer spotted in the audience was invited up to entertain with the band accompanying, delaying the jazz a little.

After that the quintet reverted to their neat arrangements of standards such as 'Ain't Misbehavin'', 'Summertime' and 'Caravan', with Butler playing with more care than the previous year. His trumpet could be both exciting and sensitive, and he had an excellent dynamic sense, but there was still a weakness for the

Benny Waters in Britain, 1980s.

exhibitionist finish to a solo, occasionally used as a crowd-pleasing gambit. Waters remained the same, each of his instruments providing a means for irrepressible, driving, warm-toned improvisations. His alto saxophone feature was a surprise: 'Those Waltzing, Crying and Laughing Blues', commencing in three-four time, with an unaccompanied chorus break leading into four-four, followed by sequences to illustrate the laughing and crying of the title. Waters' effortless swing never faltered.

I asked Benny why he had adopted alto sax at such an apparently late stage. 'Oh no, you've got it wrong; I started out playing alto, and tenor was wished on me when I was playing in Charlie Johnson's band at Small's Paradise, New York, in the mid-twenties. I was playing alto but he had this cat playing tenor who wasn't making things too good and we changed over. I also played alto when I was with the Jimmie Lunceford Orchestra in 1942. I was usually third alto except when Willie Smith was taking a vocal – on stage or on records – when I moved to first alto. I bought this alto I have now last December. The only sax I have never owned is baritone. When I led my own band at the Red Mill in New York from 1943 to '44, I even played bass sax for a novelty. They're very hard to blow, incidentally, except when very new. I was lucky enough to buy a virtually new one for $100 instead of the usual 500 to 600 dollars. I used to leave it at the club since it was far too big to take around!'

'I had some fabulous musicians in that band. There was Herman Autrey on trumpet; Eddie Gibbs on guitar (he also played one of those Hawaiian-style guitars like Alvino Rey – fantastic!); drummer Kaiser Marshall, and my wife Lorraine Faulkner on piano. She's about five years older than me and she knew more songs than I ever did. In fact, she could play any song you care to name. Before I met her she had played with Ethel Waters and

Jimmy Archey and his band, New York, 1952. Henry Goodwin (t); Tommy Benford (d); Archey (tb); Dick Wellstood (p); Waters (sop); George 'Pops' Foster (b).

had a lot of musical experience, having started out in music that bit earlier than me. I haven't seen her for years – we've been separated for a long while.'

'With Eddie in the band we didn't need a bass. He's a great player; I later got him a job with Wilbur de Paris playing banjo and they made that record 'The World is Waiting for the Sunrise'. These days he's given up guitar and banjo, plays bass. Most guitar players can do that and be proficient enough to play their first jobs in a week.'

How did Benny first come to Europe? 'I came with Jimmy Archey's band for a month in 1952 and I've stayed ever since. The band was Bob Wilber's and I replaced him, playing clarinet, when he had to go in the US Army just before we came over to Europe. That band had Henry Goodwin on trumpet, bassist Pops Foster and a great drummer who had been in Europe before – Tommy Benford. We've had some old friends in to see us here recently. Benny Carter came by and we also had Buck Clayton in to listen. Juice Wilson has been sitting in a lot recently on alto. He doesn't seem to play violin these days and Jacques says he hasn't seen Juice with his violin since 1929 in New York.'

I talked to Jacques Butler about the band changes. 'Carl Regnier, the drummer you saw last time, had to go in the army and Kansas Fields joined us in his place. He stayed about six months and then there was some kind of a hassle and he didn't show up for work on Christmas Eve, and I haven't seen him since. This new guy, an Austrian, was around to join the band and

Benny Waters, outside his home, rue Choron, Paris, September 1967. Photo by Peter Vacher.

he's settling down very nicely. The bass player's from Guadaloupe, been with us for a week, and the pianist, a Frenchman, has been with us two months.'

I asked Jacques about the early days at La Cigale. 'When I first came here [in 1953] it was a really tough joint. All the French West Indians used to gather here and there'd be razor fights and all sorts of carrying on. The owner sold out, and with the new proprietors La Cigale has completely changed character, and things are a lot quieter. I've worked here off and on for all that time. Every time I leave, the owner raises the pay a little and I find myself back on this same stand.'

It looked as though things would continue in that general way for the foreseeable future. The band was well established and popular with the local people, many of whom were French West Indians and Africans. The work was hard and the variety of music required often a little startling. The later sets, towards midnight, when the band had settled into a good groove, offered warm, swinging, mainstream jazz and Butler and Waters were always happy to respond to the interest of the genuine jazz enthusiast.

Chapter 20

Milt Buckner

Out of Detroit

Milt Buckner, 1944. Photo courtesy Milt Buckner.

Milt Buckner, the pioneer of the locked-hands jazz piano style later popularised by George Shearing, first came to London with Illinois Jacquet's trio (the other member was drummer Jo Jones) to play a season at Ronnie Scott's club in April 1971. Milt impressed everyone with his exuberance and bluesy creativity. Short and tubby, he bounced as he played, seemingly trying to swing as hard as humanly possible. I interviewed him at his hotel, and was pleased when extracts from the story he told me were eventually incorporated into Before Motown,[1] *the definitive history of jazz in Detroit.*

Milt returned to London quite often. He made many friends here and was also hugely popular in France where he toured and recorded extensively. We corresponded regularly and he introduced me to a young Frenchwoman whom he planned to marry. In July 1977, just months after that last meeting, he was felled by a heart attack at the early age of 62.

'I lost my mother when I was eight and my father when I was nine. My grandfather decided to take us all from St. Louis, where I was born [in 1915], to Detroit where my brother Ted and I each had different foster fathers. I stayed with my 'uncle' John Tobias, who played in Earl Walton's orchestra, at the Palais de Danse. Then he and his wife split up and George Robinson, the drummer in the band, took me over and raised me up. My uncle had started me on the piano when I was ten and I took it for about three years. After I went with George Robinson, I was contented for a while but then I started playing with the bands around there. I was thirteen in my first job with Mose Burke's Dixie Wang-Doodles. Couldn't swing but I could read!'

'I played with Ted Page's band for a little while and later the Harlem Syncopators. But in 1930 I went to play with Mose Burke regularly, playing for dances, from stock arrangements, some of them very good. Burke had a guy called 'Alabama' – he talked slow but he sure could play real fast trombone. Then there was Henry Strickland who could double saxophone and violin. He was a dapper sort of a fellow, looked like a little professor – he was very good too. Now Mose Burke, he was as ugly as sin, looked like a monkey, had little bow-legs. He would do buck and wing dances and he'd sing and play the old quadrilles on his violin. I was so short, I had to sit up on some Coca Cola cases on the chair. While I was playing, my feet would be dangling, so they nicknamed me 'Hoss'. I joined the union in 1930 when my [foster] dad took me down and he put my age up to sixteen so I could get in.'

'My brother's foster father had a record store and that's where we first heard Red

Nichols and the Five Pennies, Paul Whiteman, Louis Armstrong and his Hot Five, King Oliver. Detroit was mostly a dance band town; we had a very famous dance hall called the Graystone Ballroom. The Dorsey Brothers played in there, as did Jack Teagarden. But I was not big enough to go in the Ballroom then. The only time I got in was when my uncle took me there to hear Cab Calloway. That was the first time I heard a big band live and Cab was singing 'I'll Be Glad When You're Dead, You Rascal You' – I never will forget that. When I went to bed, I dreamt of the band playing that thing all night long – could hardly sleep. Next day I got up and I said to my dad, George Robinson, "I think I'm going to start learning to arrange!" I didn't know anything about instruments. He said, "I'll go down there and get a chart from the guys in the band and bring it back to you." So he got a chart and I made an arrangement of 'I'll Be Glad'. I had the trombones too high and I got all mixed up in the reeds between the way it sounds as to the way you write it. Mose Burke fixed it all up, put the instruments in the right perspective and they played it. That was my first arrangement.'

'And I made some other arrangements that we tried to play. Then I went with this young band called Stanley Miller's Harlem Syncopators. We were just a whole bunch of kids and Stanley Miller was a real nice guy. We played four nights a week up in Lansing at the ballroom there. At the end of the week Miller would line us up and hand each of us a quarter. With the rest of the

money he paid our room rent and for one meal a day. Everyone got together in one house and ate a meal, liable to be a pot of beans or a pot of spaghetti and hot dogs or some neck-bone and black-eyed peas. You could buy two cigars for a nickel then, take a girl to the movies – nickel apiece, that's a dime. You got ten cents left for the rest of the week. You could even buy a hot dog for two cents.'

'Miller left the band and Stutz Anderson took over and called it the Stutz Anderson Shufflers. We played Toledo, Ohio, and that's when I first met Art Tatum who was playing at a place of ill-repute there. They had a ballroom and Louis Armstrong and his big band were there. We got to play in the inside room as substitute band and, naturally, Pops took the outdoor place, where it's nice and cool, to play for summer dancing. We had a young trumpet player named Bill Johnson and he played just like Pops with the handkerchief and everything. One time we looked over to the side and there's Pops listening. He liked it so well he invited us to his [thirtieth] birthday party the next day at his apartment. That was the first time I met Pops. His wife Lil was with him and we had a time that day. The great Louis Armstrong. I always remember that to this day. I was the youngest in the band but they were all young: sixteen or seventeen. The guitar player was about 22 – he was the oldest one in there.'

'Sonny Heard played trombone and I used to copy all the Lawrence Brown solos for him to play, like 'The Sheik of Araby' and 'Ducky-wucky'. I used to play trombone myself. Alvin Nicholas was on bass and I remember him so well because his family was almost entirely wiped out with TB. He had to spend two years in a hospital in Detroit and while he was there he learned insurance. When he got out he went to California and got to be an official of the Golden Gate Insurance Company. But he still died awfully young – he was about 40.'

'In the saxophones we had Monk Culp; he was what we called a renegade because he played so entirely different from everybody else. Nobody wanted to hire him. He reminded me so much of how Bird was when he came to New York. But he never made it. Then there was Tubby Bowen, great big fat cat; he played with Basie later on. Now, we knew he couldn't read but you never would know it 'cause Basie's saxophone section was the best you ever heard and nobody knew he wasn't reading the music. Some guy went and told on him. Basie said, "It sound like he's reading." But he had them fooled halfway, he made them think he was playing everything. Anyway they fired him. One of our trumpets, Buster Baker, did have a little name because he played with Basie during the forties. I was doing just about all the arrangements apart from a few stocks.'

'I met Roy Eldridge back there during that time. He came to town with Horace Henderson's fine band. Roy flashed that trumpet all up. His brother Joe was playing with Earl Walton's band in Detroit and when he left the band my brother Ted got his job. Roy can play now but boy, he could play then. I remember when Dizzy was pat-

terned after Roy's style in the early forties and then he went off on that other tangent and he got his name.'

'What is it when you copy after somebody? It's like the controversy over my style. Some writer said if Milt Buckner started it, why didn't he tell somebody? So André Hodeir wrote him back and said, "We know who started it." And that rigmarole about who started it, what difference does it make anyhow? Somebody always studied after somebody else. It was a long time before I could take a solo but I would copy after Earl Hines. Then in 1932 I heard Art Tatum and I said that's the style I want to play but I couldn't play it. I was playing with Don Cox's band and we broadcast fifteen minutes every night on WXYZ in Detroit. We had five pieces and were using stock music. I would take the little notes on top with the chords in the bass and I combined the whole bunch together to make it sound like a big band. It just came easy because my hands are small and that's how I started the locked hands style to give greater fullness to the orchestra.'

'Whenever Art heard me he said, "You keep on doing that." I said, "I might as well, I can't play like you." Every time Art would come to Detroit he would look up three piano players: an old timer named 'Buckles', Lannie Scott and myself. Lannie is living in New York now and used to play with Red Allen. He was about the closest to Tatum but he wasn't as perfect – very few pianists are as perfect as Art Tatum!'

'I joined McKinney's Cotton Pickers in 1934 as arranger and assistant pianist for

$25 a week. We went to Buffalo to open the Vendome Club, a big nightclub with a floor-show. The opening night the law came in and closed the joint. The next day, it opened up again. In the show, Hertelle Collins used to do the dance of the seven veils to Ravel's 'Bolero' and the waiter, 'Fats' Johnson, would come out there with his apron on and tell jokes. He'd be comedian for the night and I built a complete thing behind him for 'Cross-eyed Kelly from P.A.', a famous song back in that day. The show was on half an hour, with a big band and chorus girls. Great thing!'

Jimmy Raschel and his orchestra, Detroit, 1935. *Left to right*: John Orange (tb); Reginald Emmett, Cedric Couch (t); Tom McNary (b); Orlando Dyer (t); George Bacon (d); Hobart McLardy (as, bs, cl); 'Scotty' (g); Willard Brown (as, ss); Arthur 'Nanny' Raschel (ts); Buckner (vibes). Inset on bass drum: Jimmy Raschel. Photo courtesy Milt Buckner.

'On trombone was Jake Wiley and 'Stump' Brady.[2] They were known as two of the fastest trombone players in the United States. They had invented solos that the two of them played together in duet. They were something – tremendously fast. We stayed two weeks at the Vendome.'

'[We were playing and] Bill 'Bojangles' Robinson came in. He must have stayed around about three or four days. He used to tell jokes and he was always bragging about what a great pool player he was. Now Stump Brady was not bad either, so the cats got high and when we closed at 5 o'clock in the morning, everybody went to the pool parlour on the corner. Bojangles says, "I'll get to 75 before you and give you the break." Stump ran up about 35 balls and miscued. Bojangles ran off 75 and he tore Stump up that morning. That was a good day; never have days like that now.'

'After we left Buffalo we drove all the way to Louisville, Kentucky, and we had to follow Noble Sissle's band. All the waiters told us we'd better be good because Sissle had been

Nub Brown's Fingers, Detroit, c.1940, including: George Robinson (d); Herb Thompson (b); Brown (t); Buckner (here shown with trombone and vibes).

there a whole year. He was doing his parading and all that stuff. We had a young guy that directed the band when Mac got tired, named Chick Carter. He was flashy and the band started jumpin' when he got up there. We stayed in Louisville for two weeks, went back to Detroit and the band broke up.'

'There was some sorry days after that. Stutz got the band together again and told us about this fellow who wanted the band for Christmas week and then he'd let us stay there through January, February and March. We rehearsed and opened up and we did one of the finest weeks ever up there. When we got through the man says he don't want us. I said,

"What about the pay for the week?" "There ain't no pay." The union did nothing.'

'That's when we started working with different bands just making gigs. Down next door to the union in Detroit is the Paradise Valley and this girl opened up a very small restaurant called Biddy's Luncheon and started selling a bowl of beans for a nickel. And for a dime you could get a whole platter of beans, a pig foot and a big piece of cornbread. Do you know, that woman got rich! They let you pour the syrup on top of the beans and you didn't care as long as you had some nourishment.'

'I went back with Don Cox's band, playing the dancing school and broadcasting every night just like I hadn't left. I guess I must have rejoined and left him about five or six times. Don Cox was the drummer.[3] We would play for the dance [at Wood's Dancing Academy], like we had to play a waltz or something but, when it came time for the ten cents a dance, we could play the introduction and the first two choruses, stop, start over again at the second ending and finish the whole arrangement where the other guys down the street were playing 59 dances an hour; so we had the best of it. Mr. Woods would come in and say, 'Now, gentlemen, I don't allow any drinking or alcoholic beverages on the premises.' He'd find the bottles hidden in the cupboards, in the back, everywhere. But he sure liked our band.'

'I left in 1935 and went with Jimmy Raschel and his Orchestra. That's when I met my wife. She was living in Defiance,

Ohio. There were only two black families in the whole town and they lived right next door to each other. The one family didn't cater too much to other people so we always stayed at Mama's house. Sometimes we'd stay with the white people that lived next door and across the street. I courted my wife for a year while doing all this playing around and I married her in 1936. We had a honeymoon down in Lexington. Right after, the band took on the name of McKinney's Cotton Pickers for a special tour. The old Cotton Pickers went by the wayside and we went under their name on this particular tour only.'

'We started with two weeks in Springfield and then put all the wives on the train and sent them back to Detroit. Then we left out on this raggedy bus. We stopped in St. Louis, and [went] from there to Kansas City. When we got there we played a dance and everybody was talking about Basie's band. "You guys ain't as good as Basie." But we went on and did our thing anyway. We'd go from K.C. to Oklahoma City, then to Tulsa and on to Dallas. Everybody was broke when we got to Dallas so Jimmy [Raschel] handed all the guys a quarter apiece. Some guy found out where you can get a foot long sausage with three biscuits on it for a nickel, and Pepsi Cola cost a nickel too, so for a dime that's what we had for dinner. We played the dance that night and while we were playing, somebody robbed the car and stole all the suits the guys had. I never will forget that.'

'We drove down to Houston. When we

got there, the man told us the job was cancelled. Jimmy called Detroit to get some more money, so we put some gas in all the cars, '34 Fords, and drove to Port Arthur. Jimmy arranged the room rent, food, cigarettes, to be tabbed until they found some of the guys were tabbing other things like whiskey. We stayed four days because the dates in Fort Worth and Galveston were also cancelled. I'll never forget the [local] schoolteachers were so nice to us; they invited us out to bridge parties and for dinner. They really treated us wonderfully. The night of the dance, all the money went right into the hotel to pay for the

Soloists with the Lionel Hampton Orchestra. *Left to right*: Buckner (p, arr.); Irving Ashby (g); Illinois Jacquet (ts); Joe Newman (t). Savoy Ballroom, New York City, 1942. Photo by P.A. Dearborn, courtesy Milt Buckner.

food and everything. So we lit out of there and went to Corpus Christi, Texas. The dance hall there was right next to a railroad track and at about 11 o'clock, you could hear a train coming, so loud that it shook the building. Everybody ran to the window and they got a big kick out of this. Every night at 11 o'clock, the only thing that happens down there – watching the trains going somewhere.

We had to drive to Amarillo, over 700 miles, for the dance the next night and then came back to Austin, the last of that particular tour. Here we were supposed to get paid. Now Jimmy Raschel was keeping a young lady in a nice apartment up there in Detroit, so he was drawing money to pay the rent and the furniture bill. When it came for us to be paid, he said the money we had drawn for our expenses left hardly enough to get home.'

'I told them I was through – I put in my notice to leave as soon as we got back to Detroit. We went into Oklahoma City and Al McKibbon's brother, Alphonso, a very fine guitarist,

Buckner's sextet with the Larry Steele Show, Atlantic City,1949. Photo courtesy mr.jazz Photo Files (Theo Zwicky).

helped us to stay at the hotel. I had an old beat-up valve trombone I was carrying all over the road and we were sitting up there with a room but no food. I went down to the pawn-shop and sold the trombone for $4 and blew it all on hamburgers and hot dogs for all the guys.'

'We went on to Kansas City, then we jumped to St. Louis and after some other dates we got to Detroit and my last night with Raschel was New Year's Eve 1936, playing a dance in Michigan. I was leaving 'cause my wife was getting ready to have a baby. I went back to Don [Cox]'s band, and we got a nice little thing going. I'd double on my marimbas, which I'd been using with Jimmy's band, till one day, the guy came to get the marimbas. I said, "How much do I owe you?" "$150 – but if you give me $25 I'll hold off for a while." Well, I was making $17.50 a week and the boss said he'd let me have the $25. How was

I going to pay him back? A dollar a week. My rent is $10 a week and it takes $5 to feed the family so I had two and a half dollars to spend on other things like doctors or going to the movies maybe once a month. So I helped that guy pack those things up and send them right on back.'

Lionel Hampton's orchestra, Paradise Theater, Detroit, late 1947. *Left to right, rear:* Earl Walker (d); Duke Garrette, Teddy Buckner, Walter Williams, Wendell Culley (t). *Middle:* Buckner (p); Billy Mackel (g); Johnny Sparrow, Morris Lane (ts); Charlie Fowlkes (bs); Bobby Plater, Ben Kynard (as). *Front:* Charles Mingus, Charlie Harris (b); Lionel Hampton (d, ldr); Leo Shepard (t); Harpo Wormack, Al Hayse, Andrew Penn, Sonny Graven (tb). Photo courtesy Milt Buckner.

'We left the dancing academy and went down to Paradise Valley and played George Nelson's Melody Lounge and stayed there a year. Then my dad said, "Why don't you come and play with Nub Brown's band?" My dad played drums. It was a fine band. I played piano and doubled on my dad's vibraharps. He liked my playing so he gave them to me. Still got them in my basement.'

'I played with my dad until 1940 and then I went out on the road with Jimmy Raschel again. When I was with him before he'd promised me $35 a week; when I left he owed me

$375! Now like a fool I was going back. I took both kids that was born then and we travelled in an old '38 Pontiac. Lionel Hampton came through Detroit to play the Graystone Ballroom and someone told him about me as I had been writing for shows a lot – I also wrote some stuff for Billy Eckstine. So Hamp asked me to make an arrangement on 'Bei Mist Du Schoen' with 'Eli, Eli' in the middle part. I wrote one of the swingin'est arrangements of 'Bei Mist' you ever heard.'

'I saw him a year later in '41. I said, "I been writing you, when you gonna pay me for that arrangement?" He said "Don't worry 'bout that." I was back with Don Cox again at the dancing school and writing for the show at the Cotton Club at the Norwood Hotel and also at Broad's Grill – only two places in town that had long shows out there. I'd do the opening, the middle part and a number for the chorus girls. Hamp heard me at rehearsal and asked me down to the joint [where he was playing].'

'At the dance I played 'Let's Take a Trip On the Bus', using my locked hands style. In the meantime [Hampton's] piano player, Raymond Walters, was talking to his wife up in the balcony. We got through and went off to intermission so they were looking around for Raymond to come back and finish the dance. It turns out that Stutz Anderson had called the law to put Raymond and his wife out as they had started a ruckus up there on the balcony. So I had to finish out the night.'

'Anyhow next day Hamp told me to come down to Broad's Grill where they were rehearsing – 'Flying Home' by the way! Raymond Walters was mad, he was arguing. I drew him on one side and said, "I don't want to take your place." He said, "No, I'll be glad to get out of the band, guys don't treat me right." So I went and played with the band. Supposed to leave [with them] in nine days but how was I going to leave?'

'I went to Don Cox and told him I had to leave as Hamp wanted me to join him. He said, "I'll let you go if you can get me Dave Spencer." He's a kid who plays locked hands just like me and he was with Tubby Bowen's band. Tubby said he could go if I could get him MacIntyre. So I had to find out where MacIntyre was and he said OK. The secretary of the union then was a good friend of mine, and he said, "We'll work it out," and that's how I was out of there in nine days.'

'I left that night and drove all the way to New York. My first time in New York – I was a happy fellow. All of them – Shadow Wilson, Vernon Alley, Irving Ashby – they took me in hand. That was a tremendous band. Irving took me up to his brother's apartment, kept me up there, fed me, slept me. I didn't know anybody, had no money anyhow.'

'We went into the Apollo for a week. Lady Day was with us; Peg Leg Bates and Jones and Foster, comedians, they were in there. We had a big show – jammed and packed all the week. After that we did some recordings including 'Now I Know' and 'Flying Home'; just four sides, with arrangements by Fred Norman. I wrote 'Nola' for the band and that was recorded in '42.'

'That year we came into the Savoy Ballroom and played four weeks. We got the highest salary ever previously been paid in there – $45 per week.'

'One Sunday afternoon, Basie was in town so they got to talking up this battle of music between Lionel Hampton, Count Basie and the Savoy Sultans. The joint was jammed all over everywhere. The Basie band had one bandstand and the Sultans had a little bandstand over there and you know they didn't have but seven pieces and they outswung us. Old Razz [Alex Mitchell] on drums and 'Bones' [Rudy Williams] on sax! We had just got a new drummer in the band, George Jenkins, to replace Shadow Wilson. He was really pumping. We just wailed. When we were playing 'Flying Home', the whole floor sank. We always say we won the battle but Basie's band said the same. That was a great day. Our featured soloists were Illinois Jacquet and Dexter Gordon. The way Hamp had that band set up there, everybody was a soloist and the top soloist of the day. I was about the most not-known in there. You could call out Marshall Royal and his brother, Ernie Royal, Karl George (he later went with Stan Kenton), Joe Newman, and the trombone section was something else with Fred Beckett, they call him the black Tommy Dorsey 'cause he could play so sweet. He died in 1945 of TB.'

'In the saxophone section, in addition to Marshall, we had Jack McVea on baritone and Ray Perry on alto, who doubled on amplified violin. Irving Ashby, our guitarist could play any classical number, one leg up on the chair on stage. The bassist was Vernon Alley, still a disc jockey out there in San Francisco. Everybody in the band was tremendous. In fact, I think Hamp had too much band for what he had to do. For I noticed after that he never tried to get that type of musician around him again. I remember one New Year's Eve show we did in New York at the Strand Theater, we had Dizzy, J.J., Max Roach, Morris Lane and Babs Gonzales, a whole gang of them there. Yeah man, quite a day.'

'In 1943 we were playing a lot of theatres. We had just played the Apollo, and Hamp said to play boogie-woogie and I just started playing. Later we were getting ready to go to Philadelphia to the Faye Theater and he said, "Why don't you write a last chorus?" So we rehearsed it that morning before we opened and that became 'Hamp's Boogie-Woogie' and he started playing the two-finger piano in there. This theatre we were playing, the balcony was swaying rather oddly (every balcony has got to have a sway when they build it) and I was scared it was going to fall right then. They called the Fire Department and they condemned the theatre and said you cannot have any more bands in this theatre.'

'That was the beginning of Lionel Hampton. We struck clear across the country. Everywhere he'd have them in the aisles, playing hookey from the school, teachers were complainin' and the subways were crowded with kids pressing downtown.'

'I came out of Hamp's band in 1948 and then I formed a big band of my own which didn't last about three months. I went back to Hamp in 1950 and I stayed with him two years and that's how I learned to play the organ. As for my big band, I came in at the wrong time. That was during the time that Basie's band shrunk, Ellington stopped travelling so much, Erskine Hawkins got a small band, Gerald Wilson broke his band up; bands were dyin' everywhere!'

'I recorded eight sides with the big band on MGM and they released six but they wouldn't release the other two 'cause I was singing on them! Perhaps the lyrics were a little too risqué. Chubby Jackson had a big band at the time so he and I had a thing they called 'Battle of Music' and we would travel up through the New England states. We did four or five one-nighters, battling each other. Promoters got all the money. I came back to Philadelphia and I formed a small band.[4] We played Boston and all around, not much happening, and I'd come back broke. That group didn't last long either.'

'I did a lot of recording with a whole lot of different guys. I recorded with Eddie 'Cleanhead' Vinson one time and we had arrangements for all the tunes until we got to the end so Sid Nathan of King Records said, "You got to do one tune to fill out the thing," and Eddie said, "Milt, you gonna start out on something there and we'll join in with you." I started on out, and they joined me on 'B-flat Blues' or something.'

'Now that was in 1950. In '54 Roy Eldridge and my trio were travelling all over together and we got into Buffalo to play a jazz joint. A [disc jockey] named Joe Rico, he's playing this one tune and they called it 'Jump 'n' Grunt', played it all day on the radio and got everybody talking about it. 'Milt Buckner's coming in with 'Jump 'n' Grunt.' No sooner I hit town, I said, "What you talking about 'Jump 'n' Grunt'; I know that's me but when did I make it?" That was the last tune on the Vinson session and the only one that did any good. I had to get a record and learn it.'

'I had my own group after Hampton in '52. When Hamp felt good, he let me go in on trombone 'cause he had to call on me a couple of times when a trombone player got drunk or messed up. I even played first trombone in Carnegie Hall. I'm proud of that.'

'I got my own trio and I tried to go along with that for a while. I didn't do too well until I got Sam Woodyard with me, and a very fine alto from Philadelphia. Danny [Turner] played with me four years but Sam, he left me in '55 to join Duke. I had to drive him to New York, take his drums out and help him up there to the hotel and get him set up. I saw him about a year later with Duke and told Duke, "Now, you take care of him," and Duke didn't pay no attention at all.'

Chapter 21

Cozy Cole

Cozy Conversing

Cozy Cole. Photo courtesy Crescent Jazz Productions.

Always fit and alert, the distinguished drummer Cozy Cole was one of the true luminaries of the swing era. Our meeting was fitted into a brief stopover at a hotel near Heathrow while he was touring Europe with Benny Carter's quartet in 1976. Although he must have been asked many of these questions before, Cozy was patient and courteous, and took care over each answer.

His steady gig at the time was with trumpeter Jonah Jones' quintet, with which I later heard him play in France at the Nice Festival. He died of cancer in Columbus, Ohio, in January 1981 aged 71.

Settled in our armchairs, we talked first about Cozy's start in music and about his unusual nickname.

'Well, my sister played piano and then I had two brothers who played piano: Jay and Ted. Another one plays drums – Herbert – that's my youngest brother. My dad was sort of a vocalist, too; he played piano by ear and he used to get the kids all surrounded around the piano and we'd vocalise.'

'I always liked the drums. In high school, in manual training, I used to make drum sticks. I didn't study, I didn't have a teacher then or anything. Of course, I took basic music in school. This was in East Orange, New Jersey, and that was the beginning of it.'

'My mother and father passed [away] when I was in high school so all of us went to stay with our grandmother who lived near Red Bank, New Jersey. That's Basie's home. I remember Basie when I was going to high school – he was around there playing piano.'

'How I got the name Cozy was playing football in high school. Out on the practice field in those days, I used to play the position of an end, and the quarterback would give you a forward pass and call you by your last name: 'Hey, you, Colesy.' So during the course of the game they weren't too particular about diction and it was just 'Cozy'. And that's how the name stuck.'

'Now listen to this: one day I was out there showing off in front of a sophomore class. I was fairly good, not professional material, of course. Anyway, on the opposing team, I knew this running back – we used to talk football. He knew every move I was going to make. So this day I caught this beautiful pass, the class got up and called out, and I looked up the line and here comes this guy at me. He looked like a giant and, boy, he was laying for me. He tackled me, and it wasn't that he hurt me; it was the scrimmage, everybody on top, and I got a dislocated shoulder. As they were carrying me off the field, goodness, I felt so bad when my class had gotten up and applauded for me, but I made up my mind: "This is my last day at football. I'm through playing football because I'll never be able to play drums if

Willie Bryant Orchestra, New York City, Spring 1935. *From left*: Edgar Battle (t); Robert Horton (tb); Benny Carter, Dick Clark (t); Cole (d); John 'Shorty' Haughton (tb); Bryant (dlr); Arnold Adams (g); Louis Thompson (b); Glyn Pacque (as); Stanley Payne (as); Teddy Wilson (p); Ben Webster (ts); Johnny Russell (ts).

I have a broken arm, broken ribs and all that." Isn't that a story?'

In 1930, while still a young man, Cozy recorded with the legendary Jelly Roll Morton. 'I'll tell you how that came about. I always loved to hang around musicians and I was around 132nd Street and Seventh Avenue in New York in the afternoon and Jelly Roll was there looking for a drummer. Well, all the drummers were busy and there I was. Somebody pointed and said, "I think the boy over there plays drums." Now, Jelly came over and asked me, "Who have you ever worked with?" I lied to Jelly. I started naming names because I wanted to make this date so bad. He said, "Oh, well, that's good enough." And so he hired me. Luckily, after I got in the studio, it wasn't anything to do but keep time. I hadn't been playing that long and if there were any solos to come up there, I knew I couldn't do it. I was just frightened to death in that studio. But the fellows that were there, all of them were very helpful. Well, I'm a newcomer, just a kid. I remember Geechie Fields on trombone and Ernest Elliott on clarinet – at the time, I didn't know that I was making history. Jelly was very, very, nice. All the musicians respected him.'

'Out in the street, he used to kid all the guys and say, "If it wasn't for me, you wouldn't be working here. I'm the one that started the whole record business." Oh, yeah? See, a lot of musicians used to get around Jelly and kid him because they knew he loved to shoot off his mouth. Especially Chick Webb. Chick was a little short guy, and Jelly's tall and he had this gold tooth here with a diamond in it and he dressed very immaculate. Everybody would just try to egg him on. A great guy – everybody just loved Jelly.'

'So that was my first time ever in a recording studio. It was wonderful. Before then I was just around not doing anything. Playing those little house parties, and putting my tuxedo on, going off around the Band Box [musicians' club]. I just loved musicians, I'd go up there and listen to them. I used to run errands for them. Then later on, I started getting private teachers. My first teacher was the drummer at the Lincoln Theatre, Charlie Brooks. Of course, after that I went to Juilliard [School of Music]. Then a very dear friend of mine, Edgar Battle, trumpet player, recommended me for my first professional job with Blanche Calloway.'

'With Blanche, that's where I got my schooling. That band taught me everything about the business. Playing shows and reading the charts and playing the dances. It was my apprenticeship in the business. We had Ben Webster, Clyde Hart on piano, Joe Keyes, trumpet, and of course, there

was Edgar Battle, too. Well, when I left Blanche Calloway I was with Willie Bryant for just a short stint while Willie was getting together. Then I was working with Benny Carter's band. At the time I was living on 131st Street. Benny didn't know me but Qualli Clark[1] – he was a copyist around the Band Box – he says Benny was looking for a drummer. He wanted Sid Catlett but Sid was out. So Qualli says, "Well, Benny, try out with the kid." I could read fairly well and then Benny looked at me, and said, "Yeah, you're doing good." In about a couple of weeks we opened in the Lincoln Theater.'

'Teddy Wilson was on piano. Benny went to Chicago to get Teddy and brought him back to New York. Keg Johnson was in the band, and Big Green. Oh yeah, a very good player. Great trombonist. We had a nice rhythm section, I thought, with Ernest Hill on bass, and Lawrence Lucie, guitar.'

'I believe a lot of musicians, me included, would have loved to have worked in Benny Carter's band for nothing, just to play his charts. That's how well liked he was musically. Other than being a great personality, a great human being, Benny's a great musician and all of the musicians respected him.'

Cozy was one of several outstanding drummers who emerged during the big band era. 'Chick Webb and Sonny Greer were my idols then. As a drummer, I just loved Chick for his approach to the drums and his co-ordination. He was very fast and had a nice foot. With Sonny, I liked his showmanship at that time. Sonny used to have all the tympanies and the chimes.

Stuff Smith's band, Onyx Club, 52nd Street, NYC, 1937. *Standing*: Clyde
Hart (p); Cole; Mack Walker (b). *Seated*: Jonah Jones (t); Bobby Bennett
(g); Stuff Smith (vln).

And a very nice personality, and very flashy. I loved that.'

Another lively character, the jazz violinist Stuff Smith proved to be a memorable
employer. 'I joined Stuff Smith in New York at the Onyx Club. Stuff was one of the greatest jazz fiddle players I've ever heard. Stuff used to knock me out every night. He was a
great artist himself but he had some some good sidemen in there. Clyde Hart, Jonah
Jones, and a boy on guitar by the name of Bobby Bennett, and Mack Walker on bass.
Later on, Ben Webster came with the band.'

'We used to sit down and rehearse and just get little things together, just little riffs. What
was so wonderful about it, everybody in there was so co-operative. And we loved to go to
work. That was the thing. Then we liked each other too. I'll tell you what we did in Los
Angeles. We played a concert with Benny Goodman. Gene Krupa, Harry James; all were
with Benny then. So we did this in the Palomar Ballroom. It was an afternoon concert.

Benny got up there and played – Gene was just beautiful in those days – so here we are with (a little) five pieces, coming on behind Benny Goodman! But we had a particular number that we played then, which was 'Stompin' At The Savoy'. We played that for fifteen minutes, and that's the only number we played on the concert. We got a standing ovation.'

'And the next day in the papers, it said the 'New King of Swing – Stuff Smith'. It was

Publicity shot for the film *The Glenn Miller Story*, 1955. *Rear*: Ben Pollack, Gene Krupa, Louis Armstrong, James Stewart, Joe Yukl, Marty Napoleon. *Front*: Trummy Young, Cole, Barney Bigard, Arvell Shaw.

just wonderful. I was with Stuff three or four years until I joined Cab Calloway in late 1938. Walter Thomas was the tenor player with Cab. I knew Walter very well and he says, "Cozy, come on here." It was a nice band. The only black bands then popular, real popular, were Cab and Duke, and they paid the most money. And then Chu Berry was in Cab's band. I loved Chu. He died too early – it was an automobile accident in 1941, I think. If he'd lived he would be another Benny Carter 'cause he could really swing and his ears were always open. He was always listening to other tenor players. Like on that Hampton record,

Cozy Cole with Ivan Rolle in Cole's band, Metropole, New York City, late 1950s. Photo courtesy Ivan Rolle.

'Sweethearts on Parade'. I think the background that Chu played then, just riffing back of Hamp, meant an awful lot to that record.'

Cozy's period with Louis Armstrong and the All-Stars brought him considerable acclaim and he was happy to pay tribute to the great man.

'I was working at the Metropole [bar] in New York when Joe Glaser, Louis' manager, called me and asked me would I like to join with Louis? Well, I would like nothing better because Earl Hines was in there, Jack Teagarden, little Barney [Bigard], Arvell Shaw and Velma Middleton. And I would say that was, as far as the small group is concerned, the highlight of my career, working with Louis Armstrong. A lot of people used to come and hear the band and say, "Well, you better get a good idea of what the band sounds like, they're unlikely to be together too long." As it was, we were all together about four or five years. The first one that left was Jack Teagarden and then Earl.'

'I don't remember *one* argument in the band. Louis was like that – he didn't want to be plagued with any arguments or anything. The only way that Louis would hire you, he's got to know you, he's got to know your character and, first of all, like your playing. And when you come in there, he has nothing to say. He would swing and he would let you do anything that you wanted to do. I enjoyed listening to him every night. He could just play and make me want to play. That was his magic.'

'Goodness, I could sit here and talk with you for the next three hours about Louis. Just so many wonderful experiences with that band – on planes talking, on buses talking, in Las Vegas at the Sands Hotel, all the Scandinavian countries, just beautiful. It's a beautiful memory. He was a great loss to the industry, by the way.'

Louis Armstrong All-Stars, Blue Note, Chicago, July 1950. Earl Hines (p); Jack Teagarden (tb); Barney Bigard (cl); Cole (d); Louis Armstrong (t, v); Arvell Shaw (b); Velma Middleton (v). Photo courtesy Manfred Selchow.

The earlier mention of Goodman's drum star Gene Krupa prompted Cozy to speak about the drum school that the two men went on to run in New York.

'I was with Louis, and there was a battle of music with Benny Goodman and Louis. Benny went back and got all the greats, all his former big band players. Helen Ward was singing, Teddy Wilson, Charlie Shavers was in the band, Israel Crosby on bass. This was for about eighteen days and during the course of that tour, Gene and I would sit together on the plane and so we were just saying that both of us were getting old for these one-nighters. I said, "Let's get a drum school." And Gene said, "Yeah, Cozy, that sounds good." So that's where we conceived the idea.'

'When we got back to New York, Gene saw his lawyers and mine, and we got together and it went just great guns there for a while. It was the Gene Krupa-Cozy Cole Drum School. Other than a great drummer, Gene was a great humanitarian, you know. This happened in 1955. We kept the school until I made the hit record, 'Topsy', and Gene called me and said, "Cozy, what the hell you staying here teaching for? Come on out on the road and make some of this money. Don't you know when you have a hit record like that, the price goes up?" '

'So that's what I did. Gene said, "When you're on the road, I'll be here [at the school].

Jonah Jones Quintet, Downtown Club, Buffalo, New York, mid-1970s. *Left to right*: Bob Fields, Jerome Darr, Ivan Rolle, Jones, Cole. Photo courtesy Ivan Rolle.

When I go on the road, you'll be here." So that went on about three or four years until my engagements with my group made me too busy. Gene was busy as well and we had kids coming to the school, and they didn't want any other teachers. "Where's Gene, where's Cozy?" they'd say. That's why we just quit.'

Cozy always stressed the value of musical education. But is it possible to teach someone to swing?

'Well, it's like Art Tatum. He was self-taught but he was one of our greatest jazz pianists. If Art would have studied, got himself a teacher, that would have slowed him down. Now there's a certain amount of feeling that you've got to have within you, which is soul. You've got to enhance that soul by learning the theory of music and add to it. Always mind why you're in that band, you're in there to swing, to keep a beat going. The young guys do some intricate things but they don't have the experience that I've had because I've played shows, in small bands; played in those little places where they would have acts and a line of chorus girls up there. See, by playing for chorus girls that teaches you how to take a drum solo. All you've got to do is just think of a dancer in front of you and it gives you something. I used to dance before I started playing drums. I was a chorus boy – Derby Wilson and I had an act together. Buddy Rich was a dancer and I think Louis Bellson was a dancer, too.'

At the time of this interview, Cozy was a member of the Jonah Jones band. 'The reason why I went back on the road is because Jonah was always on those steady gigs lasting a month or six weeks. I've been living out in Columbus, Ohio – that's my wife's home – for about twelve years. It's so relaxed after New York. Still, I'm only an hour from New York. Jonah's group has some very good players: [a] boy by the name of Jerome Darr on guitar, and Ivan Rolle on bass (he was with my band). Lannie Scott, our pianist, passed [away] and now we have Bob Fields. Jonah likes good musicians – he swings very good himself.'

Finally, Cozy talked about his remaining ambitions and picked out some favourite career memories.

'The only thing I want to do is to study some more. I've started at Capital University in Columbus on piano and arranging, and, of course, do some teaching there too. I want to learn a little bit more about the classical end of drumming. Things change, not that I'm going too far out, but I do want to advance. You've got to have an open mind so I listen to all music. I sit in with the jazz groups at Capital and the classical bands too. I would say the more you study, the more you find out what you didn't know. You love it that much: there's no disgrace in saying that.'

'Highlights? Working with Louis, also my first experience with Benny [Carter] got me off on the right foot and then working with different artists like Roy Eldridge, Teddy Wilson and Billie Holiday. On staff at CBS, I had the opportunity to play behind Frank Sinatra, Perry Como, the Andrews Sisters, and Dorothy Collins.'

'All of that, you add it into one big pile, it makes a very nice pile. It makes you just marvel that there's so many things. I'm very happy about it all.'

Chapter 22

Nick Fatool

The Good Life

Nick Fatool, California, c.1975. Photo courtesy Nick Fatool.

In 1978, I was staying at clarinettist Joe Darensbourg's home in 'the valley' north of Los Angeles while working with him on his autobiography, when he announced that he was going out for a haircut. Would I like to accompany him to nearby Van Nuys? As will be seen, Joe's 'barber' turned out to be one of the most valued big band drummers of the swing era who had gone on to achieve success in radio and studio work. Nick Fatool was also a generous host and a gracious interviewee. He died in September 2000, aged 85.

First, a domestic scene. Two men are in the yard by the swimming pool, lit by the hard California sun, the reflections from the water casting shimmering patterns across their faces. The taller of them, scissors in hand, is intent on his task, that of cutting his friend's hair. The seated man is silver-grey now and a little on the stocky side. The barber talks quietly, the accent still betraying his New England origins, moving economically as he works. He's explaining his method, and it's evident that he takes great pride in ensuring the result will be satisfactory. There's an obvious rapport between the two and a bond of friendship, well tried and trusted, can be sensed in their easy familiarity.

The alfresco haircut completed, the barber folds away the towel that had been protecting the older man's shoulders. He's lithe and tanned, carrying no excess weight and looks as though he has life the way he wants it.

No ordinary barber, in fact, but Nick Fatool, an accomplished drummer known both for fine jazz connections and for his extensive recording and soundtrack calls. His 'customer' is the clarinettist Joe Darensbourg, once of Louisiana and now, like Fatool, a resident of suburban Los Angeles. Fatool has taken care of Joe's hair for years and, of course, the two often play together – senior citizens in the music business. As we walk into Fatool's house, it's clear that his skills have brought him material success. His home is spacious, set with low settees and close-carpeted, each room a hymn to comfort. Outside, the single-storey house is screened by luxuriant shrubs and presents an aura of quiet affluence.

Fatool opens the refrigerator, takes out a shaker of ready-mixed Bloody Marys and offers drinks. It's mid-morning so we settle for beer. We're sitting around the kitchen table and he busies himself preparing food for us. He's a keen cook, too. Another Bloody Mary and talk starts to flow. Fatool's wife, Dottie, joins us and prompts her husband as he reminisces. His stories are invariably wry, often amusing, and Darensbourg chips in as Fatool lights a menthol cigarette. Seduced by the sun and the ease of these people, the onlooker could be persuaded that the jazz life is pretty rewarding after all. Fatool gently agrees, leans forward and smiles. 'It is a beautiful life. Want to know something? We probably live better than some of those movie stars that spend all their money as they make it and then

Nick Fatool, California, c.1975. Photo by Ed Lawless, courtesy Nick Fatool.

wind up busted. You know, we don't wind up broke. Joe's got enough money to burn a wet whale – if the whale ain't too big!'

But the beginning? 'How I started was, let's see, I used to beat on a chair with two rungs out of the chair. So my father used to throw me out of the house. He'd say, "Too noisy – get outta here." We had a two-storey house and my mother rented the top part to this other couple. The guy was a drummer and I used to hear the drums from down below. It sounded so good to me. You know, the sound of it, so that I kept practising and listening to him. Anyway, he owed us a month's rent: $15. So my mother said, "If you teach my son, like give him ten lessons, a dollar and a half a lesson!" He said, "I'll be glad to do it." Hell, I used to go up there every week and that's how I started. I was about ten years old.'

***

Fatool came from Miltburg, an isolated hamlet in Rhode Island. It was no great shakes of a place, by his account. 'The chief of police was the only cop in town. He was the mayor and the policeman. We had nothing. Like we had one dentist there, but he was also the man that took care of the animals. The closest house to us was a mile away. We lived about 50 to 60 miles from Providence.'

'When I was fourteen, I worked in a night club. And I had to wear spats. I bought a tuxedo, spats, shirt and everything that they wanted for $12. This was in Providence. I'd work at this nightclub, get to bed at 4 o'clock in the morning, get up at 7 and go to high school. I used to have all the music books in front of me in the algebra class. So when the guy says, "What's the shortest distance between two points?" I'd say I didn't know, and he threw me out of the class. So finally I left high school.'

'From Providence, I used to work with Bobby Hackett and then I got a job on the Providence to New York boat. This went right up the Providence River overnight, and you got to New York for the next morning. We had a trio and Bobby used to come on and just sit in with us. We'd get $10 a week but you couldn't spend it all. Everything was so cheap. So, anyway, when I got to New York, after four or five boat trips, I tried out with Joe Haymes and that's the first band I got with.'

'Joe was the most beautiful guy in the world. He had such an inferiority complex that when he talked to you, in case he'd had a drink, he'd always put his hand to his mouth so he wouldn't offend you. He always used to like a drink. He was just an arranger, really. Tommy Dorsey took his first band with all the good guys, then I joined his second band. After Joe Haymes, I went with Don Bestor. He did Jack Benny's show. Remember when Jack would say, "Play, Don"? Then I went with George Hall and after that with Benny Goodman.'

Mention of Goodman prompted the question of relationships – after all, B.G. was known to be fierce with sidemen who didn't fit the bill. Fatool was characteristically direct: 'I got along good with Benny for about a year and then he started picking on guys. Not on me especially 'cause I didn't look at him too much. Anyway, I think he liked me because Gene Krupa was such a great showman that I think he wanted a drummer just to play. I tried to play as good as I could back of Benny.'

'So he came up to me after three months and he says, "How do you like the band?" I said, "Well, Benny, it's a pleasure." How could I say anything else? It was. And he says, "I told Leonard Vannerson to give you a raise of $25." At that time I was getting $175 so he gave me a raise to $200. This is in 1939. So Leonard came up and said, "What the hell did you do to Benny there, to have him give you a raise? He's never given anybody a raise in his life." I said, "I just keep away from him. I just play as good as I can in back of him and don't say anything to him!" Leonard says, "Well, he gave you a raise. First time since I've been the manager that I can remember he ever gave anybody a raise."'

'I was about a year and a half with Benny and I enjoyed working with him,' said Fatool. 'I think Benny's just a great player and he has definitely found his own way. Then I went with Artie Shaw for a year and a half. Now, Artie's a little more of a gentleman, I would say, and another great musician. He liked to change things a bit where Benny sorta stuck with what he was doing. Artie went with strings and all that. You know, he had a helluva brass section with Jack Jenney, Billy Butterfield and different guys like that. I think 'Stardust' is about the best record I heard by a trumpet player. The way Billy Butterfield played it is just beautiful.'

From there, Nick worked briefly with Claude Thornhill's orchestra; then with Jan Savitt and Alvino Rey, before joining Eddie Miller's orchestra in California. At this point in his career, he broke into the studio scene and became a first call drummer for many leaders. He remembered those days with a mixture of pleasure and a trace of bitterness too.

'I stayed here [Los Angeles] in 1942 and I've been here ever since. I don't like bringing this up but when I was doing all the work, or doing everything I could do, they had what they call the quota. In other words, if you worked in a studio you couldn't do any record dates or radio calls. If you worked for radio, you couldn't do any studio work. I used to get called from everybody and I'd say, "Well, I'm quota'd." Do you know how much I was making? About

$150 a week, 'cause the radio shows only paid about $30 to $40. I was working the Abbott and Costello show with Freddie Rich and he wanted to hire us for a film, *A Wave, A WAC and A Marine*. He told the union, "I don't care if you fire me, I'm hiring who I like. Charge me for it." So he hired us and they fined him $1500. Abbott and Costello paid for the whole thing. They said, "We don't care, we're making enough money. We'll pay all the fines. Let him get who he wants!" That's how it was, you couldn't make over $150. It wasn't right.'

'After wartime, I did the Chesterfield Show with Johnny Mercer and the Pipers for a couple of years, and then I did the Bing Crosby show for fifteen years. Bing was beautiful. I enjoyed it 'cause Bing was so loose. Once he sang a tune, like 'Sunny Side Of The Street' – just a chorus and a half, that's all he'd sing, he'd never do it again, because he didn't want to overdo the tunes. All they'd do was change the commercials on the show. It was a fifteen-minute programme and we didn't even work! Originally, we did about 400 tunes with Bing, first with the big band led by John Scott Trotter and then with Buddy Cole and the quartet. Bing paid us $15,000 apiece for the quartet and Buddy got much more, all paid from his office. Scale then was about $5,000. So I worked ten days one year and made $15,000. With the rest of the time, I did records.'

When I asked Nick to discuss his records, he led me into the living room and took out a now-battered copy of Jonah Jones' recording with Glen Gray's Casa

Loma Orchestra. Well amplified by Fatool's imposing speakers, its swinging sounds revealed his solid drum support for the trumpeter's soaring improvisations. 'That's one I really like. I think I did about twelve with the Casa Loma and fifteen albums with Time-Life plus a whole bunch with Matty [Matlock]. I enjoyed doing these things, but I don't think I could do 'em again. Your muscles get tired. Maybe I could manage it for one night, but I couldn't do it for a week. I'd wear myself out. It's like asking Joe Louis to fight a fifteen-rounder. Better to look back and say, "Well, I did it."'

Fatool with the Benny Goodman Orchestra, c.1939. Photo courtesy Duncan Schiedt.

'The last few years, I've been doing a few jazz concerts. I do record dates once in a while but they're not very good. They either go back too far [in style] or go too far ahead. Really, I only work on weekends. I don't like to work too much. I never practise. I don't touch my drums for two weeks at a time. I'm happy when they cancel me out although I did do some stuff with Joe recently and laughed all night. And that's fun.'

Taking stock of his lengthy career, Nick said, 'Truthfully, I think it was an honour to work with every band I worked with. I appreciated it all. Hell, I don't think of myself as anything. I just say I'm lucky to be where I am. How do you ever know? If I hadn't come off that small farm, I'd probably still be digging manure out of the cellars like I did for years. There's a lot of poor guys who get stuck in small towns that have so much talent. If they ever get out, they'd expose it, but they don't have the chance. There was a lot of them that didn't get out of Providence. There was a piano player, Alphonse Antonali; he died like when he was in his late thirties. He was the most beautiful piano player I ever heard; he played like Art Tatum and those guys. Really, he did. Me, I was thrown out! Well, not thrown out exactly, but I was close to my mother and after she died, everybody left. I was the youngest of the family. Hell, I got a room in Providence for two and half dollars a week. I stayed there until I went to New York. I told myself if I wasn't worth it by the time I was 25 or 30, I'd quit and go into something else. I put a quota on time. Luckily, I got into it.'

Despite his apparently detached view of his musical contribution, Fatool loved to talk about drums and drummers, and had typically forthright views on the percussionist's role. 'I say you just try and get swinging. Try to feel the beat and if the guy is playing good you keep trying to swing in back of him. What ruins a band a lot of times is when they say a drummer can swing a band. That's impossible. The soloist has to swing and let the drummer just feel him in back of him. A soloist swings better than a drummer does. Drummers won't say that, but my opinion is guys like Bud Freeman, Louis Armstrong, they don't need a drummer! All Louis liked was a little time to keep him going.'

Leaving me to cope with that statement, Fatool moved on to speak of some favourite drummers. His enthusiasm was clear. 'I loved Chick Webb. Well, everybody liked Chick Webb. I used to watch him all the time. He was a little hunchback cat, you know. Somebody used to set him on the stool like he couldn't ever get high enough on the stool, but what he did was so perfect there. I watched Chick work down at the Roseland in Topland, Massachusetts. Taft Jordan used to play trumpet with the plunger and if it was swinging, Chick would say, "One mo'," and he'd keep it going. And if it wasn't swinging, they'd just go out and start again with a different tune. Chick could play his butt off.'

'I loved Big Sid Catlett, too. He looked like he'd break the drums but he played a solo one night at the Streets of Paris like Bobby Hackett would play a trumpet solo: so soft, tinkering around with the drums. And fast, you know, but so cute that you could order a drink while he's playing. It was soft, it was beautiful. Usually a solo will hurt your ears. I was there with Orm Downes – he was with Ted Weems – and this just knocked us out. We didn't know what the hell to do for Big Sid. He would tell you a story like all good drummers do.'

'I loved Davey Tough, Jo Jones, Gene Krupa, Buddy Rich, all the guys. And I gotta mention another drummer, Louis Bellson. He's a beautiful man and a helluva drummer. I don't like solos really but the best way to play a drum solo is the way I heard Louis do it with the Boston Pops [Orchestra] with Pearl Bailey. He just touched everything. That's the way I used to play a drum solo with Pete Fountain. You hear too many drums.'

'Another of my favourite drummers was Ronnie Verrell from England. He was with the Ted Heath band and I think he was one of the greatest drummers. No matter what he did with the Heath band, it fitted. If it was like dixieland jazz, swinging rock, anything, he'd fit himself and it was perfect. That Heath band was so precise and beautiful. If you ever see him, tell Ronnie I think he's one of the best I ever heard.'

Aside from drums, conversation with Fatool tended to encompass his abiding interest in golf. 'Well, I studied golf for about 35 years, all the little idiosyncrasies, how your hands should be, whatever comes with golf. This friend of mine has a golf course and he says, "Nick, will you help me out [teaching] till I find a qualified teacher?" I said, "Sure." So I did that for about eight years. I just did it for kicks, not to make any money, but so I wouldn't drink early. I'd go out there and I'd be there until 5 o'clock and then drink! I didn't know how to teach golf but it's like music: you teach them the fundamentals and when you get some-body that's a little ahead, you show them a little something that's forward. I love the game. Hell, I beat a lot of the teaching pros out there. I won a lot of tournaments. There was one up at Harrahs; they have 300 golfers. I beat the US Amateur champ, which was Harvey Ward. He shot 71, I shot 70. On a big course, he'd beat me. This was a smaller course.'

'I think the life I led wouldn't have been very damn good for golf because I like to drink, and you can't drink and play golf. I never did drink early, but lately, what the hell, I'm get-ting close to 70, I have a drink. I'm a good cook, but that's a little hobby on the side. So we either cook or drink or play golf or play music.'

'As to the music business, I would say give everybody equal opportunity when they play it on the air. I love concert music – I started with a concert band – and I don't mind rock and roll. Some of it is very good. I like hillbilly music. I like every kind of music as long as it's done right. So why the hell don't the stations play a variety of music? Jazz, rock, hillbil-ly: give it all a chance.'

***

'Now are you guys hungry? You want a little cheese or something?' We decline. It is time to go. Getting into the car, we turn to see Fatool in the doorway of his home, shrubs almost masking the path. He waves and says, 'Don't forget to say hello to Ronnie Verrell for me. He's a great drummer.'

Chapter 23

JC Heard

Dancer at the Drums

Like many great drummers, JC Heard was a dancer, too. In person, he was lithe, dapper, and impeccably dressed, exuding energy and confidence, and evidently at ease with himself. His comments were trenchant, and not always suitable for publication, but it was good to be in his company. The interview on which this piece is based took place at the Nice Jazz Festival in 1978 and following this I corresponded with him and saw him at the North Sea Jazz Festival in 1984, leading a sextet. His letters were always full of plans and ideas. This vibrant performer spent his last years in Detroit, fronting his impressive big band and doubt-less having a ball. He died in 1988, aged 70.

When officialdom required it, drummer JC Heard invented the forenames James Charles to satisfy the tidy mind of authority. Somehow form fillers couldn't cope with those brazen initials – nonetheless, that's how Heard was named by loving parents back in Dayton, Ohio. Some 60 years later, there was a directness about his playing and a confidence in his manner that seemed wholly in keeping with those distinctive initials. For make no mis-take, JC, as he was invariably known, was a boss drummer, fearsomely swinging and as hard driving as any percussionist on the scene. Indeed, at the Nice festivities in 1978, Heard backed pianists and small groups, jam sessions and singers, urging every performer to new heights. Even among the outstanding rhythm men assembled, his technique and skill stood out.

When we met to talk, the drummer told me of his start in show business (his phrase, not mine). He spoke in crisp, short phrases, the energy bubbling through his reminis-cences: 'Started off as a dancer at four years old. In Detroit where we lived. Kept going. I won amateur contests at six or seven. I liked the rhythm of tap dancing and I started hearing drummers. Chick Webb was one of my biggest inspirations: everybody wanted to be like him. Taught myself.'

'One day I had the chance to play when the drummer didn't show. They did the show from the pit then. Band, about six or seven pieces. And in the show was a team called Butterbeans and Susie. He was a tall, skinny guy and his wife was fat. He told me, "If you're in doubt about the tempo, just roll and the horns will pick it up and then you hear the tempo and you come on in." And it's true. Some of the best advice I ever had. I was nine or ten years old.'

Heard with Teddy Wilson's band, the Pump Room, Ambassador Hotel, Chicago, March 1942. *Left to right*: George James (bs); Wilson (p); Jimmy Hamilton (cl); Bill Coleman (t); Benny Morton (tb); Heard (d); Al Hall (b). Photo by Rising, courtesy Manfred Selchow.

Detroit played host to many bands passing through, but Heard got his first steady chance with the local small group of trumpeter Bill Johnson – 'Hell, I was the youngest guy in the band' – and their joint was soon a meeting place for visiting musicians. He remembered Benny Goodman, the Dorsey Brothers and others coming in.

The young Heard naturally wanted to play like the big band drummers he so revered: Webb, Jo Jones and Kaiser Marshall, but he had to build a local reputation first. His breakthrough came in 1939 with the celebrated pianist Teddy Wilson. 'My biggest break came when Teddy left Benny Goodman. I got this chance to go to New York. Goodman's band came to town: Teddy, Lionel [Hampton], all in the band. This is about '38. So these guys came down to our joint and Teddy heard me a couple of times. He called me up. Do I want to join his new big band? He was hot then. I couldn't have picked a bigger name to go with. Had Ben Webster and Don Byas on tenors. Bill Johnson gave me a big send-off. You never seen anything like that. Teddy's band lasted a year. Everybody got to know me in New York.'

'Teddy lost a fortune with that band. It was one of the best intonation bands in the country. No-one didn't sound better than that band for tune. But, naturally, Teddy's piano style is simple, tasteful and easy. Well, the booking agents wanted to get Teddy to be like a more rough-type thing. That's not Teddy's bag. So it didn't last.'

He then went with Benny Carter – 'King Benny, he even wrote drum parts that were magnificent' – and moved on to Coleman Hawkins' big band briefly, playing around town with different groups as the volatile war-time scene dictated. There was another exhilarating period with Teddy Wilson in Wilson's sextet at Café Society. 'In fact I used to be like a utility drummer 'round New York. Anybody come into town and their drummer got sick – especially name bands – if I was available, I could go in and cut it. I knew the style of every band. Sleep? I didn't worry about that. I used to be up two or three days at a time,' he laughed.

JC was a fervent apologist for the exciting big band days, extolling the value of varied experience for drummers and contrasting the paucity of such opportunities for young percussionists. He talked, with almost missionary zeal, of playing for chorus girls, dance teams and the like, bemoaning the lack of such awareness in the modern cats.

As an extension to his name band credits Heard cited his three-year period with Cab Calloway as particularly important. 'We had everything first-class. We changed uniforms four or five times a day: you on the stage, man, you look sharp! One of the highest paid bands in the business. I took Cozy Cole's place. That's where I learned a lot about the show business side since I had a chance to play with all the top dance teams and singers. In fact, I was with Cab when we discovered Pearl Bailey. Strictly road. Cab carried a whole show with him. I was featured. Drum solos. You got to push yourself, baby.'

JC talked knowingly about the early days of bebop – he recorded with Dizzy and Parker – and was no man to decry change. After Cab, he formed his own band with good arrangements by Jimmy Mundy, and fine people like tenorist Budd Johnson and Dicky Wells on trombone. This was to last for several action-packed years before he was called for Norman Granz' Jazz At The Philharmonic, easily the most famous concert series in jazz.

'The first [concert for Granz] I did was in '44 when Norman just came out of UCLA High School. Jam sessions. I was with Cab at the time. We had Nat King Cole on piano. It was fun. Then JATP came along in the fifties. Norman always wanted the best guys so they could blow each other's brains out. Like he had Gene [Krupa] and me. We had the drum battle. Paid good money. Chance to blow. We played

England in '53. Ronnie Scott was there playing. It was a big thing.'

'Then we had Illinois Jacquet, and he's one of the most spontaneous, most exciting tenor players that Norman ever had. He wouldn't buy anybody unless they could play in the first place. To excite an audience to this frenzy, where they go out of their minds for ten minutes: Jacquet had that. Hey, that's something man,' he enthused.

JATP visited Japan that same year – the first US jazz star visitors, hugely successful and lionised to a degree beyond belief. All concerts were sell-outs and 'drums were big' so the local promoter encouraged JC to stay on for a few extra dates. That holdover was to last for four years, with Heard at the helm of his own group working in entertainment. His picture, larger than life, was outside every concert hall where he appeared.

In short JC became a star with a 22-piece band, strings added, and his drum solos, dancing and vocals too. There were songs and, in Japan, a little comedy: 'in Japanese to make it authentic.' And then he moved on to Hong Kong, Cairo, and Australia (living there for a year) as a single song, dance and drum act.

'I was away from America for seven years from the time we first landed with Gene Krupa and the JATP.' What brought him back? 'I think I stayed away a little too long. People hadn't seen me in a long time. My mother was sick; she and my father wanted me to see them. So I came back.' In his later years, JC was travelling once more, but less exotically perhaps, contracted to the US Hilton Hotels circuit, entertaining and fronting a four-piece combo with organ, Charlie Gabriel on saxes, and Marcus Belgrave the trumpeter.

JC's drumming philosophy, epitomised each time he took the stand, went something like this: 'I want to make them play, because if I whip 'em good they'll play good, and then I'll enjoy myself.'

Chapter 24

John Hicks

Fast and Loose

John Hicks, 1990s. Courtesy John Hicks.

After a version of this piece appeared in Coda, *John's companion, Elise Wood, asked when I was going to write about his more recent musical activities. The truth is that John's desire to tell me all about his early days helped to make this interview (at the Grafton Hotel in London in August 1999) a helter-skelter experience for us both. I was fascinated by his stories, especially those relating to St Louis, an important if under-documented jazz centre.*

It is often asserted that no pianist of reasonable competence need be out of work. After all, everyone needs a piano player. Especially, of course, when the skills brought to bear are of highest quality – which brings us to John Hicks, a pianist trademarked for the constancy of his inspiration.

Hicks visits Europe often, and has appeared at Ronnie Scott's Club in London, with the Mingus Big Band, or as part of Bobby Watson's quartet. He's also regularly recorded with celebrated names, ranging from Woody Herman to Lee Morgan, Art Blakey to Jay McShann, and Betty Carter to David Murray.

Given such prolificacy, it's all too easy to see Hicks as a kind of musical chameleon. On the contrary, however, he is invariably himself: harmonically canny; his playing a heady amalgam of considered emotion and rhythmic brio; the improvisatory outcomes entirely distinctive.

When we met on a bright August morning at his hotel, Hicks, a glass of red wine to hand, was addressing a newly faxed request to play for Larry Coryell on an upcoming recording session. A ready communicator with a perceptive eye for telling detail, and frequent recourse to laughter, he talked at length about his formative experiences in music, covering periods spent in Los Angeles, St. Louis and New York. Hicks loves to digress, zigzagging away from and back to the thrust of his narrative, his conversational style a mirror image of his keyboard approach. There's the same dash and urgency when he speaks as when he plays. He is, in short, a stimulating companion.

John Hicks Jr. was born in December 1941 in Atlanta, Georgia, where his parents had both studied, his mother at Clark College (part of the Atlanta University complex) and his father, a Methodist minister, at Gavin Theological Seminary. Hicks describes Atlanta as a 'very independent place as far as black people were concerned.' Indeed, one of his great uncles was tarred and feathered by the Ku Klux Klan for advocating the foundation of a black newspaper. Clearly a product of the black middle class himself, he says, 'I don't make any bones about it. I was brought up as a decent human being where you had aspirations and there were expectations from people that wanted to see you go to the next level. And I turned out to be a piano player – I don't know if that was exactly what they had in mind!'

His father's initial post was as a chaplain in the US Navy Yards in Long Beach, California. Having first re-located 'right off Central Avenue' in 1942, the family next moved on to 'my dad's first big church, St. John's Methodist at 1009 Wilmington – the parsonage was right next door'. Hicks was seven when his mother, a schoolteacher, began his piano training. 'The first piano I actually started playing on was a player-piano. Every now and then she'd get up from the piano and put the player on and I'd be sitting there watching the keys move. I always had a good ear, and I could pick things out on my own. When my dad found out I could play the piano and read music he got a youth choir together and had me take organ lessons.'

Hicks' father had wide-ranging musical interests himself. 'My dad was a big jazz fan – his favourite band was Jimmie Lunceford. It was through my dad that I met Duke Ellington at a downtown theatre. When you went to these big theatres they would have a serial, a cartoon, the feature movie, plus you would have people like the Orioles or somebody singing, and then Count Basie or Duke Ellington. He took me to hear a lot of people. See, for him it was like a sort of release from visiting the sick and that whole thing. He was very politically involved – he was right in there with Martin Luther King and those guys.'

For a youngster like Hicks living in the tightly circumscribed black community, music was a constant. 'Straight down Wilmington Avenue, Johnny Otis had a radio show: used to play rhythm and blues, bebop and swing. Plus I had a friend who lived down the street from us and his mom was a big bebop fan. As a matter of fact, the first ten-inch LP that I ever saw in my life was at her house: Dizzy's Big Band! By that time I had moved on to another piano teacher, Mr. Parewski. I had to audition for this guy. He used to click his false teeth every time I played some funny stuff on the piano. If there was any incentive not to play anything wrong, that was it! But he was a great friend of Art Tatum and that's how I got to see Art Tatum.'

In his early teens Hicks dabbled with a number of musical options. 'I was still quite involved in church music and I was taking violin lessons along with my brother. He was really talented but I always had more of an affinity for the piano. I also used to mess around with the trombone. I played it in college – until I went to Berklee where I was uptight for some money and I pawned my trombone for $10. I never got it out so that was the end of my trombone days! In my second year in college I even had a little group that we would put together where I wrote arrangements of the TV themes for the band. But the piano seemed to take me over after that.'

The Hicks family's next port of call was St. Louis. 'I came into Sumner High School where I met all the Bowie family, and folks like [drummer] Philip Wilson and [saxophonist] Oliver Lake. Actually Oliver Lake was a late starter as far as music was concerned – I never forget because he tried to go with my ex-wife. She's also a pianist and she said, "Well, I kinda like John, he plays a little better than you." Oliver and I laugh about it now. I used to know his family – his mom used to have this restaurant – you talking about soul food? Lester Bowie's dad was a great music educator. He started off in Arkansas. As a matter of fact the late Richard Boone used to be one of his students.'

Hicks immersed himself in choral music at Sumner – there was no swing or jazz band – and made it to the all-city choir, looking to hone his jazz skills where he could. 'At that time everything that you did on that level was on your own. After finishing sports I would go over to [the musicians' union] Local 197 on Newstead and Delmar, a big white building; on the first floor there's a piano and a rehearsal room. I would go to the piano and hang out with people like John Chapman, Oliver Nelson and Sam Malone, a pianist who turned me on to a gig with [saxophonists] Johnny Griffin and Lockjaw Davis, because Lloyd Mayers' wife was sick and he had to go back to New York. I took his place for a couple of weeks based on a recommendation from Sam Malone. That's another funny story: because when I get to the gig, it's in East St. Louis; it was a big club called the Blue Note. It was a Sunday afternoon, I walk in and there's this guy sitting at the piano with a saxophone in his lap and he's playing the piano. I thought, "I don't think I can play all that stuff – what am I doing here?" It was Johnny Griffin! That got me

nervous. I was just mesmerised by these guys. I remember Johnny saying, "Wait till one of these women breaks your heart, you'll play the blues a lot different then. You're a happy blues player right now." I never forgot that! Jaws [Eddie Lockjaw Davis] was one of the hardest guys to follow; I used to think, is this guy playing backwards or what?'

Like others of his St. Louis generation, Hicks gained valuable performing experience in blues bands like those led by Little Milton and Albert King. As a youngster he spent his summers on the road with Milton, travelling the South and the Mid-West, working constantly, once playing four gigs over an eighteen-hour period. Gigs usually started every night at 9 p.m. with an after-hours follow-on until 5 a.m. – hard work when you had to go to church on Sunday morning ahead of playing a matinee later that day. It impressed him that the band's hornmen were into Sonny Rollins and keen to transcribe Charlie Parker solos. Oliver Sain was the musical director and saxophonist Julius Hemphill (also from Sumner High) – 'this cat was already *there*, he was writing stuff you wouldn't believe' – was a colleague.

Hicks recalled that his first gig with Milton was at the Moonlight Bar in St. Louis. 'The lady that owned the club, she looked at me when I came in. I had my little shorts on, dressed pretty hip for the day, and she says, "Aren't you Reverend Hicks' son? What are you doing in here? You're too young, we serve liquor in here." So I immediately pulled out my wallet and showed her my union card and I said, "I'm the piano player." She says, "You go home and get a note from you mother to say that it's OK for you to play in here."'

Hicks moved to New York in the autumn of 1963 (singer Fontella Bass took his place in Milton's band). He had completed his course at Lincoln University and a year at Berklee School of Music in Boston before leaving for a 'gig on the road with a singing group' and returning to St. Louis for yet more study. 'I did have some gigs of my own in St. Louis and I was in a couple of different bands, like a big band led by one of Miles' [Davis] friends, trumpeter Bobby Danzie. But the music scene in St. Louis was kinda tapering off. Miles, Clark Terry and Oliver Nelson urged me to go.'

Hicks in Milan, c.1972 with Clifford Barbaro (d); Charles Tolliver (t) and Clint Houston (b). Courtesy John Hicks.

Armed only with a 'lunch pail and some tuna-fish sandwiches', Hicks headed for Brooklyn and lodged with St. Louis bassist Bill Davis for $8 a week. Within hours of his arrival he was hired to play that same night with singer Big Maybelle at the Purple Manor club on 125th Street, eventually doubling up on a gig with tenorist Joe Farrell and the late Art Blakey Jr. on drums. Then he met trumpeter Tommy Turrentine, 'who turned me on to the gig with Al Grey and Billy Mitchell. They had come out of Count Basie's orchestra and wanted to do their own thing. That's my first gig on the road, from just coming to New York. We went to the Pennsylvania Dutch country. Great band: we had Tommy on trumpet, Ali

Jackson on bass and Billy Butterfield on drums. Tommy was strung out, but he was always serious about the music.'

It was Cedar Walton, pianist with Art Blakey's Messengers, who recommended Hicks to Blakey. 'Cedar knew me from St. Louis when the Messengers band played a big concert down on Franklin Street, and then he heard me on some gigs in New York. The audition [for Blakey] was playing tunes in the book – you had to know, or at least be able to hear what was going on. You had one time to play with the music, then Art would ceremoniously collect all the music and lock it up in his drum case. He would just bear down on you and say, "Play!" You had to get something out of working in that band, and the people that you were playing with, like Lee Morgan or John Gilmore. Another phenomenal guy – he had his own style. Now you have people that you can't tell one from the other, and that's a problem.'

'My first tour with the Messengers was for two years and then I came back in the seventies with Eddie Henderson, and played right here, in Ronnie Scott's.' The next important association for John Hicks was with the ever-inventive singer Betty Carter. Of her he says, 'It was like playing with a horn player. She was so adventurous, she'd change keys, she'd change tempos, and she'd change metres. Betty was like a well-kept secret, too – her success was by word-of-mouth then.'

Conversation with the mercurial Hicks is a little like going into free-fall, as there's no knowing where you're going to land. A reference to Mary Lou Williams brings forth a mini-torrent of memories from when she introduced him (and his pianist wife Olympia) to the sights of New York. Talk about Billy Strayhorn (Hicks has a tribute album to Strayhorn on High Note) sparks off memories of a chance meeting with Billy and Coleman Hawkins in Beefsteak Charlie's and a later engagement with Hawk. A mention of Thelonious Monk prompts recollections of all sorts of chance encounters with the enigmatic innovator. Wheeling a piano on a dolly back to his apartment on West 87th Street with fellow-pianist Walter Davis, the two saw Monk, 'standing on the corner, with a top coat and a fez on.' The upright now installed in the Hicks' apartment with Thelonious present, 'Monk immediately sits down to the piano. Doesn't even take his coat off. Just played 'In Walked Bud'. Went through it like a dissertation on how to change the harmony under a basic melody.'

This allusion to Bud Powell reminds Hicks of when he played opposite Bud (with trombonist Bennie Green) at Birdland. 'I says, "Hi Bud, how you doing?" He says, "Give me a dollar." So he goes around the corner and gets a glass of wine with the dollar. After about three or four days [Bud's minder] François [Paudras] says, "John, I know you love Bud but when he asks you for a dollar *don't* give him a dollar." Now, this is my hero! But just to watch Bud, that was another great experience.'

There are few players who have successfully run the gamut of the music (and its key personalities) as completely as

Hicks – taking in his stride choral music, blues accompaniment, R&B, easy-going swing, hard-edged modernism, and shouting big bands. Which brings us to Woody Herman.

Hicks was called to join Woody's big band on April 4, 1968, by road manager Bill Byrne 'through Albert Dailey who was one of my good friends, and lived across from me on 87th Street, down the street from Andrew Hill. We had a helluva block! I was with Woody almost two years and my son was born during that time. [Herman tenorist] Sal Nistico was my son's godfather. Oh, Sal was a sweet player.' Herman was always supportive of his black sidemen, as Hicks recalled. 'I never forget Lafayette, Louisiana, when Woody invited Harry Hall, one of the trumpet players, and me to eat some gumbo with him in the hotel restaurant and the guy says, "I'm sorry Mr. Herman but *these* guys have to eat in their room." And Woody says, "Listen, I was playing here before you were born; if they don't eat with me, I'm not making the gig. Now give me a table by the window so we can look out on the water!"'

About the only time Herman gave Hicks any pointers was for the *Light My Fire* album when he suggested that Hicks 'play a little more in the style of rock, which was cool because I already had a background in blues bands. But I was glad that he mentioned it to me, just to put it in perspective. It's always good to know what people want. Being with Woody gave me a sense of programming, how you present what you have. He had a way of doing it. Actually, I

made as much from writing arrangements for Woody as I got for playing the gigs!'

After further sojourns with Betty Carter and Art Blakey, Hicks started working with younger musicians, including future stars like saxophonists Chico Freeman, David Murray and Arthur Blythe. This pattern continues to the present day. Something of a jazzman for all occasions, like a Hank Jones for our time, he's as likely to appear with the Mingus Big Band (he was the band's first pianist) as he is to play with Bobby Watson or Murray. Never one to eschew sideman opportunities, Hicks divides his time between fronting his own trio and acting as a first call player in the studios and on bandstands around the world. Nor does he reject his roots in the church, usually taking time out to play the organ at his local church in New York on the first Sunday of the month when he's in town. 'I'm still a believer,' he says. Hicks knows that his other journey, the musical one, has a way to go: 'I'm not there yet and it's going to take more [effort] on my part. What I have always perceived as my life's goal is, first of all to have respect for myself and, at this point in my life, to make a fairly decent living. I've dedicated my life to this music and I know I have integrity. It's been a struggle but I have my own standards.'

When it comes to composition, he says, 'There's certain things that I have done that I would like to build on, like my trio and strings album [that came out] on a small label, and all my original compositions.' His partner, the flautist Elise Wood, plays an active role in his musical life, 'taking care of

Hicks (*right*) with Jay McShann, St Louis, 1999. Photo courtesy John Hicks.

my paperwork, booking the gigs,' and, of course, appearing on record with him. He says his enthusiasm has stayed high, 'You can't have a low flame on it.' As we finish our conversation, Hicks' eyes light up as he talks about his granddaughter, a gifted young pianist. How does she see her granddad's place in things? 'She says, "Papa John, how you play so fast?"' How indeed?

Chapter 25

Hank Jones

Mr Elegance

Hank Jones, July 1983. Photo by Tony Kreppel.

One of the most widely recorded of jazz musicians, Hank Jones lives in upstate New York and continues to perform in the city's best clubs and and tour abroad. This piece is based on an interview conducted in 1983 while he was playing at the North Sea Festival. Self-effacing and relaxed, Hank Jones seemed happy to talk about his early days in Detroit and to reflect on his desires and aims.

Hank Jones is the kind of pianist whose playing attracts adjectives that read like character references. Words like 'tasteful', 'elegant', and 'distinguished' jostle for priority in any hack's writing about this jazz elder's keyboard creativity. Encounter him in person and it's clear that the style is the man. His demeanour is gracious, the tone of his conversation humorous yet reflective, with a line in modesty which belies his status as one of the finest, most consistent artists of his generation.

When I asked him why his appearances in Britain had been so few he said, 'People have to become aware of who I am and I don't suppose too many people are, at this point, and then I have to practise a lot to justify that interest.' In fact, Jones performed here as long ago as 1948 when he accompanied Ella Fitzgerald on tour and he has also appeared in one-off concerts fronted by Benny Goodman or with occasional all-star line-ups.

The doyen of an important jazz family (the late Thad Jones and Elvin Jones were his brothers), he was born in Vicksburg, Mississippi in 1918 but is forever associated with the Detroit school, although as he pointed out, his people were actually resident in nearby Pontiac.

Jones accounted for the emergence of so many great jazzmen from this area in typically down to earth fashion: 'There was so little going on in Detroit that everyone worked very hard to get out,' he laughed. 'Detroit, as you know, is an automobile manufacturing city. When business is good and they're making lots of cars and trucks, then the town lives. It booms and comes alive. When automobile manufacturing goes down, as it is today, the town dies. It's that up and down prosperity cycle that affected Detroit and maybe affected the musicians. There's a basic instability in a city like Detroit.'

Music was always a formative influence. 'My mother played enough piano to accompany choirs in church and my father sang in the church choir. I had three sisters who sang and two sisters who played piano. Some of my younger brothers also played. My mother used to buy all sorts of records. We had a lot of blues records during that period. Later on, we began to get records by Duke Ellington, Earl Hines, Jimmie Lunceford.'

Jones began his piano studies at nine. He met 'a very fine musician when I was growing up. His name was Jimmy Parker. He was one of those musicians who played every instrument in the orchestra. He was about two years older than I was. When I was thirteen, having just been playing the piano about three years, we were both in a small band in Pontiac. It had a drummer named Bernard Brown; Sam Parr, a guitarist; myself; Jimmy doubled on trumpet and sax, so whenever we had another saxophone player, we had a section! Later on, I played with people like [tenorists] Wardell Gray and Lucky Thompson in Flint, Michigan, when I was about twenty. This was in a territory band led by Benny Carew, playing dances and small clubs in the area. Wardell and Lucky both had tremendous talent and improvisational ability even then. At one time or another, I played also with Art Mardigan, the drummer who went with Woody Herman and there was another saxophone player named Marion Davida who, for a short time, came to New York and played with some of the bands. All these people were from Detroit.'

Hearing Teddy Wilson on records by Benny Goodman's trio provided Jones with his first inspiration: 'He was an idol of mine but Art Tatum is definitely my all-time idol on piano. With people like that as guides or role-models, at least you have a point at which to aim.'

Bebop remained a closed book until Jones made it to New York in 1944, having spent part of the war in a defence plant, making wings for the Vought Corsair fighter. 'I didn't even hear bebop until I came to New York. The records hadn't reached

Pontiac. Nothing reached Pontiac!'

His first name band experience came when he went out on the road (and recorded) in 1944 with the great trumpeter and vocalist Hot Lips Page. 'Lucky Thompson had come to New York at least a year and a half before I did. He was working with Page with a small band at the Onyx Club on 52nd Street. Lips needed a piano player and Lucky put in a good word for me so I had a job waiting when I came to New York. I was lucky in that respect. I worked for a short time with Lips on 52nd Street and then went on tour with his big band. Spent three months in the South, doing one-nighters. We came back to New York after the tour and went back into the Onyx Club. Lips was strongly influenced by boogie-woogie so I had to play a great deal. He always used to introduce me as "the young man from the West – our boogie-woogie artist," and I didn't know one boogie-woogie lick from another! Unfortunately, Lips liked the sauce too much, used to drink quite a bit. I suppose musicians then thought they had to do something to combat the hardships that they faced on an everyday basis.'

Jones went on to work with Andy Kirk's big band, John Kirby's small group and the Billy Eckstine Orchestra before his time with Jazz At The Philharmonic and Ella Fitzgerald. His playing had begun to change, to take more from bebop. 'From Monk, it was his harmonic concept. The way he voiced his chords, that's what I liked about Monk. He used progressions that were not conventional. I liked the jazz

Jazz at the Philharmonic at Amsterdam Airport. *Left to right*: Jones, Roy Eldridge, Flip Phillips, Dutch promoter, Norman Granz, Max Roach, Lester Young, Oscar Peterson, Irving Ashby. Photo courtesy mr.jazz Photo Files (Theo Zwicky).

lines that Bud Powell and Al Haig played. A stylist has to go his own route, that's one of the essentials. Today, what I'm doing is playing what I would like to consider is me. This is probably a distillation of whatever or whoever I've heard up to this point in time. I don't see myself going in a different direction now, but I would like to develop to the limit of my ability. Certainly you would like to have whatever you do be current in the idiom. You don't want to be dated.'

Hank Jones has enjoyed an exceptional career. He spent fifteen years on the staff at CBS, accompanied Broadway shows and has performed with every jazz artist of consequence, including his illustrious brothers. He continues to make excellent recordings. For all that, when asked to ponder his many achievements, this consummate professional says only, 'I should have practised more.'

Chapter 26

Nappy Lamare

Crosby Days

Nappy Lamare with Bob Crosby and his band, 1930s. Photo courtesy Max Jones Archive.

Floyd Levin and Barry Martyn brought the touring show A Nite in New Orleans *to London in May 1975 and I trooped out to their hotel in Upper Norwood to see who among the musicians might want to talk for publication. Banjo player Nappy Lamare was sharing a room with the acerbic trumpeter Wingy Manone and proved far more amenable than his companion when I suggested an interview. We talked at some length and this piece uses selected extracts from Nappy's story. A few years later, Joe Darensbourg and I called on Nappy at his home in Van Nuys, California, and spent a cordial day together, visiting Disneyland and eventually sharing a bottle of Nappy's corn liquor. The hangover was memorable. . . Nappy kept working as a freelance into the 1980s and died in Newhall, California, in May 1988.*

Joseph Hilton 'Nappy' Lamare was a New Orleans native, born in 1907, with French blood in the family. Jazz soon caught his attention. 'I used to listen to bands. I didn't know who they were at first: guys like Kid Punch [Miller], Kid Rena and [Alphonse] Picou. We used to dance a lot and hire their bands. I just liked music,' he smiled.

Nappy's brother, Jimmy, played sax. He himself tried to play trumpet but in one of those timely twists of fate, swapped instruments with an aspiring banjoist. Within a month the fourteen year-old Nappy was working his first job – 'We called ourselves the Midnight Serenaders' – and a famous jazz career was underway. Early associates included other fledgling hot music stars such as drummer Ray Bauduc, tenorman Eddie Miller and clarinettist Irving Fazola – all later, with Lamare, to gain fame with the successful and jazz laden Bob Crosby Orchestra. The city seems in retrospect to have been teeming with outstanding musicians of both races, and, interestingly, some crossing of racial lines took place in those segregated days. Nappy explained, 'I studied with a coloured guy, Sonny, on banjo. He was a good player. I still use things today that he taught me. He had what I wanted – the beat. I never did really care for the full ringing style banjo; a lot of times you hear guys playing and it really hurts my ears. I'll choke every beat, it swings really, and this cat taught me all that. Then there was a white guy named Gillette who played with the Wolverines and I heard a break he did and I got an idea from that. Then I started playing with Ray Bauduc's brother and he'd draw all these things out and teach me. He'd play and I'd rush home and try to do the things he'd done. "Practise, practise," he emphasised.'

Nappy left the Crescent City for good in 1929. In his words, 'There was nothing there,' and an uncle encouraged him to go: first to Chicago with trumpeter Johnny Bayersdorffer, where he found no work, and then to New York and employment on guitar with Billy Burton, a violinist, who played in Atlantic City. Soon Nappy was in fast company and not for wholly musical reasons either. 'All the bands would come to town and they knew there was a New Orleans guy down the street. They'd come and see me as they thought that coming from New Orleans I must have some golden leaf [pot]. I didn't, but I got to know so many musicians that way.'

Joe Darensbourg Band, September 1978. *Left to right*: Dick Cary (t); unknown (d); Darensbourg (cl); Lamare (bj); Eddie Miller (ts). Photo courtesy Joe Darensbourg.

Few could spend time with Nappy without talking about his days with the Ben Pollack and Bob Crosby orchestras, a halcyon period evidently, and one for which he retained the warmest feeling. I asked him to tell me about his introduction into the Pollack ranks.

'Ben Pollack hired me on 48th and Broadway in New York – they used to hire guys on the street then. Let's see, Eddie Miller, Charles Spivak and myself, we all went to Benny at the same time. And Jack Teagarden, who I knew from Louisiana, Sterling Bose and Ray Bauduc from New Orleans, they were in the band too. Ben was working at the Park Central

Hotel and then we went out on the road. I stuck with the guy; no pay, no transportation, just young and wanted to play.'

'We went to California, played at Sebastian's Club where Louis Armstrong was. Then we decided we weren't doing quite enough: Pollack had his wife singing and she'd crack the notes, and Jack wanted to leave so we all packed up our music books and one by one we quit. That's when we went to New York, did some radio work with Ruth Etting – we were all members of the New York local [union] and Red Nichols used us too.'

'We rehearsed so all we needed was a front. We didn't know who to get. Then they suggested Bob Crosby. He was young, had a good sense of humour. A real nice guy. It turned out he was a real good M.C. In fact we were talking about that the other day and Bob was remembering how Ray [Bauduc] told him to just start waving his arms and then he'd pick up the tempo. That was the beginning of that.'

The Crosby band and its many great soloists satisfied Nappy's musical needs until the impact of the Second World War brought the music business to near seizure in 1942. There were frequent recordings – a novelty like 'Big Noise from Winnetka' selling in the thousands – and the Bobcats too, a small New Orleans style band-within-the-band which sowed the seeds of the jazz revival. Were there any special memories from the Crosby days? 'Yeah, like when Ray Bauduc popped Fazola in the mouth. Oh, did Ray feel sorry; he cried, 'cause he split Fazola's lip. No, there were a lot of good things. Everything was good.'

During the war years Lamare worked on the Chesterfield radio show out of California, where he had moved with his family after the Crosby break-up. Later he part-owned and ran his own nightclub on the Coast and then co-led a fine dixieland band with his erstwhile Crosby chum, Ray Bauduc. At the time I interviewed him, he was playing banjo as often as not, taking in sessions in the TV studios and recordings. Then there was Disneyland, trio jobs with friends like clarinettist Joe Darensbourg, and occasional reunions with Crosby colleagues. He even played Fender bass if required.

Looking back, Nappy seemed to have enjoyed it all but it was to the Crosby days that he turned most readily; 'The guys got along so good. Why, I'm closer to them now than my own brothers. Yes, they were good times.'

Chapter 27

Junior Mance

All Blues

Junior Mance with Marty Rivera (b), Café des Copains, Toronto, 1983. Photo courtesy Junior Mance.

I interviewed pianist Julian 'Junior' Mance in 2001 for Coda, *which seemed appropriate as Mance has recorded often for Sackville Records, a label originally linked with this Canadian magazine. The interview was a delight all the way and Junior's ready help with pictures and willingness to clarify details added immeasurably to its value. He's a gracious and urbane man, who puts you at your ease and looks for ways to please you. It's a privilege to present at least part of his story.*

I was bowled over by Junior Mance when I first heard him with Dizzy Gillespie's feisty quintet in 1959. Years later, I was able to show him a photograph taken backstage at the Hammersmith Odeon in London during that tour. I felt just as enthusiastic about his appearance at the Brecon festival in 1993 with Lionel Hampton's Golden Men of Jazz alongside Clark Terry, Sweets Edison and James Moody. For all his veteran status – Mance was born in October 1928 – he remains a soulful improviser, animated and hard-swinging. There's something upbeat about his philosophy that pleases audiences and inspires his accompanists. He seldom moves far away from a blues feeling in his interpretations even when handling a standard or a classic bop original.

Recently he formed an informal partnership with two young British musicians, bassist Andy Cleyndert and drummer Steve Brown, that led to a pair of extensive UK tours, the second of which ended in February 2002. It was Junior who pressed for this follow-up tour – a tough-sounding schedule of fifteen one-nighters in a row – and Cleyndert who again handled bookings and travel, also issuing a CD on his own Trio label, using recordings made on Mance's earlier visit. A further live CD was issued after the 2002 dates to add to the impressive roster of Mance albums already on the market, referred to by their instigator, ironically, as '43 of the best-kept secrets in jazz.'

Talking over a pasta lunch at his London hotel midway through the 2001 tour, it soon became clear that Mance's bandstand persona is matched by his real-life generosity of spirit. As in so many conversations, each subject led to another, but first we spoke about his continuing willingness to travel given his other commitments, notably in the teaching sphere. Pointing out that he's 'no spring chicken', he explained how he juggles tours and concerts with his participation in the jazz programme at New York's New School University. That said, Junior was keen to highlight his continued desire to perform provided that he can select his opportunities with care, and look for comfort wherever possible. He knows, too, that the merit of his teaching is directly linked to his standing as a creative artist.

Mance tutors a blues ensemble course for instrumentalists and a class for blues vocal-

ists, helping to prepare students for the cut and thrust of artistic life. 'We're teaching performance,' he emphasised. 'The premise is to turn out *performers*.' So what does he himself get from teaching? He smiled. 'I learn a lot! We always get youngsters coming in with
something new. See, when Chico Hamilton and Arnie Lawrence first asked me to be a part
of the programme, I said, "I don't know, I've never taught, I don't have teaching credentials." They said, "That has nothing to do with it – we want professionals, somebody who's
doing it." So they asked me to "try it for a week or two, and if you don't like it you can quit
and we'll understand." I've been there fourteen years now – I liked it the *first day*!' What's
more, Mance's contract is flexible; he can take off whenever he wants, provided he can

Lester Young at the Blue Note Club, Chicago, 1949, with Mance (p), Tex Briscoe (b), Jerry Elliott (tb), Roy
Haynes (d) and Jesse Drakes (t). Photo courtesy Junior Mance.

supply 'a viable substitute'. Mance's spoke of his preferred deputy, bassist Carline Ray, late
of Ruth Brown's band and the widow of the celebrated bandleader Luis Russell. 'I'm telling
you, she knows so much music. She not only plays bass, she plays guitar, she sings, and
she teaches classical piano. She's 76 years old and a Juilliard graduate. She has a ball,
and the students love her.'

  Junior takes huge pride in the achievements of his former students. 'Listen, I have three
who now have record contracts. One of them is Jesse Davis, alto saxophonist, another is

Brad Mehldau, piano player, and the other one is Larry Golding who turned to organ after he graduated.' Speaking of Mehldau, how had Mance helped him? 'I knew he was going to be great. I wouldn't say that I taught him; we did, like, workshops, fine-tuning certain things. When I first started working with him, he was more of a Wynton Kelly style player, then he learned how to broaden his other talents.'

Why is teaching so important to Mance? 'It's an old worn-out phrase, but it's a great feeling to give back something. And it's something I'm going to continue to do.'

When it comes to his own performances, Mance likes to pick and choose. 'I don't care if the guy's the greatest musician in the world, if his personality or attitudes are wrong, I won't work with him. I have to get along with the person off the stage as well as on the stage.' Which brought us to Japan, another regular destination. 'I go to Japan at least once a year, sometimes two or three times. I've been doing the 100 Golden Fingers tour over there since 1989. We do about a month tour with ten piano players from the States, and one bass player, Bob Cranshaw, who's been there from the beginning, and one drummer. It's Grady Tate now, used to be Alan Dawson before he passed away. The first tour, we had John Lewis, Hank Jones, Tommy Flanagan, Ray Bryant, Kenny Barron, Monty Alexander, Lyn Arriale, Harold Mabern, Cedar Walton and myself. Right now I'm the senior member 'cause John and Tommy have gone, and Hank doesn't want to do any long tours anymore.'

No interview with Junior Mance would be complete without reference to the blues. 'I love the blues,' he affirmed. 'I came from a town [Chicago] which was very blues-oriented, more so than now. When I was coming up the real blues players were blues singers like Muddy Waters, Tampa Red, Memphis Slim, all those people. My first love on piano was boogie-woogie; my first heroes were, like, Pete Johnson, Meade Lux Lewis and Albert Ammons. Ironically, I got my real professional jazz training under Albert's son, Gene Ammons.'

'I was born in Chicago but I grew up in Evanston, which is just like a suburb of Chicago. My mother was very much into the blues, had all the blues records; there was always blues in the house. My father – Julian Mance Sr. – was more into big bands, and he was a stride pianist but only at home. When I think about it now, he could have been professional. His favourite big band, until the day he died, was Count Basie. He took me to meet him when I was ten years old. Basie came to the Regal Theater in Chicago. It was the first live band I'd seen. I was so enthralled. There were three shows in those days, so we stayed for all three and then we got ready to leave, but we weren't heading in the direction of the train station to go back to Evanston, we went in another direction. My dad went to the backstage entrance and asked to speak to 'Mr. Basie'. Basie came down and he talked to me for about 20 or 30 minutes right there in the lobby, encouraging me. That stayed with me. Many years later, at the original Birdland, where

Basie usually worked for the whole month of December, they drew such big crowds, they thought they'd hire a trio to get a turnover [of the audience] so they hired my trio. Basie remembered me, and we became good friends.'

'I started playing professionally in Chicago when I was about thirteen. Upstairs, over us, lived this good saxophone player. His name was T.S. Minns. He had a gig one night and his piano player got sick. His gig consisted of piano, drums and saxophone. He had heard me practising and he thought I knew enough. At least I knew how to play the blues and I knew things that had 'I Got Rhythm' changes which a lot of saxophone players played, so I made the gig that night. I learned a lot from him. In fact his regular piano player never came back! This was during the summer, too, when I was out of school, so I had the gig all summer. It was at what they called a roadhouse, a cafe outside of Evanston on the highway, so there was no chance of anyone coming in and giving him a summons for hiring somebody too young.'

'Then I started getting gigs around Chicago, playing with bands that played the local dances. I was even working in clubs from the time I was about sixteen, on the South Side. That was another no-man's land, for the law anyway. The music was basically jazz because that was the only thing that was around, especially in the black community. There were always quartets, trios, in some of the smaller clubs, and sometimes they had a floor show; you'd have a tap dancer, and maybe what we used to call a shake dancer. That's a scantily clad woman who comes out, and she shakes! And usually you'd have a blues singer. Those three elements. I remember there was one singer named Doctor JoJo Adams, he was very good. I also remember this great harmonica player who played blues; he was more of a soloist, they called him Rhythm Willie,' Mance laughed.

Club gigs on the South Side brought him into contact with any number of great tenor players. 'I worked with Von Freeman a lot. He and Gene Ammons were great friends. Also with Tom Archia; he and Gene did a double saxophone thing for ages. Tom was a beautiful guy, everybody loved him. Died young. He was a heavy drinker – a guy who could be drunk, and still be on his feet, you wouldn't know that he was drunk, and just put everybody away playing the horn.'

Another formative experience for the young pianist came when he joined Jimmy Dale's orchestra, a locally-based big band. 'The leader of the Jimmy Dale Band was a guy named Harold Fox; he was a tailor. He used to be a trumpet player; never played in the band but he knew music. He knew all the musicians too, and in those days all the big bands had uniforms, so he would make outfits for a whole band in exchange for letting someone copy their book of arrangements. That way we had Stan Kenton arrangements, we had Woody Herman arrangements, we had Count Basie arrangements, we even had Billy Eckstine's big band arrangements, Dizzy's band, and Duke's band. They all wore Harold Fox uniforms. We rehearsed every week and the band was so tight. We had a who's-who of jazz in that band, it's where I met Gene Ammons who was playing tenor, and people like Lee Konitz, and [bassist] Eugene Wright, and the best of the locals.'

The full story of South Side jazz in the 1940s has yet to be told, and Junior was anxious to pinpoint a number of Dale sidemen who deserve attention if only belatedly. 'Some guys, especially in Chicago, they didn't want to be recognised or known, they were just

100 Golden Fingers, Japan, 1993. *Left to right*: Bob Cranshaw (b); Alan Dawson (d); and pianists Marian McPartland, John Lewis, Hank Jones, Mance, Tommy Flanagan, Dave McKenna, Ray Bryant, Roger Kellaway, Duke Jordan and Kenny Barron. Photo courtesy Junior Mance.

happy playing the music. Which I was too, but I listened to so many people on recordings and never got a chance to meet them; that's why I wanted to come to New York so as I could see these people in person.'

Trumpeter Gail Brockman played in the Dale band, but is forgotten now. 'He's one of the finest trumpet players, went with Earl Hines and with Billy Eckstine's band; there he was playing most of the lead, the high notes, sort of blew his chops out and that's when he became a very lyrical player. By the end he wanted to just settle down.' Then there was Hobart Dotson, also a Dalesman: 'He is respected as one of the best trumpet players – could play any style. He could play with a bebop band, with a dixieland band, he could play with Mingus' band. He was just that flexible. And he had a good sound for big bands, too.'

'We had such a good time in that band,' Mance enthused, lamenting that it never recorded, and adding that, 'we only had two gigs that lasted more than one night, otherwise Harold just got single gigs. The band went to Detroit and played a club for a week but Harold couldn't go so Gene fronted and the band also went to St. Louis and played a club there. Oh, the band did go to New York and play the Apollo and Gene fronted that too. I think Harold came and he was there for a few days but then he had to get back to his tailor shop.'

Mance feels that he came of age when he joined tenorist Gene Ammons' band. One incident stayed in his mind, as it precipitated a major change of direction for him. 'We were at a club right next door to the Regal Theater, called the Congo Lounge. Bands would come in to play the Regal, and Gene would know everybody in the band, and afterwards he would invite them to come on down to the Congo. Their last show would be over 11 o'clock latest, and we didn't start playing until 10 o'clock. The hours for playing clubs in Chicago were, like, from 10 till 4 a.m. and 10 to 5 a.m. on Saturdays, so they'd come down, and man, we had some great sessions. I was in seventh heaven. All the people that Gene knew were, like, very quality players. Even Charlie Parker would come down when he was in town.' Given that Gene's father, the pianist Albert Ammons, was an early Mance hero, did he get to know him? 'Yes, he often used to come, when I first joined the band, and listen to Gene when we were working in the little clubs in Chicago. Albert was a father to me,' he said, adding that 'Gene's brother Edsel is a bishop in the AME church – I think he's still alive. They were close.'

Lester Young came to Chicago minus a piano player to play a dance – Bud Powell had missed his flight from New York – and Mance was asked to sub but he couldn't,

'because I was working. So that night, after the dance, Lester and his manager came by the Congo to listen and his manager came over and said, "Lester would like to have a word with you." So Lester offered me the job. I said, "Let me think about it." They stayed the rest of the evening. Before we started on the next set I said, "Gene, I want to talk to you. Lester Young has offered me a job in his band." Well, Gene idolised Lester, so Gene said, "What! Take it! Now I'll tell you what happened to me." That same day, Woody Herman offered Gene a job and Gene was playing around in his mind what he was going to do. He wanted the job with Woody because it would enhance his name. So he said, "Why don't you take it, and then I'll go on the road with Woody?" So after the next set I told Lester, "Yes, I'll take it," and Gene called Woody, and we both left town at the same time.'

Lester Young is the subject of endless scrutiny, especially today, with Douglas Henry Daniels' massive study,[1] and I was happy to stay in Mance's slipstream as he reminisced about his time in the tenorist's sextet. 'With Lester, playing in that band was different, but it was so wonderful. Lester was not like a bandleader, he was like one of the guys, and he was very generous with his solos. He would let everybody solo. Some people, even some jazz players, they came to hear Lester Young, not the rest of the band. When he was asked why he was so generous with the solos, Lester said, "It's because they can play. You might not like me but you might like somebody else in the band." That was his philosophy,' Mance explained.

Young's bass player, Tex Briscoe, decided to retire and Mance recommended Leroy Jackson from the Ammons band as his replacement. 'Leroy and I were really, really, tight as buddies, the same age, and I said "I gotta guy for you." So Lester sent for Leroy and he liked Leroy the first set. Leroy and I stayed until the band broke up.'

'There were times when Lester had to work with Norman Granz. As the only two guys that weren't from New York, Leroy and I were staying in the same hotel that Lester was staying in, the Marden Hotel. It was full of musicians: Charlie Parker lived there, Deke Watson of the Inkspots, Harold West, the drummer. So anyway, when Lester had to go out

Cannonball Adderley Quintet at the Bohemian Caverns, Washington DC, 1955. Nat Adderley (c); Mance (p); 'Specs' Wright (d); Sam Jones (b) and Cannonball Adderley (as). Photo courtesy Junior Mance.

with Granz, he'd pay our costs and then give us some money to keep going. He was never gone more than two weeks.'

'Jerry Elliott was on trombone; he was the same age as Leroy and me. Jesse Drakes was the trumpet player and Roy Haynes was the drummer. Roy left after about a year and joined Sarah [Vaughan], and Leroy and I had heard Connie Kay, so we told Lester, "We know a good drummer." And Connie stayed until the band broke up. We played places like Birdland or the Savoy Ballroom. That was like working a club because you didn't go into the Savoy, not just for one night. You'd be doing a whole week or two, alternating with a big band, usually Buddy Johnson – marvellous band – or Lucky Millinder, who also had a great band. Lester was a favourite there.'

Questioned about Young's famously reclusive persona, Mance said, 'Don't forget now, he was such an outstanding personality, everybody wanted to get close to him. He wasn't one to have people around him that just wanted to hang around him, you know. Even some of the writers, he didn't take kindly to, 'cause they asked him all kinds of dumb questions.'

Young relied on his manager, Charlie Carpenter. 'Business was the one thing that

The Dizzy Gillespie Quintet, 1959. *Left to right*: Teddy Stewart (d); Mance; Gillespie; Leo Wright (as and fl); Art Davis (b). Photo courtesy Junior Mance.

somebody else had to plan. We never rehearsed, it was almost like a session every night, but the horn players would get together and work on different things. Sweets Edison told me about the Basie band in the thirties: he said there was no book. Like one guy would set a riff, and their ears were so good the whole section would pick it up in *harmony*. That's how Lester liked it. We played everything, mostly standards, and things like 'Lester Leaps In' or 'Jumping with Symphony Sid'. For the time, the money was good and it was prestige to work with Lester Young for those two years.'

Young broke up the band ahead of a long engagement with Jazz At The Philharmonic and Mance made for Chicago to rejoin Gene Ammons. He was saddened to see that most of his fellow bandsmen were 'strung out'. Asked how he managed to stay clean, Mance said, 'I got drafted into the army. I guess that what's saved me. Gene Wright and I were the

Lionel Hampton and The Golden Men of Jazz, 1991. *Back row*: Grady Tate, Arvell Shaw, Mance. *Front row*: James Moody, Al Grey, Hampton, Harry 'Sweets' Edison and Clark Terry. Photo courtesy Junior Mance.

only two in the band that wasn't using drugs. I just never did.' He added that junkies 'hurt nobody but themselves. All the people that were like that, they were great people, not just as musicians but as people. Especially Charlie Parker, and I worked a lot with him at a club in Chicago called the Bee Hive. I was in the house trio, Israel Crosby was the bass player, and a local drummer named Buddy Smith was the leader. I learned a lot from Charlie Parker and Coleman Hawkins, the two of them, like standards that I didn't know. I'd ask them, "What key shall I play it in?" And the answer was always, "Make it easy on yourself." They meant that they could play any tune in any key.'

'I'll never forget Charlie Parker. He told me, "You need to come to New York." And I said, "I'll be there soon." And then when I did show up, I ran into him on Broadway in the day-time, and he said, "Well, I see you finally made it." When I said I was going to New York, the local guys said, "You gonna what? Are you crazy, those New York musicians will eat you up." In other words, Chicago musicians had a sense of awe about New York. In reali-ty, most of the Chicago musicians were better than a lot of New York musicians. Once I got there, I realised that. In no time, man, I was working and every time I came to Chicago, the same musicians came back on me. "What's it like, man? Boy, you went there and you made it." I said, "Yeah, it's great, you should be there."'

Mance was drafted into the army and encountered band sergeant Julian 'Cannonball' Adderley. 'To make a long story short, Cannonball saved my life, I like to say. I decided to go into the Service Club and sit in with the band, and that's when Cannonball said, "Are you coming to the band?" And I said, "No, because I don't play a marching instrument." So he got together with the band commander and they pulled some strings. They weren't exactly legal, either, by army standards but he got me a job as a company clerk in the band, working in the office doing the clerical work. That got me out of an infantry training company that was shipped to Korea and only about five or six people survived.'

'Cannonball and I were room-mates. He was head of band training. His brother Nat was in the band, Curtis Fuller was in the band. Our band was still segregated, and they had two other [white] bands, but we all hung out together; the only time things were segregated was when we were playing marches. By the time I got out three years later in '53, the whole army was integrated. I played the Bee Hive again for a year, then I left there to go on the road with Dinah Washington because I wanted to come back to New York.'

'Everybody says Dinah was so hard to get along with, but I never had any problems. I was with her for two years, one of the greatest gigs I ever had. Wynton Kelly felt the same way. I learned a lot about accompanying, learned more about the blues.' Mance was reunited with Adderley in 1956. 'They wanted to say he was the new Charlie Parker but he wasn't. He didn't play Bird to me, he was himself, which is great in itself.'

Talking comparisons like this prompted Mance to return to his views on jazz education. 'Don't be a copycat, don't imitate solos, that's what I teach at my improvisation class. Erroll Garner told me, "Always look like you're enjoying what you're doing." And I tell my students, "Jazz is fun, this is a fun type of music."'

'And when it stops being fun, I'm out of it.' Napkin folded, bill paid, Mance was on his way, still smiling and looking forward, no doubt, to yet more bandstand fun.

Chapter 28

Wilfred Middlebrooks

Ella's Bassist

Wilfred Middlebrooks in the UK with Paul Smith's quartet, 1962. Photo by Brian Foskett.

Bassist Wilfred Roland Middlebrooks toured with Ella Fitzgerald for five rewarding years. When I visited him at his hotel in London in 1961, he proved to be an accomodating and engaging interviewee. We met again the following year and some of this later interview material has been included here.

After he tired of travelling the world as part of Ms Fitzgerald's accompanying unit, Middlebrooks returned to Los Angeles in 1963 to play locally. He later found regular employment with the US Post Office for whom he worked from 1978 to 1995, while continuing to perform at weekends, often with pianist Paul Smith. At present he still freelances. Wilfred's recollections demonstrate yet again how little we know about the fine territory musicians who committed themselves to jazz without gaining any kind of wider fame.

'I'm from Chattanooga, Tennessee, and I was born 'round July 17th 1933. My father was a bass player also – not in jazz though, because jazz was not too strong in Tennessee at that time. There were some good jazz musicians around but they were always out on the road. My father stayed home and played with local people; never anyone well known. I guess you could say that their style was something like Lionel Hampton today. He was a family man and drove a taxi during the day; my mother played piano and I have an uncle, a schoolteacher, who could play some piano too. My family believed in everyone starting on piano and I began going to a teacher when I was nine or ten years old.'

'I first picked up the bass around the age of twelve – there was always my father's bass to try and play! My grandmother used to play a little piano and all of a sudden I'd feel like getting up and playing something. She'd strike a groove playing stride piano so I'd get me a stool and climb up to the bass and just fool around with it a little, feeling pretty good. I really didn't know about positions, so that any time she'd play something I'd slide my hand down and say, 'This sounds like what she was playing.' And finally I would find those notes that she was playing in her left hand. So I started from there, playing by ear. Then my father decided to send me to a teacher because he wanted me to know the right way to play the instrument.'

'I grew up with Leslie Spann, the guitar player. I remember when he first started, when neither of us could play a note. He's the only one [that] people know from my time in Chattanooga – we were also very close to Phineas Newborn, the piano player from Memphis, Tennessee. He always studied so hard and has great talent.'

'I left home at the age of fifteen to play my first professional job on string bass with a stage show. Incidentally, I'm taking a bass to my father in Chattanooga after this tour. He always has to borrow one for gigs because when I left I took his bass with me. First he knew was when I sent a card from San Antonio, Texas. He was going to come after me but I travelled too fast! I had heard so much about the road from guys that went out and came back that I decided to try it. I just fell in love with the whole idea of travelling. The show travelled mostly through the southern states and around New York, playing the vaudeville theatres. We had a seven-piece band that would normally play for the dancers [and] then do two or three band numbers in a jazz style and accompany the acts in the show. I met quite

Middlebrooks in London, March 1961. Photo by Ian Powell.

a few good musicians that were a big help to me; most of them were experienced in jazz and some had played with Lucky Millinder. Those guys had wanted to stay near their homes to be with their families and they would come out with a show every once in a while. At that time I knew certain things about the bass but I still had a whole lot to learn so I started to listen to Ray Brown on records and the way he was playing fascinated me. He was my favourite then and today he's my teacher.'

'In the band was Ernest 'Punch' Miller, a trumpet player from New Orleans, a nice fellow and a good musician. We were together quite a lot and he used to show me things on the bass that people like Pops Foster used. They were simple but swinging and I still use them today. After the show we'd have jam sessions and Punch would play – differently to the others but still good. I remember he always used to sit behind me in the bus.'

'They used to give us two or three dollars at a time to buy meals but we never saw any regular money. They certainly took advantage of us. I didn't care too much about a salary as I was just interested in the experience but I never knew how the older guys managed.'

'After a couple of years with the show, I quit in New York and joined [saxophonist] Tab Smith. He was working around New York and spent a lot of time at the Savoy Ballroom. With him we played what I call semi-jazz: swing-time stuff very closely related to jazz. As you know, Tab was an ex-Basie man and this was a Basie-type combo. All I wanted to do was swing and working with Tab really taught me about swinging and pushed me further into jazz. I don't know whether I thought of myself as a jazz musician at this time but meeting New York musicians helped me to learn a lot about jazz. I finally got to Birdland; I was really too young to get in but somehow I looked older than I was and I managed to get through and hear Charlie Parker, Dizzy Gillespie, Curley Russell and those guys.'

'There were six pieces in our band, Tab himself played alto and tenor and we had a very wonderful tenor player out of St. Louis, Charles Wright. The trumpet player was Irving Woods, a very good musician who used to be with George Hudson's band, again out of St. Louis. Lavern Dillon was our piano player and he was a swinger, very close in style to the jazz played today. He had tremendous talent and technique and I think he was the first one that started to really get me into more of a jazz feeling. He'd play some things that I don't seem to have been close enough to at the time, but he eased me into these things without me knowing and I got to where I enjoyed trying to play these difficult things. There were times when he would play and I would get nervous, I thought he was playing over my head, which he really was. We were always together – he was blind and I used to take care of him. I wish I could find him now and I've often tried to contact him. He has a style all his own, which swings so beautifully, and he deserves to make records. Our drummer was Walter Johnson of the old Fletcher Henderson band, a wonderful musician. I've always been the youngest member in each group that I've worked with and I've been very fortunate in having good drummers like Walter to put down a good swinging beat and make it so easy each time for me.'

'We went all down through the South with that band, playing for dances and doing an occasional concert. That's when I was first introduced to concert work. We never did play for a white dance. There was only one time that we played for a mixed audience and that was in Little Rock, Arkansas. It was a coloured dance with the whites upstairs and we were fortunate enough not to have any trouble. I made records for the first time with Tab, for United, a small Chicago label.'

'I stayed with Tab [for three years] until I was drafted into the Service in 1953, and the group always stayed the same during my time. I was in the army from 1953 through March 1955, and I stayed at Camp Stewart, Georgia, all that time. The Camp is right out of Savannah, Georgia, about 400 miles from my home town so I got a chance to go home every week. After basic training I got put into the band where I was fortunate enough to meet pianist Wynton Kelly and later Phineas Newborn. Both of them helped to push me further into what you could call the jazz feeling and I had to learn a completely different musical environment to play with them. I wanted to play with those fellows, and as they were strictly jazzmen I either had to get with it or leave it alone.'

'I played tuba in the marching band, and [met] a good teacher who helped me a lot. I played string bass in the dance band, of course, and we'd play nice jam sessions – there were lots of very good musicians in the band. Today these men are unknown because they stayed in the South. I remember Kenny Clarke, a pianist, and an alto player named Edwin Winder, both beautiful jazz musicians with a good technique.'

'I went back with Tab Smith after I got out of the Service and travelled with him to California. By that time there had been one change in the group. Chauncey Locke was playing both trumpet and piano. Locke was a very beautiful player and I learned a lot from him. I stayed with Tab about two weeks, just long enough to get to California and then Chauncey and I left the band together. He stayed there and he's living in California right now. I had decided that I wanted to concentrate on jazz and I went there with that purpose – I'd heard so much about the place and all the jazz there.'

'I started to work with Buddy Collette's quintet and then I met Bill Holman and Mel Lewis and worked with their group quite a while. Buddy's group had Gerald Wilson playing trumpet (he also had a big band), a wonderful guitar player Al Viola – an Italian – and a beautiful drummer named Earl Palmer. I guess I worked with Buddy about two years – we stayed around Los Angeles playing the jazz clubs – Jazz City, the Jazz Cellar – and we'd also give concerts in different high schools. Although I was mainly with Buddy I did a lot of freelance work with Bill and Mel's quintet, or with Art Pepper (what a wonderful tone), Frank Rosolino, Herb Geller, or occasionally Sonny Stitt.'

'In 1958 I got a phone call from Norman Granz asking me to join Ella. I left town with her and I've been working with her ever since. I never knew how Norman came to call me – there must have been a recommendation from someone! If we're off at all I usually go home and do a few jazz gigs with Buddy Collette or Bill Holman.'

'Working with Ella has improved me as

a jazz player and it's work that I enjoy. She's a great musician, reads well, knows something about piano and plays a harmonica beautifully. The programme changes constantly, from ballads to uptempo things, and each song requires something from the bass. She's also a very sincere and very humble person and don't think of herself as a big star at all. She carries her audience wherever we go – there are never any problems. I love playing in the quartet – especially with a great drummer like Gus Johnson. With these guys there's something new every night.'

'I made my first real jazz recordings with Frank Rosolino in 1958 for Bethlehem, and Sonny Clark, piano, and Stan Levy, drums, were on that date with us. Right after the last European tour I did a date with King Pleasure for HiFi Jazz, which was a real ball. He's a wonderful character and we had some fine musicians on the session. Earl Palmer was on drums, a very versatile player who plays all types of studio work, Matthew Gee on trombone, Harold Land and Teddy Edwards on tenors and Gerald Wiggins (a pianist who I've worked with many times). We had a nice feeling and the date was a swinger. I also did an album out on the coast a few months back with Johnny Hodges and Ben Webster.'

'I've done a little bit of studio work – including records with Doris Day. I never had the ambition to settle for this type of work. You have to be there all the time and I still like moving around too much. I love to be on the road and I like the life that I live now. I've made three European tours with Ella now and I'm looking forward to many more. These days I enjoy seeing all the different countries; right now we're off for a two-week tour in Israel. When I get older I might settle for the studios – but I've a few years before then!'

'I don't care too much for big band work although I've done a little with Gerald Wilson's big band out in Los Angeles. They're good for your reading and keep you on your toes but my favourite is a trio, where you can really hear the bass. Once I even worked as a duo with Gerald Wiggins and that really felt good.'

'Other bass players? Ray Brown was about the first I heard and he's still my top favourite. He searches for improvement in his playing, in his knowledge of the instrument, and he practises all the time. My favourite big band is Count Basie but I love Ellington too – such a beautiful composer. I love playing his tunes – every one tells a story and some are very moving.'

'Yes, I've listened to Ornette Coleman but I'm not far enough advanced to understand it – I don't put it down, but it's not for me. His drummer, Billy Higgins, plays altogether different from the records: he's a real bass player's drummer; melodic with wonderful time. I worked with Eric Dolphy's band at the Club Oasis on the coast, backing singers and dancers and I know that Eric felt restricted by the nature of the music. He had a professor for each instrument he plays and could sit in any symphony as though he'd been there all his life. Now he's come to New York and he just seems to have let loose with something completely new. We have to remember that [jazz] still has to swing. I really learned to swing with Tab Smith – it was just all rhythm. I had lessons from Professor Fritz from the Chattanooga School of Music but I still had to learn how to swing.'

'My ambitions? To continue to improve on the instrument and to work for the betterment of jazz musicians generally. I also want to take up the tuba again. I'm also going to get hold of one of Ray Brown's new jazz cellos and work on that. He's got one with him now and was using it on the Continent.'

'I really love that bass, you know. I remember once I was without it while I was having a case made for it. I was miserable, I couldn't relax and I walked through the house I don't know how many times. It was just supposed to be there and wasn't. I was waiting for this guy to call and tell me to come over and pick my bass up. Finally I called him and said, "Look, I'll be right over and you can just take a chance on it fitting. You've had it long enough." But just not to see it there – normally I'd walk through the room and any time I'd go back through there, I'd pick it up and play something.'

'Not having it around, I thought I'd go stone crazy.'

Chapter 29

Gene Rodgers

Recording Body and Soul

Gene Rodgers, New York City, 1960. Mercury Records photo.

Pianist Gene Rodgers knew London in the 1930s when he toured the UK with a musical act and recorded with Benny Carter. He returned 50 years later with the Harlem Blues and Jazz Band, a group of big band veterans based in New York, organised and promoted by Al Vollmer. Rodgers presented an imposing figure and was at pains to stress his readiness to play and sing as a soloist. On tour with the Harlem Blues and Jazz Band in April 1981, he was able to demonstrate his impressive jazz credentials to the full and it was then that I taped his life story.[1] This short piece, however, is based on a later interview and concentrates on his association with Coleman Hawkins. Rodgers was courteous and helpful but you sensed that he might be hard to handle if the situation turned against him. He died on 23 October 1987 in New York aged 77.

The course of jazz history is marked by significant recordings that encapsulate a vital stage in the development of the music. They set a standard, unwittingly perhaps, for the immediate period ahead. One example of this would be Louis Armstrong's 'West End Blues'. Another, indubitably, would be Coleman Hawkins' version of 'Body and Soul' made in October 1939, which created a frame of reference for all jazz tenor saxophonists for years thereafter. Indeed, another tenorist of that generation, Benny Waters, told me that Hawkins' superb extemporisation had so affected him that he felt compelled to make a sax section arrangement of the entire solo for Claude Hopkins' Orchestra, while attempting to play it himself out front. It was, he assured me, virtually impossible to do it justice.

Another key witness to the importance of that recording was the pianist on the session, Gene Rodgers, to whom I spoke when he returned to London for a solo tour. At that time, we met in the comfortable ambiance of the London flat where he was staying while appearing at the Pizza on The Park. I asked the burly New Yorker how his association with Hawkins began.

'I was working in a place called Nick's in New York with Zutty Singleton and Edmond Hall, who was one of the most fluid clarinettists that one could ever imagine. We had a fine little thing going but one day I got a call from a young lady that you may have heard of: her name was Hazel Scott. She said, "Hey Gene, what you doing? Coleman Hawkins just came back from Europe and he's looking for a piano player. I suggested you. What do you think?" I said, "Well good grief! I would love to go with Coleman." So I told Zutty about it and Zutty was quite upset. He says, "Man, you can't do that. We got a helluva thing going here." So I says, "Yeah, Zutty. But I gotta look out for myself a little." Then he says, "Why

can't you see if you can get me with it?" I
said, "I don't think so because I don't even
know if I'm in there yet. Why don't you let
me see what happens?" Anyway I went
and saw Coleman and when I finally knew
I was with the band I gave my notice to
Zutty.'

'We were working at a place called
Kelly's Stables on 52nd Street for quite a
while, just as a small group. I remember
Billie Holiday sang with us for a small stint
there. One day Coleman said, "Gene, we
have a recording date so why don't you
write one of the tunes? I'm gonna write
something." I used to be up his house all
the time. Coleman loved the piano. He very
seldom picked up his saxophone at home;
he always went to the piano and figured out
everything he had in mind.'

'So we recorded quite a few tunes,
including a thing called 'Fine Dinner' and
then Coleman arranged something. Now
this was the day of the 78s, when time was
a prime concern. So after we had done the
whole record date there seemed to be
three minutes lacking, so Coleman says,
"Jeez, we gotta do something else. What
the hell we gonna do?" I remember him just
as if it happened yesterday. He reached
over and he got a bottle of cognac, took a
good healthy sip; then he laid it down
and he got right under the middle of the
microphone and he said, 'Gene, make an
introduction on 'Body and Soul' and take
the first chorus.'

'So I made the introduction that became
the legend with the record. I don't know
where it came from, I put my hands down

and it just came out. I took the first chorus
and then Coleman came in and he played
it out. Now what happened was, it was too
long so they cut it and he said, "Gene, I'm
sorry. We're gonna have to cut your first
chorus; just make the introduction."'

'I wasn't the least upset because this
was just like a throwaway to make up the
time so, of course, I made the introduction
and Coleman came in and that was it.
Everybody said "so long," we got our
cheques and went on about our business.'

'The next thing we knew, when that
record hit the market, it was like a forest
fire. We had a date to play the Apollo
Theater and this is where the augmenting
of the band came about 'cause we needed
a larger band. When I peeped out of the
side of the curtain there from the stage, I
was shocked. Every saxophone player was
in the audience, Benny Carter; Vido
Musso, who was a great tenorman; Ben
Webster; the whole front line was nothing
but saxophone players sitting there. We did
our show and finally Hawk said, "Gene,
'Body and Soul'," and we played it. It was
the identification of the band from then on.'

Had Gene his own explanation for the
extraordinary success of 'Body and Soul'?
'Well I think that the reason for that was this
was a record that Coleman made from his
heart. There was no shackles of an
arrangement, he just stood up there flat-
footed and played with no interruption. His
eyes was closed and he played as if he
was in heaven. That picture will always live
with me.'

After the Apollo engagement Hawkins

kept his big band on the road for a while. With little recorded evidence it's difficult to evaluate its worth. Just how good was the band?

'We had this tremendous first trumpet player, Bill Dillard; he's still in New York today. He's in a different field, he's an actor now although he still plays. And we had five or six arrangers including Andy Gibson, Buster Tolliver and Buster Harding. These were top arrangers for those days and they used to write way above Ds, Es and Fs, which was very high for trumpet, and Dillard would just sit there with his legs crossed and hit those terrific notes. Anyway Bill got into something with Coleman about money. He wanted more, and

The Harlem Blues and Jazz Band, The Ginger Man, New York City, early 1980s. Left to right: George James (as); Rodgers (p); Peck Morrison (b); Al Casey (g); Eddie Durham (tb); Bobby Williams (t).

Coleman didn't agree with it, and he left the band. His replacement had a previous reputation as being a fine first trumpet player, but his playing had deteriorated. He went out on the road with us and we started playing the usual dances all over creation, but the band didn't have the sparkle it once had. I personally think that was the downfall of the band.'

'See, Coleman was a marvellous musician but as far as being a bandleader was concerned, he was always up in the clouds. He was not, definitely not, a businessman. Some times on pay nights you couldn't even find Coleman. He was gone off somewhere and the man that had the place would say, "Well, who'm I going to pay? Coleman isn't here." So I finally went to Hawk and said, "Hey, Hawk, gosh sakes, you never here to get the salary so why don't you give me power of attorney and let me collect the money? I know how

Coleman Hawkins Orchestra, Fiesta Danceteria, New York City, May 1940. *Rear, left to right*: Rodgers (p); Johnny Williams (b); Arthur Herbert (d); Lawrence Lucie (g). *Front*: Ernie Powell (ts); Eustis Moore, Jackie Fields (as); Kermit Scott (ts); Hawkins (ts); Claude Jones (tb).

much everyone gets." In fact we were all getting the same money. So he said, "OK, that's a good idea." Just to get it off his back, you know. See, sometimes right after the show or the last set he wouldn't say goodnight to anybody, he's gone; he's in a cab surrounded by a bunch of floosies. The women Coleman was attracted to were numerous.'

'There was some air checks [broadcast recordings] that came from the Savoy and I've just very recently heard them and it was a phenomenal band. Hawk could blow over the entire band: this one man would stand there with three trombones, five trumpets and six saxophones blaring to the top of their lungs and he'd just blow over them all. He had tremendous power.'

Towards the end of his life the great tenor saxophonist appeared to have lost much of his extraordinary zest for living. Although Rodgers was not associated with Hawk in his later years, he kept in touch with his activities and remembered a last TV appearance with sadness.

'He looked terribly dissipated. It was inevitable because Coleman was a man that really enjoyed life to the fullest degree. I've never met an individual that lived as fast. He lived for the moment strictly. But his performance on the bandstand was just superb. The power and exuberance that he portrayed was breathtaking.'

Although principally known as a solo pianist, Rodgers worked with early New York bands (including recording with King Oliver) and later with Erskine Hawkins, before taking film work in Hollywood and enjoying solo residencies around New York and Connecticut. An accomplished performer, he was open to contemporary influences, although reserving his greatest admiration for Art Tatum. His musical perspective remained fresh and his keyboard skills were of a very high order indeed.

'I'm not ultra-modern,' he said, 'but I've always listened to the younger jazz musicians. My playing is strictly influenced by anything that I can handle that the modern kids are doing today.'

Chapter 30

Cousin Joe

New Orleans Joys

Cousin Joe in London, early 1980s. Photo by Dave Bennett.

Cousin Joe, then known as Smilin' Joe, made quite a name for himself in the 1940s with a series of blues recordings whose lyrics, penned by him, were both funny and touching. After years in comfortable obscurity, he resurfaced in the 1960s and began to tour internationally. He came to Britain first in 1964 with the American Blues Caravan and returned many times over the next twenty years or so. I caught up with him at his London hotel in 1978 and listened as he told me his story. Every time I suggested a question, he dismissed it, saying, 'I know what you want to hear,' and carried on regardless. Always colourful and popular, Joe saw himself as a blues entertainer and raconteur, and he excelled as both. He died in October 1989 aged 81.

One of the fascinations of jazz lies in the extraordinary compression of its development: from Buddy Bolden to Ornette Coleman in a mere half century or so. The music evolved in that very short period from the artless to the artistic: primitive origins yielding at headlong speed to the highly sophisticated demands of today.

The resulting kaleidoscope of styles left casualties – men unable to reconcile themselves to change and often sadly neglected as a result. Others, made of sterner stuff, rolled along regardless, giving the enthusiast the chance to evaluate and enjoy representatives of each era in a kind of convenient juxtaposition. By the 1970s, time for this was running out but some interesting survivors remained – durable veterans like Cousin Joe, the blues pianist and entertainer from New Orleans, who became a regular musical tourist to Britain and mainland Europe.

Having caught Joe at a London gig and enjoyed his wry, sometimes sardonic, way with the blues, I sought him out at his hotel and asked him to talk about his life and career. Joe, it turned out, was anxious to spill forth his exotic story. By then a senior citizen but still youthful in demeanour and appearance, his carmine three-piece, pendant, leather topcoat and soft cap combined to make him look like a Storyville professor translated to another time. Yes, a sharp dude and a hustler too.

He sported a few 'names' in his time: his given title was Pleasant Joseph – that forename recalling a past Governor of Louisiana – but he answered willingly to his billing as Cousin Joe, Pleasant Joe or even Cousin Joe Pleasants, happily barnstorming his way across half a continent.

Originally from Wallace, Louisiana, Joe was brought to the Crescent City as a small child and talked racily of his family's gambling connections. Contrasted with this was his recollection of his parent's religious leanings: 'My people, they were all strict Baptists. My daddy could sing, man, but he never sang nothing but spirituals and my grandmother too, 'cause she taught him. Now, she never went to school but could read type, but couldn't read writing. She learned how to read from the newspaper – isn't that miraculous! Well, that's a gift from the good Lord. Like my mother [who] couldn't read or write but she would always catch the right streetcar every time. Just from the sound. Amazing!'

Cousin Joe in New Orleans, 1930s.

'So He must have given me a gift too, in the music field, because I first started in the Baptist Church when I was seven years old. I was a child prodigy – I used to write gospels and my daddy used to have 'em printed. We'd ride on a little train, called an excursion, from New Orleans to Wallace, going and coming. No music. My dad used to start to clapping and I'd start to singing, and my dad was selling them gospels for ten cents apiece and he would get rid of about a thousand. Both ways. I ain't never seen no money though,' Joe added, smiling at the memory.

At school he acquired a ukulele, the ideal accompaniment to his vocals, and said that his appearances at college football games earned him his professional name: 'Girl, name of Alma Collins, we were at school. She says, "Pleasant, how come you never get angry, you always smiling. I'm gonna call you Smiling Joe. That's where that started.'

'After that I got a job – I was about seventeen. Here's an old Russian guy, got a shoe-maker shop on Rampart and Canal and I saw the shoeshine stand, nobody on it, so I went to work. You take half, you give 'em half. I worked there a long time until in come two guys named Hats-&-Coats and Green, they was dancers, out of this world. I used to bring my ukulele to work when there wasn't much to do and we'd be singing together, harmony, so these cats say, "Come on with us." They had a little boy, his name was Earl Palmer, that became a drummer later. He was the greatest dancer in New Orleans. He was about seven or eight years old, I'd carry him on my back to his mother. She wouldn't let him go with nobody but me. We could get in all the white places like Louis Prima's and make that

Cousin Joe, New Orleans, 1970s. Crescent Jazz Productions photo.

money. Why they hired me: I could play the ukulele for them to dance so they wouldn't have to split with the band. I learned how to dance too. I got my dancing shoes right there with Fred Astaire: aluminum taps,' he affirmed, grinning wickedly.

Joe's recollections of New Orleans in the 1930s coincided with the onset of the depression and were studded with references to the rampant racial segregation that characterised the Paris of the South. In Joe's words, 'White people for pleasure. Negroes to play for them.'

At about this time Joe set up home with the beautiful Eva, Spanish-Indian, and her children – 'They all recognise me now as Papa Joe' he said – and made a living playing the uke and singing at Saturday night fish-fries and parties, his developing popularity apparently giving him the opportunity to leave his dancer friends and go his own way.

'I got me a piano player, Mitchell Frazier. What a player he was! He had a left hand so big he could span a twelfth, better than Fats Waller. He was a master, but he drank so much wine, stuff kill him. We'd play for parties, 50 cents apiece. Then my girl got me a job where she was working – when I used to do my dance, they had to sweep the floor free of sawdust so my taps could hit. After that I got to be known all over town. From there I got a job at the Black Gold club, a place not far from where I live now, after a fellow got killed in there, split down the middle with a ham knife. That was in the Garden District; I worked there a long time.'

'I had a band and I bought me a six-string guitar for $7 and didn't know how to tune it even. I had one in the band – you might have heard of him – Cap'n John Handy, clarinet and alto, he played with me. 'Round about '34. I was leading the band with my guitar and doing most of the singing.'

Pursuing his links with important jazz musicians, Joe told me next of his association with Billie and Dede Pierce, celebrated names to traditionalists, at a club called the Kingfish, this leading to an engagement at the Gypsy Tea Room which was then 'the hottest club in the city. I was producing the shows, I had my act with my guitar; we had two or three comedians, like vaudeville. They even gave me my own apartment upstairs,' he enthused.

From there, Joe joined the Jazz Jesters from Cincinnati, indulging in four-part harmony, strictly cabaret from his account, taking in further unusual experiences including the Texas Centennial in Dallas in 1936. There he claimed to have met Jack Benny, movie producer Frank Capra and assorted millionaire oil-men whose patronising attitude to black entertainers seems ridiculous now but must have appeared sinister then. Nevertheless Joe, always the hustler, came back to New Orleans richer by $900.

Ever the follower of fortune, he moved on to New York at agent Joe Glaser's behest, ostensibly to join the Ink Spots. But they had broken up because 'they had a fight on the stage at the Zanzibar, Deke Watson and them. Joe gave me $85 and a round trip ticket to New York. I had to audition and I depped for them for a while, and I was ready to come back home. So Danny Barker, the great rhythm guitar man, he told me, "You ain't going home; you stay on 52nd Street." Mondays they had jam sessions, and Leonard Feather asked would I like to record for Aladdin. We had Harry Carney on baritone, Al Sears, and Jonah Jones on trumpet.'

'Hot Lips Page was the only one singing the blues on 52nd Street then. Charlie Parker and Dizzy Gillespie was at the Three Deuces; me, Billie Holiday, Tiny Grimes and his band was at the Down Beat. Then in comes Sidney Bechet and asked me to play guitar in his band so I worked nine months with him. The world's greatest soprano saxophone player, nobody could compare with him.'

This band worked in New York and Boston, included the important bassist Pops Foster and a fine West Indian pianist named Egbert Victor, and preceded a period of exhilarating activity for Joe as he recorded (often with pianist Sammy Price) for many labels, major and minor, using his own quite idiosyncratic blues lyrics. With Joe's uncertain feeling for chronology, it was sometimes difficult to pin him down on actual dates but his five-year stopover in the Big Apple took in the war-time epoch, a sort of halcyon time on 52nd Street. He also spoke of his work with saxophonist Harold Dejan in the late 1930s, on the steamship *Dixie*, in a band including the legendary Burnell Santiago, a pianist fit to compare with Earl Hines, according to Joe.

After the war his role as singer-entertainer continued in New Orleans as before, often with bands, short-lived probably, and later in New York again, but this time in the burgeoning Greenwich Village folk-scene of the 1960s.

When I asked Joe to explain how he came to substitute piano for guitar, he gave

Cousin Joe in a chance encounter with Hal Singer, Nancy, France, 1970s. Photo courtesy Hal Singer.

me a characteristically candid account, lacing his story as ever with an extra superlative or two. 'Well, my piano player, Alton Purnell, he worked seven years with me and then his brother Theodore played saxophone with me too. One night I'm looking for Alton to come to work and he calls me up and tells me he's in Chicago. So I put the guitar down and from the chord changes on the guitar I could start to play the changes on the piano so the club owner said to me, 'You supposed to have five pieces, you ain't got but four.' When Alton did come in he was loaded and I said, 'We like brothers but I'm going to give you two weeks notice – I'm gonna give you *all* two weeks notice, then I'm going on my own.'

'I hired a drummer and for three pieces I was getting more money than [rhythm amd blues pianist] Paul Gayten and his band, more than [vocalist] Annie Laurie. $400 a week, man. I worked five years in the Pools Patio and four years in the Mardi Gras Lounge and the last eight years at the Court of The Two Sisters, and that's when I retired, in 1972, at 65.'

Retirement was clearly a relative term to someone who spent lucrative months every year in Europe, bringing the stagecraft gleaned from his vivid career experiences and a rainbow of memories to bear on new audiences. For all his self-deprecatory comments on his own keyboard expertise, it was always idiomatic, the perfect foil for his blues, whose themes invariably poked fun at man's pretences and vanities.

Notes

Chapter 1 Sonny Cohn

1. The King Fleming band comprised Johnny Thompson, then playing alto and clarinet; James Couch, alto and business manager; James 'Tom' White, tenor; Harold Tyler and Cohn, trumpets; Wilbur Hathaway, trombone and piano; Leroy, drums, later replaced by Dan Deans.
2. Captain Dyett's band included Chauncey Jarrett, Geraldine Springs, altos; a tenor; Sam Dean, trombone; Melvin Moore and Cohn, trumpets.
3. Red Saunders' band included Saunders, drums; Cohn; Antonio Cosey, later replaced by Nat Jones, alto; Leon Washington, tenor; Mickey Simms, bass; Porter Derico, later replaced by Rudy Martin, piano.
4. The reorganised Saunders band included Porter Kilbert, first alto; Leon Washington and Everett Gaines, tenors; Harlan 'Booby' Floyd and Joe McLewis, trombones; Earl Washington, piano; Jimmy Richardson, bass; Charles Gray, first trumpet; Cohn; Nick Cooper, trumpet and arranger.

Chapter 4 Art Farmer

1. Clora Bryant and others, *Central Avenue Sounds: Jazz in Los Angeles*, Berkeley: University of California Press, 1998.

Chapter 6 Grover Mitchell

1. The size of Harper's band varied. Sometimes it was an eight-piece with three reeds, three rhythm, trumpet and trombone. The trumpeter was often ex-Benny Carter bandsman, Edwin 'Youngblood' Davis. Later, Tommy Turrentine took his place. Joe Harris was the drummer.
2. At the time Bradshaw had a hit record, *Who*, featuring Prysock.
3. Trombonist Sam Hurt from Dizzy Gillespie's band later replaced Cooper in Paul Williams' band but left, in turn, to join Lloyd Price.
4. Mitchell provided information on the personnel of his rehearsal band used by Earl Hines: 'Our lead alto, Clarence Warren, from Oklahoma, was very good. The original baritone was Fred Purtle, replaced later by Jimmy Lomba. Tenor and alto respectively were Dave Madden and Herb Lorden, both with Harry James. The other trombones were Lulu Parker, later with Stan Kenton, and Ike Bell who had played trumpet with Count Basie. Our lead trumpet, Art Walker, used to play lead for Earl Hines' old band, and a kid who played in Hal McIntyre's band, Len Haggard, had most of the solos. Then there was Ron Smith and the fourth chair fluctuated. We had Frank Fisher for a while. Cedric [Heywood] was the piano; Dick Crawley, guitar; Melvin Boyd, bass and Ray Fisher, Earl's drummer, completed things. Our singer was Mary Stallings, tremendous, later with Billy Eckstine.'
5. Cedric Heywood was later replaced by Portuguese pianist, John Marabuto; Ray Fisher was replaced on occasion by Cuz Cousineau, and, for a period, Walter Perkins.
6. Henderson Chambers was added to the Basie band in January 1964; Henry Coker was replaced by Al Grey in October 1964, and the section stayed this way until Richard Boone succeeded Chambers in May 1966. In September 1966 Grey left to join the Sammy Davis entourage, and was replaced by Harlan 'Booby' Floyd from Chicago.
7. *Count Plays Duke* was issued on Mama Records, MMP 1024, and won a Grammy.

Chapter 7 Warren Vaché

1. Warren Vaché Sr., *The Unsung Songwriters: America's Masters of Melody*, Lanham (Maryland) and Oxford: Scarecrow Press, 2002.

Chapter 8 Britt Woodman

1. Charles Mingus died in 1979 but the Mingus Big Band continues to play his music.
2. Buddy Collette with Steve Isoardi, *Jazz Generations – A Life in American Music and Society*, London and New York: Continuum, 2000.

Chapter 10 Teddy Edwards
1. Clint Eastwood's film *Bird* (1988) starred Forest Whitaker as Charlie Parker.

Chapter 13 Illinois Jacquet
1. Count Basie, as told to Albert Murray, *Good Morning Blues – The Autobiography of Count Basie*, London: Heinemann, 1986.

Chapter 17 Hal Singer
1. *Financial Times*, 31.10.1079.

Chapter 20 Milt Buckner
1. Lars Bjorn with Jim Gallert, *Before Motown*, Ann Arbor, Michigan: University of Michigan Press, 2001.
2. McKinney's Cotton Pickers included Kelly Martin on drums; Milt's brother Ted, alto; Cecil Lee, lead alto; Milton MacNeil, tenor; Todd Rhodes, piano; Cat Morrison, bass, and Elwood Peters, trumpet. Frank Fry, who also played trumpet, was described by Buckner as 'the first of the high note men that could read and play up there.'
3. Don Cox's band included Buckner, piano; Clarence Ross, trumpet; Alvin 'Fats' Wall, alto, and Arvell Hutchinson, bass.
4. Milt Buckner's band included Billy Mitchell, tenor sax; Julius Watkins, French horn; Bruce Lawrence, bass; Eddie Grant, drums, and Bernie Mackey, guitar.

Chapter 21 Cozy Cole
1. H. Qualli Clark, cornetist with the Tennessee Ten, which also included bassist Ed Garland, later became an arranger with Pace & Handy Music Company, and was the co-composer of 'Shake It And Break It'.

Chapter 27 Junior Mance
1. Douglas Henry Daniels, *Lester Leaps in: The Life and Times of Lester 'Pres' Young*, Boston: Beacon Press, 2002.

Chapter 29 Gene Rodgers
1. Published as 'Looking Back, Looking Ahead', *The Mississippi Rag*, Vol. 10, No. 3 (January 1983).

Published Sources

The chapters in this book have been adapted from the author's articles previously published as follows:

Milt Buckner, 'The Milt Buckner Story', *Jazz & Blues*, December 1972.

Sonny Cohn, 'The Sonny Cohn Story', *Jazz Journal*, September 1963 .

Cousin Joe, 'Durable Veteran – Cousin Joe', *Jazz Journal International*, April 1980.

Cozy Cole, 'Cozy Conversing', *Mississippi Rag*, April 1978.

Willie Cook, 'Willie Cook', *Jazz Journal International*, September 1983.

Kenny Davern, 'Straight Talk from Kenny Davern', *Mississippi Rag*, May 1997.

Harry Edison, 'Harry 'Sweets' Edison', *Coda*, March/April 2000.

Teddy Edwards, 'Teddy's Ready', *Coda*, October/November 1986.

Art Farmer, 'Art Farmer: The Final Interview?', *Coda*, November/December 2000.

Nick Fatool, 'A Day With Nick Fatool', *Mississippi Rag*, June 1981.

Herb Hall, 'Hallmarks', *Jazz Journal International*, August 1981.

Scott Hamilton, 'More Fun Than Ohio', *Jazz the Magazine*, December 1992.

JC Heard, 'Heard About J.C.?' *Melody Maker*, November 4, 1978.

John Hicks, 'John Hicks: Something To Live For', *Coda*, July/August 2002.

Illinois Jacquet, 'Full Mettle Jacquet', *Jazz the Magazine*, February 1993.

Hank Jones, 'Have You Met Mr. Jones?' *Jazz Magazine*, May/June 1994.

Herbie Jones, 'Herbie Jones', *Jazz Journal*, March 1967.

Nappy Lamare, 'Nappy Lamare', *Footnote*, February/March 1976.

Junior Mance, 'Jammin' With Junior', *Coda*, September/October 2002.

Wilfred Middlebrooks, 'Ella's Bassist', *Jazz Monthly*, February 1963.

Eddie Miller, 'In Praise of Beauty', *Melody Maker*, November 25, 1978.

Geezil Minerve, 'Minerve: Blues Is Like Love', *Melody Maker*, March 22, 1975.

Grover Mitchell, 'The Grover Mitchell Story', *Jazz Monthly*, May 1970, and 'Grover Indulgence', *Boz (Jazz Express)*, June 1998.

Vi Redd, 'Vi Redd', *Jazz Journal International*, May 1996.

Gene Rodgers, 'Bean, Body and Soul' *Jazz Times*, May 1982.

Hal Singer, 'Hal Singer: A Career Profile', *Jazz Journal International*, November 2000.

Warren Vaché, 'Warren Vaché: Horn of Plenty', *Jazz Magazine*, November/December 1994.

Eddie Vinson, 'Vinson's Blues', *Melody Maker*, August 12, 1978.

Benny Waters with Jacques Butler, 'Montmartre Mainstream', *Jazz Journal*, February 1963, and 'La Cigale 1963', *Jazz Monthly*, January 1964.

Britt Woodman, 'Britt Woodman', *Coda*, September/October 2001.

Index

New from Northway

Some of My Best Friends are Blues (2nd edition)

by Ronnie Scott with Mike Hennessey

with a new foreword by Pete King

Original illustrations by Mel Calman and

contributions by Benny Green and Spike Milligan.

Reviews of first edition:

'In the train journey sense, it's a Good Read. However, beyond all the anecdotes and the wonderful lines. . . and the hints of Ronnie's East End childhood, there's something deeper. It took Ronnie Scott's account of his early struggles to make me see one of the fundamental differences between jazz musicians and the rest.' *Sunday Telegraph.*

'One of the best books about jazz, and its characters, ever written.' *Music Week.*

'I laughed a lot.' *Melody Maker.*

'With its array of outsize characters and crisp anecdotes the book is genuinely entertaining, even for non-jazz buffs.' *Financial Times.*

'An enthralling book about a memorable character.' *Jazz at Ronnie Scott's.*

Northway Publications ISBN 0 9537040-6-8 £6.99

Joe Harriott – Fire in His Soul

by Alan Robertson

Jamaican alto saxophonist Joe Harriott had no doubts about his talent and abilities – and with good reason. A brilliant instrumentalist, he gained legions of admirers for his fiery playing in Britain and beyond. His unique concept of free form heralded the emergence of contemporary European jazz. Later, with John Mayer, he pioneered fusions of jazz and Indian music. Alan Robertson's book, based on extensive interviews with many of those who knew Joe best, gives for the first time a full account of the triumphs and tragedies of Harriott's remarkable life.

'Robertson's research is meticulous and far-reaching. . . An important work: a detailed assessment of a seminal but long neglected artist.' *Independent on Sunday.*

'Robertson tells Harriott's story warts and all. . . a wonderful read.' *Jazzwise.*

'Joe Harriott was the most vital saxophonist to emerge from the British scene of the 1950s and 60s. . . This text. . . is fighting fresh, direct, necessary.' *The Wire.*

'A long overdue and welcome homage to a sadly neglected and original musician.' *Jazz Journal International.*

'The method Robertson takes is simply, clearly, to present the evidence, meticulously gathered from written and oral sources. . . and, mercifully, avoid the judgemental and tendentious.' *Jazz Rag.*

Northway Publications ISBN 0 9537040-3-3   £11.99

Bass Lines: A Life in Jazz

by Coleridge Goode and Roger Cotterrell

A 'prince' among bassists, Coleridge Goode has recorded with Django Reinhardt, Stéphane Grappelli, Ray Nance, George Shearing and countless other jazz stars. Here, with jazz writer Roger Cotterrell, he recalls his childhood in Jamaica and arrival in Britain in the 1930s, the lively wartime London club scene, the Ray Ellington Quartet of Goon Show fame and his long association with Joe Harriott. A contributor to many of the most exciting jazz developments of the past half century, Coleridge Goode is a thoughtful witness to a fascinating part of jazz history.

'the story of a man's resilience as well as an artist's ingenuity, of Goode's steely determination to find his place in a society in a state of flux and play music that was both in and out of step with its shifting demographics.' *Independent on Sunday*.

'packed with entertaining information.' *Cadence*.

'rich with anecdotes and one man's observations on the music he loves.' *Jazz Review*.

'in addition to the warm character of the narrator, there is much valuable information here about a huge swathe of jazz in Britain.' *Jazzwise*.

'un contributo essenziale alla storia del jazz inglese ed europeo.' *Musica Jazz*.

Northway Publications ISBN 0 9537040-2-5   £9.99

Other jazz books from Northway

Notes from a Jazz Life

by Digby Fairweather

Jazz cornetist, band leader and broadcaster Digby Fairweather tells of his life and career with candid, warm and hilarious anecdotes.

Illustrations by Peter Manders and Humphrey Lyttelton. 183 pages.

£7.99
ISBN 0 9537040-1-7   2002

Gold, Doubloons and Pieces of Eight

by Harry Gold

The autobiography of saxophonist and band leader Harry Gold – a wonderful memoir of the early years of jazz in Britain.

207 pages plus 39 gloss photos.

£10.99
ISBN 0 9537040-0-9   2000

forthcoming

A History of Jazz in Britain 1919-50 (2nd edition)

by Jim Godbolt.

*

Nat Gonella: The Georgia Boy from London

by Ron Brown with Digby Fairweather.

*

Out of the Long Dark - A Biography of Ian Carr

by Alyn Shipton.

Northway, 39 Tytherton Road London N19 4PZ,
email info@northwaybooks.com